MUSIC / CULTURE

A Series from Wesleyan University Press

Edited by George Lipsitz, Susan McClary, and Robert Walser

PUBLISHED TITLES

My Music by Susan D. Crafts, Daniel Cavicchi, Charles Keil, and the Music
in Daily Life Project

Running with the Devil: Power, Gender, and Madness in Heavy Metal Music
by Robert Walser

Subcultural Sounds: Micromusics of the West by Mark Slobin

Upside Your Head! Rhythm and Blues on Central Avenue by Johnny Otis

Dissonant Identities: The Rock'n'Roll Scene in Austin, Texas by Barry Shank

Black Noise: Rap Music and Black Culture in Contemporary America
by Tricia Rose

Club Cultures: Music, Media and Distinction by Sarah Thornton

Music, Society, Education by Christopher Small

*Listening to Salsa: Gender, Latin Popular Music, and
Puerto Rican Cultures* by Frances Aparicio

Any Sound You Can Imagine: Making Music/Consuming Technology
by Paul Théberge

Voices of Bali: Energies and Perceptions in Vocal and Dance Theater
by Edward Herbst

*A Thousand Honey Creeks Later: My Life in Music from Basie to
Motown—and Beyond* by Preston Love

Musicking: The Meanings of Performing and Listening
by Christopher Small

CHRISTOPHER SMALL

Musicking

THE MEANINGS OF
PERFORMING AND
LISTENING

WESLEYAN UNIVERSITY PRESS

Published by University Press of New England

Hanover and London

WESLEYAN UNIVERSITY PRESS
Published by University Press of New England,
Hanover, NH 03755
© 1998 by Christopher Small
All rights reserved
Printed in the United States of America   5 4 3 2 1
CIP data appear at the end of the book

Contents

Musicking

Prelude
Music and Musicking

✳

In a concert hall, two thousand people settle in their seats, and an intense silence falls. A hundred musicians bring their instruments to the ready. The conductor raises his baton, and after a few moments the symphony begins. As the orchestra plays, each member of the audience sits alone, listening to the work of the great, dead, composer.

In a supermarket, loudspeakers fill the big space with anodyne melodies that envelop customers, checkout clerks, shelf assistants and managers, uniting them in their common purpose of buying and selling.

In a big stadium, fifty thousand voices cheer and fifty thousand pairs of hands applaud. A blaze of colored light and a crash of drums and amplified guitars greet the appearance onstage of the famous star of popular music, who is often heard on record and seen on video but whose presence here in the flesh is an experience of another kind. The noise is so great that the first few minutes of the performance are inaudible.

A young man walks down a city street, his Walkman clamped across his ears, isolating him from his surroundings. Inside his head is an infinite space charged with music that only he can hear.

A saxophonist finishes his improvised solo with a cascade of notes that ornament an old popular song. He wipes his forehead with a handkerchief and nods absently to acknowledge the applause of a hundred pairs of hands. The pianist takes up the tune.

A church organist plays the first line of a familiar hymn tune, and the congregation begins to sing, a medley of voices in ragged unison.

At an outdoor rally, with bodies erect and hands at the salute, fifty thousand men and women thunder out a patriotic song. The sounds they make rise toward the God whom they are imploring to make their country great. Others hear the singing and shiver with fear.

In an opera house, a soprano, in long blond wig and white gown streaked with red, reaches the climax of her mad scene and dies pathetically. Her death in song provokes not tears but a roar of satisfaction that echoes around the theater. As the curtain descends, hands clap thunderously and feet stamp on the floor. In a few moments, restored to life, she will appear before the curtain to receive her homage with a torrent of applause and a shower of roses thrown from the galleries.

A housewife making the beds in the morning sings to herself an old popular song, its words imperfectly remembered.

So many different settings, so many different kinds of action, so many different ways of organizing sounds into meanings, all of them given the name *music*. What is this thing called music, that human beings the world over should find in it such satisfaction, should invest in it so much of their lives and resources? The question has been asked many times over the centuries, and since at least the time of the ancient Greeks, scholars and musicians have tried to explain the nature and meaning of music and find the reason for its extraordinary power in the lives of human beings.

Many of these attempts have been complex and ingenious, and some have even possessed a kind of abstract beauty, reminding one in their complexity and ingenuity of those cycles and epicycles which astronomers invented to explain the movement of the planets before Copernicus simplified matters by placing the sun instead of the earth at the center of the system. But none has succeeded in giving a satisfactory answer to the question—or rather, pair of questions— *What is the meaning of music?* and *What is the function of music in human life?*—in the life, that is, of every member of the human species.

It is easy to understand why. Those are the wrong questions to ask. There is no such thing as music.

Music is not a thing at all but an activity, something that people do. The apparent thing "music" is a figment, an abstraction of the action, whose reality vanishes as soon as we examine it at all closely. This habit of thinking in abstractions, of taking from an action what appears to be its essence and of giving that essence a name, is probably as old as language; it is useful in the conceptualizing of our world but it has its dangers. It is very easy to come to think of the abstraction as more real than the reality it represents, to think, for example, of those abstractions which we call love, hate, good and evil as having an existence apart from the acts of loving, hating, or performing good and evil deeds and even to think of them as being in some way more real than the acts themselves, a kind of universal or ideal lying behind and suffusing the actions. This is the trap of reification, and it has been a besetting fault of Western thinking ever since Plato, who was one of its earliest perpetrators.

If there is no such thing as music, then to ask "What is the meaning of music?" is to ask a question that has no possible answer. Scholars of Western music seem to have have sensed rather than understood that this is so; but rather than directing their attention to the activity we call music, whose meanings have to be grasped in time as it flies and cannot be fixed on paper, they have quietly carried out a process of elision by means of which the word *music* becomes equated with "works of music in the Western tradition." Those at least do seem to have a real existence, even if the question of just *how* and *where* they exist does create problems. In this way the question "What is the meaning of music?" becomes the more manageable "What is the meaning of this work (or these works) of music?"—which is not the same question at all.

This privileging of Western classical music above all other musics is a strange and contradictory phenomenon. On the one hand, it is claimed to be an intellectual and spiritual achievement that is unique in the world's musical cultures (for me the claim is summed up by the reported remark of a famous scientist who, when asked what message should be included in a missile to be fired off in search of other intelligent life in the universe, replied, "We could send them Bach, but that would be boasting"); on the other hand, it appeals to only a very tiny minority of people, even within Western industrialized societies; classical music records account for only around 3 percent of all record sales.

We even see it in the way the word *music* is commonly used; we know what kind of music is dealt with in the music departments of universities and colleges and in schools and conservatories of music, and we know what kind of music an upmarket newspaper's music critic will be writing about. In addition, musicology is, almost by definition, concerned with Western classical music, while other musics, including even Western popular musics, are dealt with under the rubric of ethnomusicology (the real musical study of Western popular musics, in their own terms rather than those of classical music, is only just beginning and does not yet dare to call itself musicology).

The contradiction extends to the nature of the music itself; on the one hand, it is regarded as the model and paradigm for all musical experience, as can be seen from the fact that a classical training is thought to be a fit preparation for any other kind of musical performance (a famous violinist records "jazz" duets with Stéphane Grappelli, and operatic divas record songs from Broadway musicals, all without apparently hearing their own stylistic solecisms); and on the other, it is regarded as somehow unique and not to be subjected to the same modes of inquiry as other musics, especially in respect to its social meanings; brave spirits who have attempted to do so have brought the wrath of the musicological establishment down on their heads. Even those who try to right the balance by comparative study of other human musics most often avoid comparisons with Western classical music, thus emphasizing, if only in a negative way, its uniqueness and implicitly privileging it in reverse, although it is in fact a perfectly normal human music, an ethnic music if you like, like any other and, like any other, susceptible to social as well as purely musical comment.

So it is that while scholars of music may disagree of any number of matters, there is one matter on which there is virtually unanimous agreement, all the more powerful for being for the most part undiscussed and unspoken. It is that the essence of music and of whatever meanings it contains is to be found in those things called musical works—works, that is, of Western classical music. The most succinct modern formulation of the idea comes perhaps from the doyen of contemporary German musicologists, Carl Dalhaus (1983), who tells us, flatly, that "the subject matter of music is made up, primarily, of significant works of music that have outlived the culture of their age" and that "the concept 'work' and not 'event' is the cornerstone of music history." Any history of music will bear out Dalhaus's contention. They are primarily histories of those things which are works of music and of the people who made them, and they tell us about the circumstances of their creation, about the factors that influenced their nature, and about the influence they have had on subsequent works.

It is not only historians who assume the primacy of musical works but also musicologists, whose purpose is to ascertain the real nature and contours of musical works by recourse to original texts, as well as theorists, whose purpose is to discover the way in which the works are constructed as objects in themselves, and aestheticians, who deal with the meaning of sound objects and the reasons for their effect on a listener. All are concerned with things, with musical works. Even the recent area of study known as "reception history" deals not, as one might reasonably expect, with performance itself but with the changing ways in which musical works have been perceived by their audiences during the term of their existence. The part played by the performers in that perception does not come into consideration; when performance is discussed at all, it is spoken of as if it were nothing more than a presentation, and generally an approximate and imperfect presentation at that, of the work that is being performed. It is rare indeed to find the act of musical performance thought of as possessing, much less creating, meanings in its own right.

The presumed autonomous "thingness" of works of music is, of course, only part of the prevailing modern philosophy of art in general. What is valued is not the action of art, not the act of creating, and even less that of perceiving and responding, but the created art object itself. Whatever meaning art may have is thought to reside in the object, persisting independently of what the perceiver may bring to it. It is simply there, floating through history untouched by time and change, waiting for the ideal perceiver to draw it out.

It is for the sake of that unchanging, immanent meaning that paintings, books, pieces of sculpture and other art objects (including musical works and the scores that in some not quite understood way are supposed to be the bearers of them) are cared for, lovingly exhibited in air-conditioned museums (and concert halls), sold for exorbitant prices (the autograph score of Schumann's Piano Concerto in A Minor was sold in London in 1989 for nearly one and a half million dollars), printed in luxurious editions, pursued to the creator's manuscript (and performed in "authentic" versions). The critic Walter Benjamin encapsulated the idea in one memorable sentence: "The supreme reality of art," he wrote, "is the isolated, self-contained work."

This idea, that musical meaning resides uniquely in music objects, comes with a few corollaries. The first is that musical performance plays no part in the creative process, being only the medium through which the isolated, self-contained work has to pass in order to reach its goal, the listener. We read little in music literature about performance other than in the limited sense of following the composer's notations and realizing them in sound, and we are left to conclude that the more transparent the medium the better.

There are even those who believe that, since each performance is at best only an imperfect and approximate representation of the work itself, it follows that music's inner meanings can never be properly yielded up in performance. They can be discovered only by those who can read and study the score, like Johannes Brahms, who once refused an invitation to attend a performance of Mozart's *Don Giovanni*, saying he would sooner stay home and read it. What Mozart, the supreme practical musician, would have had to say about that one can only imagine. We note the corollary to *that* idea, which is seriously held by many musical scholars and even musicians: only those who can read a score have access to the inner meanings of music. One wonders, in that case, why we should bother performing musical works at all, when we could just sit at home, like Brahms, and read them as if they were novels.

As for performers, we hear little about them either, at least not as creators of musical meaning. It seems that they can clarify or obscure a work, present it adequately or not, but they have nothing to contribute to it; its meaning has been completely determined before a performer ever lays eyes on the score. Composers, especially in the twentieth century, have often railed against the "liberties" taken by performers who dare to interpose themselves, their personalities and their ideas between composer and listener. Igor Stravinsky (1947) was especially vehement in this regard, condemning "interpretation" in terms that seem as much moral as purely aesthetic and demanding from the performer a rigidly objective approach called by him "execution," which he characterized as "the strict putting into effect of an explicit will that contains nothing beyond what it specifically commands." The eagerness with which many composers took up electronic composition from the 1950s onward was motivated at least in part by the prospect of dispensing altogether with the services of those troublesome fellows.

The second corollary is that a musical performance is thought of as a one-way system of communication, running from composer to individual listener through the medium of the performer. This is perhaps just another way of stating the first, though it brings a change of emphasis, for it suggests that the listener's task is simply to contemplate the work, to try to understand it and to respond to it, but that he or she has nothing to contribute to its meaning. That is the composer's business.

It suggests also that music is an individual matter, that composing, performing and listening take place in a social vacuum; the presence of other listeners is at best an irrelevance and at worst an interference in the individual's contemplation of the musical work as it is presented by the performers. A flowchart of communication during a performance might show arrows pointing from composer to performers and a multitude of arrows pointing from performers to as many listeners as are present; but what it will not show is any arrow pointing in the reverse direction, indicating feedback from listener to performers and certainly not to composer (who in any case is probably dead and so cannot possibly receive any feedback). Nor would it show any that ran from listener to listener; no interaction is assumed there.

A third corollary is that no performance can possibly be better than the work that is being performed. The quality of the work sets an upper limit to the possible quality of the performance, so an inferior work of music cannot possibly give rise to a good performance. We all know from experience that that is nonsense; performers are always capable of turning trivial material into great performances. Adelina Patti could reduce an audience to tears singing "Home Sweet Home," while the wealth of meanings that Billie Holiday was able to create with her performances of the tritest of popular songs is both legendary and documented on record. Were it not so, then much of the culture of opera would collapse, for who would tolerate the musical and dramatic absurdities of *Lucia di Lammermoor,* for example, or of Gounod's *Faust* if it were not for the opportunities the old warhorses give singers to show off their powers?

But I should go further and shall argue later that it is not just great performers who are capable of endowing such material with meaning and beauty. However trivial and banal the work may be that is the basis of the performance, meaning and beauty are created whenever any performer approaches it with love and with all the skill and care that he or she can bring to it. And of course it is also possible to give a beautiful performance without any work of music at all being involved, as thousands of improvising musicians have demonstrated.

A fourth corollary is that each musical work is autonomous, that is to say, it exists without necessary reference to any occasion, any ritual, or any particular set of religious, political, or social beliefs. It is there purely for what the philosopher Immanuel Kant called "disinterested contemplation" of its own inherent qualities. Even a work that started its life as integrally attached to a myth and to the ritual enactment of that myth, as, for example, did Bach's *Saint Matthew Passion,* which was intended as part of the Good Friday obsequies of the Lutheran Church, is today performed in concert halls as a work of art in its own right, whose qualities and whose meaning for a modern listener are supposed to depend solely on its qualities "as music" and have nothing to do with the beliefs that Bach believed he had embodied in it.

My musical friends scoff at me when I say I can hardly bear to listen to the piece, so powerfully and so cogently does it embody a myth that to me is profoundly antipathetic. "Don't bother about all that," they say, "just listen to the marvelous music." Marvelous music it is indeed, but marvelous for what? That is a question that seems never to be asked, let alone answered. Other musical cultures, including our own past, would find such attitudes curious; Bach himself, could he know about them, might well feel that his masterpiece was being trivialized.

Neither the idea that musical meaning resides uniquely in musical objects nor any of its corollaries bears much relation to music as it is actually practiced throughout the human race. Most of the world's musicians—and by that word I mean, here and throughout this book, not just professional musicians, not just those who make a living from singing or playing or composing, but anyone who sings or plays or composes—have no use for musical scores and do not treasure musical works but simply play and sing, drawing on remembered melodies and rhythms and on their own powers of invention within the strict order of tradition. There may not even be any fixed and stable musical work, so the performer creates as he or she performs while the listeners, should there be any apart from the performers, have an important and acknowledged creative role to play in the performance through the energy they feed (or fail to feed), selectively and with discrimination, back to the performers.

But even within a literate musical culture such as the Western classical tradition the exclusive concentration on musical works and the relegation of the act of performance to subordinate status has resulted in a severe misunderstanding of what actually takes place during a performance. That misunderstanding has, as we shall see, had in turn its effect on the performance itself—on the experience, that is, of the performance, for both performers and listeners—an effect that I believe to have been more to impoverish than to enrich it. For *performance does not exist in order to present musical works, but rather, musical works exist in order to give performers something to perform.*

That being so, a musical performance is a much richer and more complex affair than is allowed by those who concentrate their attention exclusively on the musical work and on its effect on an individual listener. If we widen the circle of our attention to take in the entire set of relationships that constitutes a performance, we shall see that music's primary meanings are not individual at all but social. Those social meanings are not to be hived off into something called a "sociology" of music that is separate from the meaning of the sounds but are fundamental to an understanding of the activity that is called music.

The fundamental nature and meaning of music lie not in objects, not in musical works at all, but in action, in what people do. It is only by understanding what people do as they take part in a musical act that we can hope to understand its nature and the function it fulfills in human life. Whatever that function may be, I am certain, first, that to take part in a music act is of central importance to our very humanness, as important as taking part in the act of speech, which it so resembles (but from which it also differs in important ways), and second, that everyone, every normally endowed human being, is born with the gift of music no less than with the gift of speech. If that is so, then our present-day concert life, whether "classical" or "popular," in which the "talented" few are empowered to produce music for the "untalented" majority, is based on a falsehood. It means that our powers of making music for ourselves have been hijacked and the majority of people robbed of the musicality that is theirs by right of birth, while a few stars, and their handlers, grow rich and famous through selling us what we have been led to believe we lack.

This book, then, is not so much about music as it is about people, about people as they play and sing, as they listen and compose, and even as they dance (for in many cultures if no one is dancing then no music is happening, so integral is dance to the musical act), and about the ways in which they—we—go about singing and playing and composing and listening. It is also about the reasons we feel the urge to do these things and why we feel good when we do them well. We could say that it is not so much about *music* as about people *musicking*.

So far as I know the word *musicking* does not appear in any English dictionary, but it is too useful a conceptual tool to lie unused. It is the present participle, or gerund, of the verb *to music*. This verb does have an obscure existence in some larger dictionaries, but its potential goes unexploited because when it does appear it is used to mean roughly the same as "to perform" or "to make music"—a meaning that is already well covered by those two words. I have larger ambitions for this neglected verb.

I have proposed this definition: *To music is to take part, in any capacity, in a musical performance, whether by performing, by listening, by rehearsing or practicing, by providing material for performance (what is called composing), or by dancing.* We might at times even extend its meaning to what the person is doing who takes the tickets at the door or the hefty men who shift the piano and the drums or the roadies who set up the instruments and carry out the sound checks or the cleaners who clean up after everyone else has gone. They, too, are all contributing to the nature of the event that is a musical performance.

It will become clear as we go along how useful this verb—and especially its gerund—is (the added *k* is not just a caprice but has historical antecedents), and I shall use it from now on as if it were the proper English language verb that I hope it will become.

I have to make two things clear. The first is that to pay attention in any way to a musical performance, including a recorded performance, even to Muzak in an elevator, is to music. The second is related but needs to be stated separately: the verb *to music* is not concerned with valuation. It is *de*scriptive, not *pre*scriptive. It covers all participation in a musical performance, whether it takes place actively or passively, whether we like the way it happens or whether we do not, whether we consider it it interesting or boring, constructive or destructive, sympathetic or antipathetic. The word will remain useful only for so long as we keep our own value judgments clear of it. Value-laden uses that I have heard, such as "Everyone ought to music" or "You can't call listening to a Walkman musicking," distort its meaning, weaken its usefulness as an investigative tool, and plunge us back into futile arguments about what music or musicking is. Value judgments come later, if they come at all.

Apart from favoring the idea that music is first and foremost action, the word has other useful implications. In the first place, in making no distinction between what the performers are doing and what the rest of those present are doing, it reminds us that musicking (you see how easy it is to slip into using it) is an activity in which all those present are involved and for whose nature and quality, success or failure, everyone present bears some responsibility. It is not just a matter of composers, or even performers, actively doing something to, or for, passive listeners. Whatever it is we are doing, we are all doing it together—performers, listeners (should there be any apart from the performers), composer (should there be one apart from the performers), dancers, ticket collectors, piano movers, roadies, cleaners and all.

I am not, of course, so silly as to see no distinction between what the performers are doing and what the cleaners are doing; they are obviously doing different things, and when we want to distinguish between the two sets of activities we already have adequate words with which to do so. In using the verb *to music*, on the other hand, we are reminded that all these different activities add up to a single event, whose nature is affected by the ways in which all of them are carried out, and we have a tool by means of which we can begin to explore the meanings that the event as a whole is generating. We take into account not just what the performers are doing and certainly not just the piece that is being played or what the composer, should there be one, has done. We begin to see a musical performance as an encounter between human beings that takes place through the medium of sounds organized in specific ways. Like all human encounters, it takes place in a physical and a social setting, and those, too, have to be taken into account when we ask what meanings are being generated by a performance.

That being so, it is not enough to ask, *What is the nature or the meaning of this work of music?* To do so leaves us trapped in the assumptions of the modern Western concert tradition, and even within those limits, so narrow when one considers the whole field of human musicking, it will give answers that are at best partial and even contradictory. And of course, if there is no fixed and stable musical work, as is true of many cultures, then the question cannot even be asked. Using the concept of musicking as a human encounter, we can ask the wider and more interesting question: *What does it mean when this performance (of this work) takes place at this time, in this place, with these participants?* Or to put it more simply, we can ask of the performance, any performance anywhere and at any time, *What's really going on here?* It is at that point, and not before, that we can allow our value judgments full rein—if we wish to do so.

In framing that question, I have placed the words "of this work" in parentheses to remind us that there may not necessarily be a musical work but that when there is, then the nature of that work is part of the nature of the performance, and whatever meanings it may in itself possess are part of the meaning of the event—an important part but only a part. I do this in order to reassure those who fear that I am going to ignore the part that the nature of the work plays in the nature of the performance or even that I am going to deny its existence altogether. Of course not; those set sequences of sounds we call works, or pieces, of music form an important part of the musical economy of the modern world, from the Ninth Symphony of Beethoven to "Rudolph the Red Nosed Reindeer."

But they are not the whole of musicking and in fact are not even necessary for it to take place, as can be seen from the large number of human musical cultures in which there is no such thing as a musical work, in which there are only the activities of singing, playing, listening—and most probably, dancing.

Thus we see that the second question does not exclude the first but rather subsumes it, into a larger and more comprehensive question. In addition, if the definition of musicking I have offered takes in all the activities that affect the nature of that event which is a performance, then that must include preparing for it. That means that composing, practicing and rehearsing, performing, and listening are not separate processes but are all aspects of the one great human activity that is called musicking. And if the meaning of the work is part of the meaning of the event, then the opposition between "work" and "event" expressed by Carl Dalhaus does not exist.

By expanding our questioning to the total performance we can escape from the assumptions of the Western concert tradition as it exists today, which continue to dominate the ways in which we think about music; and we can see that tradition, as it were from the outside, as a small and these days (it was not always so) tranquil (some might even say stagnant) lagoon of the great restless ocean of human musicking. We may see also that, when viewed from outside, it is less isolated from that great ocean than those who look only from inside may think and perhaps also that whatever vitality we can continue to find in it today is, as it always has been, produced by the quickening effect of the life-giving water of that great ocean.

Any theory of musicking, which is to say any attempt to explain its meaning and its function in human life, that cannot be used to account for all human musicking, no matter how strange, primitive or even antipathetic it may seem to our perceptions, is not worth the paper it is written on. It is not just a question of why the *Saint Matthew Passion* of J. S. Bach and the Ninth Symphony of Beethoven are great works—which they undoubtedly are, once we accept the premises on which they were composed. It is not even just a question of why people like to sing and to hear

"Rudolph the Red Nosed Reindeer" or "Does Your Chewing Gum Lose Its Flavor on the Bedpost Over Night?" or why drunken ol' pals like to gather around the piano and sing bawdy songs together in rustic harmony. It must also explain why it is that taking part in a performance of the *Saint Matthew Passion* or the Ninth Symphony or "Rudolph the Red Nosed Reindeer" arouses in some a powerful and joyful emotional response while in others it induces only boredom and irritation.

But the theory must go further, and be able to explain why Indonesians enjoy taking part in performances of gamelan music, why the Ewe of Ghana like to play, sing and dance to Afro-Cuban popular music as well as the *adzida* dance, and why many, but by no means all, African Americans like to sing and to hear gospel songs. It must also be able to explain why so many white people go for African American blues, some of them even becoming successful and admired practitioners, why rap has become an important and influential way of musicking on both sides of the American color barrier, and how it is that reggae got big in Japan.

It must be able to explain, in fact, not just why members of one social and cultural group differ in their ways of musicking from members of another group but how it is that members of one culture can come to understand and to enjoy, and perhaps creatively misunderstand, the musicking of others. It must explain also how some musical cultures become dominant, sometimes across the whole world, while others remain confined to the social group within which they originated. And of course it must be able to explain why people like to music at all.

There is no dearth of studies, many of them brilliant and illuminating, of musicking's social function, that show the ways in which musicking functions as a social and even a political act. Nor do we lack for studies of the dazzling series of interactions, fusions, crossovers and hybridizations that are taking place today between musicians the world over. In this book there is no way in which I could possibly deal with all these phenomena even if I had the knowledge and experience to do so. Nor am I trying to give an account of what musicking has become in our time or of how it got to be that way; I shall have little to say about recording, broadcasting or what has become known as the music industry.

My purpose here is different—at the same time more modest and more ambitious. It is to propose a framework for understanding all musicking as a human activity, to understand not just *how* but *why* taking part in a musical performance acts in such complex ways on our existence as individual, social and political beings. What I am proposing is a way of interpreting what we already know about human musicking, a *theory of musicking* if you like.

Who needs a theory of musicking? Surely, such a thing is too academic to be of either interest or use to ordinary people?

Everyone, whether aware of it or not, has what we can loosely call a theory of musicking, which is to say, an idea of what musicking is, of what it is not, and of the part it plays in our lives. As long as that theory remains unconscious and unthought about, it not only controls people and their musical activities, limiting and circumscribing their capabilities, but also renders them vulnerable to manipulation by those those who have an interest in doing so for purposes of power, status, or profit. It is one of my aims in this book to make readers more aware of the the nature of their "theories" of musicking and thus be in a better position to take control of their musical lives. A theory of musicking, like the act itself, is not just an affair for intellectuals and "cultured" people but an important component of our understanding of ourselves and of our relationships with other people and the other creatures with which we share our planet. It is a political matter in the widest sense.

If everyone is born musical, then everyone's musical experience is valid. That being so, a theory of musicking, if it is to have any basis in real life, must stand up to being tested against the musical experience of every human being, no matter who he or she may be or how the experience was acquired. For that reason I shall write in terms that are as closely tied to concrete musical experience as I can make them, and I ask in turn that every reader test everything that I have to say against his or her own experience.

So if the meaning of music lies not just in musical works but in the totality of a musical performance, where do we start to look for insights that will unite the work and the event and allow us to understand it?

The answer I propose is this. The act of musicking establishes in the place where it is happening a set of relationships, and it is in those relationships that the meaning of the act lies. They are to be found not only between those organized sounds which are conventionally thought of as being the stuff of musical meaning but also between the people who are taking part, in whatever capacity, in the performance; and they model, or stand as metaphor for, ideal relationships as the participants in the performance imagine them to be: relationships between person and person, between individual and society, between humanity and the natural world and even perhaps the supernatural world. These are important matters, perhaps the most important in human life, and how we learn about them through musicking is what this book is about.

As we shall see, the relationships of a musical performance are enormously complex, too complex, ultimately, to be expressed in words. But that does not mean that they are too complex for our minds to encompass.

The act of musicking, in its totality, itself provides us with a language by means of which we can come to understand and articulate those relationships and through them to understand the relationships of our lives.

That being so, we need to look as well as listen around us during a performance, to find out what relationships are being generated in the performance space. To show the kind of questions we might ask of a performance, I shall be examining carefully an important event in Western musical culture, namely, a symphony concert as it might take place in a concert hall anywhere in the industrialized world. I am going to try to deconstruct it, which is to say, to decipher the signals that are everywhere being given and received, and to learn the meaning not just of the musical works that are being played there but of the total event that is a symphony concert. I have three reasons for taking this event as an example.

The first is that it is likely to be an experience that most readers of this book will have undergone at least once, and you will therefore be able to check my observations against your own.

The second is that a symphony concert is a very sacred event in Western culture, sacred in the sense that its nature is assumed to be given and not open to question. I know of few writings that so much as attempt to describe it in detail, let alone question its nature. I shall therefore, and I cheerfully admit the fact, find it a pleasurable task to examine it and to ask the forbidden question, *What's really going on here?*

I have to pause here, remembering the response of some critics to my earlier attempts to deconstruct a symphony concert. It seems that I need to explain that to do this is not to anathematize or in any way pass judgment on either the event or the works that are played during its course. To try to tease out the complex texture of meanings that a musical performance — any musical performance, anywhere, at any time — generates is *not* reductive or destructive. Quite the contrary; it is to enrich our experience of it. And after all, at the very least, the ceremonies of the concert hall must, to the unbiased eye and ear, appear as strange as did those rituals of Africa and America which the first European travelers encountered and just as much in need of accounting for. As I said earlier, it is an ethnic music like any other.

Nor, in asking of a symphony concert the question *What's really going on here?* am I suggesting, as some critics seem to think, that what is going on is something sinister, something "dehumanizing" or "authoritarian" (two words recently used in this regard by a critic). It is no part of my purpose to characterize symphonic or indeed any other performance in such crude reductive terms. I simply want to show the kind of questions that we might ask of it, and I cannot help wondering if those who show such resistance to asking questions of a symphony concert might not themselves be a little afraid that they will uncover meanings they would rather not know about.

Another caution that I have learned from my critics is that I am not making the logically quite unjustified jump from deconstructing a symphony concert to characterizing (and apparently, by implication condemning) classical music as a whole. As those critics have kindly pointed out to me, there are other kinds of event within the classical music culture: chamber music concerts and opera, for example, as well as solo recitals and record evenings; and while they clearly possess many features and meanings in common with symphony concerts, they also differ from them, as can be seen from the fact that their respective audiences, while they overlap, are not identical. To those critics I can only repeat that my intention is not to give a blanket characterization of classical music but simply to show the kinds of questions one can ask of a particular kind of musical performance.

All that said, I have to confess that there is a third, more personal reason for taking the symphony concert as example. It arises from my own continuing ambivalent relationship with the Western classical tradition, with the works that are assumed to comprise it, on the one hand, and, on the other, with the institutions through and in which it is disseminated, performed, and listened to today. Despite the fact that I grew up half a world away from its heartland, I was brought up in that tradition. I learned to play its piano repertory, I listened to records and went whenever opportunities presented themselves (very rarely up to my twenties) to attend performances of the symphonic and chamber repertory; opera did not come my way until I was too old to succumb to its charms. I still get a feeling in the seat of my pants every four minutes or so when I play my magnificent new CDs of wonderful old warhorses like the *Emperor* Concerto or the Rachmaninov Second Concerto, when I used to have to get up and turn over the twelve-inch, 78-rpm record.

It is my heritage and I cannot escape it, and I understand well the continuing urge on the part of performers, as well as of musicologists, theorists, and historians, to explore those repertories and learn their secrets. I myself continue to love playing such piano works of that tradition as are within the reach of my modest technique and take every opportunity to do so, both in public and in private.

But from the moment when I began to attend large-scale public concerts, I have never felt at ease in that environment. Loving to hear and to play the works but feeling uncomfortable during the events at which they are presented has produced a deep ambivalence that has not lessened over the years. Now, in my seventy-first year, I have come nearer to pinning down what is wrong. I do not feel at ease with the social relationships of concert halls. I can say that they do not correspond with my ideal of human relationships. For me there is a dissonance between the meanings—the relationships—that are generated by the works that are being performed and those that are generated by the performance events.

I have no desire to impose these feelings on anyone who might read this book, and I hope that by acknowledging them right at the start I can avoid even the appearance of wanting to do so. I strongly suspect, however, that I am not alone in feeling as I do; if so it may be that my exploration of my ambivalent feelings might be of use to others besides myself, including perhaps, mutatis mutandis, those who feel at ease in the concert hall environment but not in certain other musical environments—a jazz or rock concert, for example.

In any case, I do not regret the dissonance, which has over the years been a rich source of feelings and ideas, nor do I feel any resentment against the culture for what is apparently my own self-exclusion from it. It is this continuing ambivalent fascination with the culture of the concert hall that leads me to frame a question—a subquestion, if you like, of that which I framed a few pages back: *What does it mean to take part in a performance of Western concert music in a concert hall in these closing years of the twentieth century?* I shall be devoting a substantial part of this book to an exploration of this question.

There must be a link between the nature of symphonic works and the nature of the events at which they are played. That link is flexible, as we can see from the fact that most of them were first played to different audiences and under different conditions from those under which they are played and listened to today; but it must, on the other hand, exist, since only works from a certain specific repertory are displayed at modern symphony concerts. One does not hear "Rudolph the Red Nosed Reindeer" there, or "Black and Tan Fantasy" or "Please Please Me"; they are heard in other places, under other conditions. That leads me to a difficult question, which I hesitate to ask but must ask: *Is there something built into the nature of the works of that repertory that makes performing and listening to them under any circumstances go counter to the way I believe human relationships should be?* Do they sing a siren song? Or to put it in newspaper headline terms, *Was even Mozart wrong?* Many people whose views I respect would answer those questions with a firm yes.

Nevertheless, I feel the case for the prosecution has yet to be proved. The various counsels for the defense, in schools, music colleges, and universities, may be overemphatic in defense of their client and overeager to claim privilege for it, but we are not in a court of law, and an adversarial stance does little good for either side. Besides, as long as they center their argument on music objects and ignore the music act, centering on music rather than musicking, the cycles and epicycles keep spinning merrily, and the question can never be answered. Maybe that is why they do it. In any case, that is one reason the question must be asked in a new way.

It seems obvious to me that performing these works under certain circumstances generates different meanings from performing them under others. For instance, when I, an amateur pianist using material provided by Josef Haydn under the name of Piano Sonata in E-flat and charging nothing for admission, play the piano to a couple hundred of my fellow citizens of the little Catalan town where I live, people from a variety of occupations that could be called working-class as well as middle-class, most of whom I know and who know me, at least by sight in the street, I think we are together making different meanings from those made when a famous virtuoso pianist performs from that same material to an anonymous paying audience in a big concert hall. At the same time, since we are both playing from the same material, making more or less the same sounds in the same relationships, there must also be a residue of meanings that are common to both performances. Maybe if we knew completely where the differences and the similarities lay, we should understand completely the nature of musical performance. In any case the first step is taken when we ask the question *What's really going on here?*

But do not expect from me any final or definite answer to that or any other questions that I may raise in this book. In the first place, I do not think there *are* final and definite answers to any of the really important questions in human life; there are only useful and useless answers—answers, that is, that lead in the direction of enrichment of experience or of its impoverishment. And in the second place, it is one of the assumptions on which I write that you, the reader, are perfectly capable of coming up with your own answers, just as you are capable of doing your own musicking. All I hope to do is help frame the questions, for if questions are not framed properly, then there is not much hope of coming up with right, or useful, answers.

There will be times when, in order to make a question clear, I have to propose an answer—and I do have answers of my own, many of them strongly felt, that I do not intend even to try to keep under wraps. But as I used to say to my students, I don't care whether or not you agree with my answers, so long as you see that there are questions to be asked.

The majority of this book, then, will be taken up with a description, as fine-grained as I can make it, of the ceremony in Symphony Hall and of the human and sonic relationships (and the relationships between those relationships) that are being generated there. I wish it were possible to run at the same time, in counterpoint as it were, a parallel text that explains why I believe it is important to understand the nature of these relationships. But (and it is one of the themes of this book) while the gestures of musicking can articulate many kinds of relationship at once, words, on the other hand, can deal with things only one at a time, and there is no way they can be made to bear the cargo of multiple simultaneous meanings that the gestures of musicking can do. I shall therefore be obliged to pause from time to time in my description and to interpolate three interludes, which I hope will gave a more theoretical understanding of my search for the meaning of a musical performance. They are only loosely attached to the description that precedes them, and readers who wish to continue following the description uninterrupted could leave them to one side and come back to them later.

So let us begin by looking and listening carefully around us at this symphony concert. It does not matter too much where it is taking place, for it is an international ceremony; that is part of its nature. It might be taking place in New York, London, Tokyo, Wellington, Taipei, Minsk, Reykjavik, or Denton, Texas. Wherever the Western scientific-industrial culture has gone and wherever a middle class has grown prosperous from its activities, there we shall find symphony concerts taking place and concert halls built to house them.

CHAPTER I

A Place for Hearing

*

The chances are that it is a modern building, built since the Second World War. The last fifty years or so have seen a doubling of the number of professional symphony orchestras in the world, as the Western classical music tradition has moved into regions where it was previously unheard, and an explosion of concert hall building has taken place to house those orchestras and their performances. Countries and cities that wish to signal their entry into the "developed" world often do so through the construction of a "center for the performing arts," of which the centerpiece is a big concert hall, and through the establishment of a symphony orchestra to play there. In addition, many cities in the older industrial countries have decided that their existing nineteenth- or early-twentieth-century hall is too small, or insufficiently specialized, or that it projects an image that is not up to date and have commissioned replacements. So today modern concert halls greatly outnumber older ones.

As we approach the building, our first impression is likely to be of its great size. It is a landmark in the cityscape, and even its external appearance tells us that it was built with no expense spared, probably in the forefront of the design and building technology of its day. It stands most likely on a prominent site, on a rise perhaps, in a park, beside a river or harbor, or as the focal point of a complex of civic buildings. It is probably located slightly apart from the commercial center of the city, possibly surrounded by gardens and fountains, and at night it will almost certainly be floodlit. In the winter darkness it blazes with light inside and out, a beacon of culture in the philistine world of commerce that surrounds it, welcoming the initiated with dignity and discreet opulence but making no attempt to attract the vulgar with those flashing neon signs and brightly colored posters which one sees outside cinemas and other places of popular entertainment.

Every building, from the tiniest hut to the biggest airport terminal, is designed and built to house some aspect of human behavior and relationships, and its design reflects its builders' assumptions about that behavior and those relationships. Once built, it then has the power to impose those assumptions on what goes on within it. A conventional school building, for example, with its rows of boxlike classrooms joined by corridors, its assembly hall, its gymnasium and its staff room, is built in accordance with certain assumptions about what young people in our society ought to learn and how they ought to learn it. But it also enforces those assumptions, making difficulties for those who might have different ideas. Even so everyday a structure as a family house or apartment makes, and enforces, certain assumptions about family life and its relationships, about childhood, privacy, cleanliness and sex.

The scale of any building, and the attention that is paid to its design and appearance, tell us much about the social importance and status that is accorded to what goes on within it. The decline in the importance of rail transport is clearly mirrored in the modest appearance of most twentieth-century railroad stations in comparison with the splendor of those built in the great era of nineteenth-century railroad building, when the railroad signified a quantum leap in human mobility and speed of travel. Today their splendor has passed to airport terminals.

Some buildings lend themselves to uses, to the housing of sets of relationships, that were not foreseen by their builders. The great Victorian railway engineer Robert Stephenson could never have dreamed that the magnificent roundhouse he built for one of his new London terminals would in the 1960s begin a new life as a versatile performance space. Such new careers for buildings depend on their not having been designed too rigidly for their original function. For while some buildings leave room for a variety of activities and relationships, others impose their structure very firmly on what goes on within them.

Modern concert halls fall mainly into the latter category. They are highly specialized buildings, designed down to the last detail to house not just musical performances but performances of a very specific kind. The architects who design them, and the committees of civic authorities who commission and approve the designs, are for the most part members of the social group that tends to take part in such events. They know how people are supposed to behave there and will shape the building in ways that will encourage that behavior, at the same time closing off the possibility of behaviors of different kinds.

Perhaps the most interesting thing about this building may be that it is here at all. For musicking, even large-scale musicking, does not *need* a building such as this. Human beings have been musicking for as long as there have been humans and have done so mainly without feeling the need for a specialized building to house their activities, certainly not for anything on so grand a scale as this, anything so opulent or so impressive. If the cathedrals and palaces that in Europe in earlier times were the scenes of many such performances were grand and opulent, if was not for the sake of the performances themselves but for the religious or aristocratic ceremonies of which the performances were no more than a part.

The grandeur of this building is something else, and it tells us loudly and clearly that the performances that take place here are an important social activity in their own right, not just as part of another ceremony or event. It tells us also that those who consider them important have the confidence and possess, or at least control, the wealth and the power to actualize that belief in architectural form.

If the idea of an event that consists entirely of a musical performance, with no other social function than playing and listening to music, is a modern one, so is the building that is built expressly to house such an event. The large purpose-built concert hall is essentially a nineteenth-century invention. Only a handful were built before the turn of the nineteenth century, and almost all were tiny by present-day standards. Even many of the big nineteenth-century halls that are now used from time to time for symphony concerts, like London's six-thousand-seat Royal Albert Hall, were intended, and are still used, as multipurpose places of assembly, symphony concerts taking place among balls, political rallies, boxing matches, and the like. These are the halls that, even though they may have served very well for symphonic performances for more than a hundred years, are now being replaced by more specialized buildings. This means that virtually all musical works composed before the late eighteenth or early nineteenth century, and many later ones as well, are out of their original setting when they are played in a concert hall.

The architectural style of older concert halls, even those which have been built outside Europe, first in the Americas and later in more remote colonies such as my own country (Wellington built itself a fine one in Italian baroque style in 1904, barely sixty years after the first British settlers arrived in New Zealand), generally emphasizes a continuity with the past of European culture. It may be plain classic, exuberant baroque, Renaissance, or a mixture of these, so the building may remind us of a Greek or Roman temple, of an Italian Renaissance palace, a French château, or even, in the case of Barcelona's dazzling Palau de la Mùsica Catalana, an art nouveau fantasy world straight out of the pages of William Morris's *News from Nowhere* (an appropriate evocation perhaps for a building that was built for their own performances by a workers' choir in the early twentieth century, before socialism became a dirty word).

I cannot remember seeing a concert hall built in Gothic style, possibly because its association with a mystical, theocentric culture is felt to be out of place in the rational, humanistic world of classical music. Despite the widespread use of Gothic Revival in the nineteenth century for anything from railway stations to London's Houses of Parliament, neither of the two great Gothic Revival architects, Gilbert Scott in England and Viollet-le-Duc in France, ever got to build a Gothic concert hall.

The entrance facade is impressive (in older buildings a tall classical colonnade surmounted with a pediment like a Greek temple is a favorite device) and is intended to make entry into the building an event of importance. We pass through the doorway into a lobby with a row of ticket windows, the only visible sign in this big building of a link with the everyday world of commerce and money. We have had the foresight to pay in advance the money that entitles us to take part in the event, so, armed with the tickets that are the symbol of that entitlement, we walk past the windows, where a line of people is waiting to pay and be admitted.

At an inner door we show our tickets to an attendant who stands guard to ensure that only those entitled to do so will enter. He takes the tickets, returns the stubs that bear the numbers of the seats we have been allotted, and politely motions us on. Passing through the door, we find ourselves in a grand ceremonial space. Now we have entered another world, apart from that of our everyday life.

The space extends around us, lofty and sumptuous. If it is in an older building, it will most probably be formal and rectangular, matching in style the building's exterior, lit perhaps by big chandeliers and decorated with statuary and mirrors. In more recent halls, it may well be asymmetrical, with staircases rising in unexpected ways, ceiling sloping this way and that and even curved, with angled walls that trick the sense of perspective, all carried out with up-to-date skill and technological daring that is clearly intended to place the building and what goes on within it squarely within today's up-to-date technological culture.

There are bars for coffee, snacks and alcoholic drinks. On the walls and display stands there are posters, some advertising future concerts and others giving the entire schedule of performances for the season. There are glossy program booklets on sale or free distribution telling us about tonight's conductor and soloist, listing the pieces to be played, and giving such background information as is thought to be necessary for full appreciation of them. We buy a booklet and thumb through it, more interested at this moment perhaps in the crowd of people who, like ourselves, are waiting for the concert to begin. There is a quiet buzz of conversation. Although there are chairs and tables, most people seem to prefer to stand and keep their ability to move around.

This, we know, is not the space where the performance is to take place but a transitional space through which we pass in the progression from the outer everyday world to the inner world of the performance. It is at first hard to understand why a mere transitional space should be so big and grand; it must have added considerably to the construction cost. Nevertheless, its spaciousness and grandeur tell us that it is an important part of the building, where an important part of the event takes place. It is a criticism I have heard made of the otherwise excellent church-turned-concert-hall, St. John's, Smith Square in London, that it has no transitional space between the outside world and the auditorium, even though it does have a place for socializing in the crypt. Traditionally, churches do not, of course, have foyers; those modern churches that do may speak of a change in the nature of the ceremonies that take place there.

The foyer is a place to eat and drink and socialize, to see and be seen. There is nothing wrong, of course, in wanting to socialize or to see and be seen; where we are seen to be, like where we are not seen to be, or seen *not* to be, is an important element in who we are. Musical performances of all kinds have always been events to which people go, at least in part, to see and be seen; it is part of the meaning of the event. In the ceremony that is to take place here, socializing and listening are kept strictly separate from each other and are allocated separate spaces.

A grand ceremonial space such as this imposes a mode of behavior on those who are unaccustomed to it. They become somewhat self-conscious, lowering their voices, muting their gestures, looking around them, bearing themselves in general more formally. They may even feel something like awe. But frequent concertgoers who are accustomed to the place cease to feel the need for such submissive behavior, and with it their demeanor changes. The muted gestures are replaced by gestures of body and voice that are not only relaxed but *signal* relaxation, gestures that say, in effect, to anyone who is watching and listening, *I am at ease in this place and with this occasion.*

One can observe similar patterns of behavior in other grand ceremonial buildings—a great church, for example, where it is the visiting unbeliever who creeps quietly around while the priest and the pious talk and joke unconstrainedly, or in a palace, an important government building or the headquarters of a big organization. All have their initiates and their outsiders, and from their behavior as they move around the building it is generally not too difficult to tell who are insiders and who outsiders, who are privy to its rituals and who are not.

It would not be stretching matters too far to call this building a sacred space. Certainly, it is the site of events that are of more than ordinary importance in the minds of those who built it and those who use it. In their minds those events need no justification; they ought to take place, and that is that. The impression of a sacred space is reinforced by witnessing the indignation of those classical music lovers who see their hall being let, perhaps by a management desperate for income in these straitened times of vanishing subsidies, for rock concerts and other kinds of events in which the rules of symphony concert decorum do not apply.

So in the foyer we take time out to assure ourselves that we are indeed present, that we belong in this place. Even if we have come alone and know nobody, we can still feel a part of the event as we buy a cup of coffee or an alcoholic drink and look around us as we sip. Among those present we might recognize celebrities—a famous violinist, the music critic of a quality newspaper, even perhaps an eminent politician. The latter may be taking cocktails with a group of expensively dressed men and women whom we can assume to be executives, and their wives, of the corporation that is sponsoring tonight's concert. They will be pleased that it is so well attended and will be occupying boxes or the two front rows. Their sponsorship, and their interest in being seen here tonight, give further confirmation that this is an event of importance in the modern world, not only, it seems, of high culture but also of commerce. All appear casually at home in this place. We remember our manners and do not stare.

A few minutes before the appointed starting time of the performance, a discreet electronic signal sounds to warn us that we should take our seats. The concert will start on time, and those who are not in their seats by then will, like the foolish virgins of the parable, find themselves shut out, at least until the end of the first piece. We mount the stairs and, following the instructions on the ticket stub, find our door and pass through into the auditorium itself.

If the entry to the foyer was impressive, that into the great inner space is dramatic. Now we have really crossed the threshold into another world, and that world opens up around and above us and envelops us. The very air feels different. Beneath the lofty ceiling sparkling with lights, row after curved row of seats separated by aisles extends across the raked floor, while above are galleries with more rows of seats. All face in the same direction, down the rake of the floor toward a raised platform at the end. This platform is itself tiered, and on it are seats facing the audience or, rather, facing concentrically toward a small dais at the front center of the platform. Behind the dais is a waist-high desk, and on it lies the score of the first piece to be played tonight, waiting for the conductor and the musicians who will between them bring the piece into existence. It is this dais and desk that together form the focus, the center of attention, of this whole vast space.

Auditoriums vary greatly in shape and size, from symmetrical boxes with galleries along the sides and at the end, through fans, horseshoes, ellipses, and parabolas to free-form spaces with cascades of seats spilling down on all sides toward the musicians' platform. They range from the plain, austere and colorless to the riotously ornate and many-colored. They might incorporate, on the one hand, features of classical, baroque, or rococo architecture: columns and pilasters, swags, cornices and pediments and even caryatids, lunette windows high up, coved and vaulted ceilings, big ornate chandeliers and maybe allegorical fresco paintings or mosaics on the walls or ceiling, or on the other hand, the common stock of modern or postmodern architecture: daringly cantilevered balconies and boxes, tentlike ceiling, asymmetrical seating, curved or strangely angled walls, cunningly concealed or brutally visible lighting, sound reflectors hanging apparently unsupported above the platform, even perhaps jokey postmodernist references to the motifs of classical or vernacular architecture, like the square-mullioned windows, resembling those in a child's drawing of a house, that confront one in the auditorium of Dallas's postmodernist Meyerson Center. (It is not only the horseshoe shape of that auditorium that reminds one of a traditional opera house; the foyer, the place for seeing and being seen, is larger and grander than the auditorium itself, while the architecture of aristocratic privilege reappears unexpectedly in the row of boxes, each with its minute retiring room barely big enough to hang a mink coat, that forms the first tier of the balconies.)

Auditoriums may be lined with wood, with plaster, with colored hangings and sculpted panels, even perhaps, as a relic of the once-fashionable "new brutalism" of the 1960s, with raw concrete still bearing the imprint of the wooden shuttering into which it was poured, or any of these in combination. In general, discreet colors are favored: pastel, ocher or white for the plasterwork; the rich tones of natural wood; hangings in the colors of natural dyes; seats upholstered in deep red, slate blue or soft sea green, with aisle carpets in matching or tastefully contrasting colors.

What they all have in common is, first, that they convey an impression of opulence, even sumptuousness. There is wealth here, and the power that wealth brings. But on the other hand, there is a careful avoidance of any suggestion of vulgarity. What is to happen here is serious and important and will not appeal to the vulgar. Second, they allow no communication with the outside world. Performers and listeners alike are isolated here from the world of their everyday lives. Commonly, there are not even windows through which light from outside may enter. Nor does any sound enter from that world, and none of the sounds that are made here will be allowed to escape out into it.

We take our allotted seats, which for tonight's concert are in the middle of a row between two aisles. When the other seats in the row are taken, we shall have to stay here for the duration of the performance; there will be no moving around. Since all the seats face in the same direction, we can talk only to our neighbors in the same row and, with more difficulty, to the person immediately behind or in front of us. If the foyer was a place for socializing, this is strictly a place for looking, listening and paying attention. It is indeed an auditorium, a place for hearing. The word itself tells us that hearing is the primary activity that takes place in it, and here indeed it is assumed that performing takes place only in order to make hearing possible.

The modern concert hall is built on the assumption that a musical performance is a system of one-way communication, from composer to listener through the medium of the performers. That being so, it is natural that the auditorium should be designed in such a way as to project to the listeners as strongly and as clearly as possible the sounds that the performers are making.

No large space, of course, can be without some sonic resonance, and over centuries musicians and listeners alike have come to accept, and eventually to feel the need for, a certain amount of resonance in the sound as an element in the communication. Those who composed for performance in the great and very resonant Gothic cathedrals wrote into their masses and motets an allowance for the enormously long time, sometimes several seconds, that it takes for each sound to die.

But concert music from the seventeenth century onward has been written with less resonant spaces in mind; the resonance must not be so strong or so prolonged as to blur the logic of the progression from one note or one chord to the next. Great care, even today as much intuitive as it is scientific, goes into the acoustic design of concert halls to give them enough resonance but not too much. Halls such as London's Royal Festival Hall that are found to be to insufficiently resonant may resort to discreet boosting of their resonance by using electronic delay circuits, but this last-resort use of modern technology is felt to be somehow out of place in the performance of symphonic music. It is felt somehow to be cheating, and it does not advertise its presence.

All other considerations are subordinated to the projection and reception of the sounds. In particular, care is taken so that listeners will not be disturbed by the presence of others as they listen. For this purpose the auditorium floor is raked to give uninterrupted sightlines, the audience is fixed in the seats and knows it is to keep still and quiet; the program booklet politely asks us to suppress our coughing, and nobody enters or leaves during a performance. The very form of the auditorium tells us that the performance is aimed not at a community of interacting people but at a collection of individuals, strangers even, who happen to have come together to hear the musical works. We leave our sociability behind at the auditorium doors.

The auditorium's design not only discourages communication among members of the audience but also tells them that they are there to listen and not talk back. The performance is a spectacle for them to contemplate, and they have nothing to contribute to its course. Such occasions as the famous riotous premiere of Stravinsky's *Rite of Spring* in Paris in 1913, one of the last occasions in the history of the Western concert tradition when the audience talked back to the performers, are now well in the past. Today's concert audiences pride themselves on their good manners, on knowing their place and keeping quiet.

Nor does the design of the building allow any social contact between performers and listeners. It seems, in fact, designed expressly to keep them apart. It is not only that the orchestra musicians enter and leave the building by a separate door from the audience and remain out of sight when not actually playing, but also that the edge of the platform forms a social barrier that is for all practical purposes as impassable as a brick wall. Not even the wraparound design of certain modern auditoriums, such as Berlin's Philharmonie or Toronto's Roy Thompson Hall, can disguise the fact that a concert hall houses two separate groups of people who never meet. The technology of the concert hall has produced a gain in acoustic clarity, but that clarity is balanced by a loss of sociability. That, of course, is the way of technologies; none comes without its price. It seems that our contemporary classical music culture feels that the gain is worth the loss.

The great building, then, dramatizes and makes visible certain types of relationships. It isolates those within it from the world of their everyday lives, it brings some together and keeps others apart, it places some in a dominant position and others in a subordinate position, and it facilitates communication in one direction but not in the other. These relationships are not god-given but were brought into existence by human beings for reasons of which they may not even be conscious but which, I believe, model or enact ideal human relationships as those taking part imagine them to be. The relationships of the building are not, of course, the total meaning of the event, being only one strand of the immensely complex web of relationships that is the performance. But they do establish some general limits, or parameters, for those relationships which can be, and are, brought into existence every time a musical performance takes place there.

We can learn much about what *is* by considering what *is not*. A building for musicking that must surely have encouraged a different set of relationships was opened in London in 1742. Its interior was portrayed by Canaletto in a painting that hangs today in London's National Gallery. It was the Rotunda in Ranelagh Pleasure Gardens.

I have discussed pleasure gardens and their musicking in another book as a "feature of London's social and musical life . . . until well into the nineteenth century. They must have been agreeable places, to which admission could be gained for a modest charge, where the finest musicians of the day were pleased to appear and some of the best musicking could be enjoyed by all regardless of social class, not as a solemn ritual but as part of an enjoyable social scene which included eating, drinking, promenading, and, occasionally, watching fireworks. They catered to a public that was not at all selected in terms of social class, and the single public enjoyed a single repertory known to all—folk music, songs, operatic and orchestral music alike" (Small 1987).

The Rotunda at Ranelagh was a remarkable and beautiful building, the grandest music room in the two hundred or so pleasure gardens of eighteenth-century London. It could not be more unlike a modern concert hall. Canaletto's painting shows a big circular space three stories high and a 150 feet in diameter with, in the center, an enormous and ornate octagonal fireplace, open on all sides, whose chimney doubles as central support for the roof. In the whole big space there are no seats.

Warm sunlight pouring in through the second-story windows and an open door shows us at floor level a continuous row of tall arcaded niches; above them is a colonnaded gallery, and above that is a row of arched clerestory windows. Big candelabra of shining brass hang from the ceiling, with a smaller one in each ground-floor niche. It must have been a glittering scene at night. At each compass point there is a two-storied arched and pedimented doorway, one of which has been blocked off to make a canopied orchestra platform on which Canaletto shows us, not very distinctly, an orchestra playing. It might be Mr. Handel directing one of his organ concertos or a concerto grosso; or that remarkable phenomenon, the eight-year-old Wolfgang Amadeus Mozart, presenting a piano concerto of his own composition; or the regular music director, Dr. Thomas Arne, directing his new symphony—they all performed there. Whatever it is they are playing, we can be sure it will be a piece that modern concert audiences sit in stillness and silence to listen to.

But that is not what the people in this picture are doing. They are standing or walking about, talking in pairs and in groups, or just coming and going, in much the same way as people do in the foyer of a modern concert hall. It appears that the building has not caused socializing and enjoying music to be divided into two separate activities as does a modern concert hall, and the members of the audience seem to be perfectly capable of doing both things at the same time. We have to assume that they were no whit less sophisticated or discerning in their musical judgment than modern audiences, since this is the period, around 1760, that is generally regarded as one of the high points in the history of the Western tradition.

Most of those present seem, at least to our eyes, to be treating the performance as background to their other social activities—there is even in the foreground a couple of small boys engaged in a bout of fisticuffs—but there is a knot of people gathered around the musicians' platform, as in a later day jazz enthusiasts would gather around the bandstand in a dance hall when one of the great bands was playing for the dancing. If the musicians are part of the social scene and do not dominate it, it is to large extent because of the circular shape of the building, which allows no direction to be the dominant one. Even the musicians' platform is unobtrusive; it looks like the afterthought that we are told it was, since the musicians were originally placed at the center of the space. Another detail emphasizes what is to our eyes the informality of the scene: in the niches around the circumference can be seen diners seated at tables. In one niche I think I can even see a waiter bending over obsequiously, taking the order. It looks like a very agreeable scene.

As we listen today, in the concert hall or on record, to the early piano concerto of Mozart, the organ concerto or concerto grosso of Handel, or the symphony of Arne, we might recall that, while the patterns of sound we hear are more or less the same as the audience in Canaletto's painting was hearing, they are an element of an experience that is very different— not better, necessarily, or worse but different. That audience took from the performance what they wanted, and we take from it what we want. Like any other building, a concert hall is a social construction, designed and built by social beings in accordance with certain assumptions about desirable human behavior and relationships. These assumptions concern not only what takes place in the building but go deep into the nature of human relationships themselves.

CHAPTER 2

A Thoroughly Contemporary Affair

As we wait for the orchestra to assemble on the stage, it is worth taking a look behind the scenes in the hall. A concert hall is a very complex place, and just to contemplate the technology and the logistics of the events that take place here can tell us much about their nature.

Very little takes place here spontaneously. Every event needs a great deal of planning and organization, both inside the hall and outside it; and an extensive infrastructure, most of it invisible to the audience, has to be brought into action if the event is to take place at all. In the first place, programs have to be planned and artists engaged well in advance of the concert. These days artists who have drawing power are probably members of the international jet set and may have to be engaged as much as years ahead.

This is quite unlike the situation that prevailed in Europe up to well into the nineteenth century, when a musician might arrive in a town or city, contact some of the musically most influential people there, and arrange a series of concerts, all within a matter of days. There were even handbooks for traveling musicians, giving the names of such people; the composer Carl Maria von Weber compiled one in the 1820s for every town of any size in Germany. No musician would give a whole concert on his own; local performers, amateur and professional, would be called in to collaborate and possibly the local orchestra with whom he would play a concerto of his own composition, the orchestra playing generally at sight or with at most a single rehearsal. Among the first to give entire solo performances was Franz Liszt, in the 1840s, who at first called them "monoconcerts" before settling on the term more familiar to us, "recital."

Artists with the kind of charisma that gives them real drawing power today would appear to be as scarce as diamonds and as hard to cultivate as orchids. The critic Norman Lebrecht (1991) notes that the shortage of star conductors is becoming a real problem for orchestras today, with a consequent inflation in fees. But orchids thrive in the rain forest without human assistance, and diamonds lie around in many places waiting to be picked up; in the same way one is led to wonder if the scarcity of stars is not created and maintained artificially. If the number of young aspirants emerging from music colleges and conservatories every year, possessing technical powers that would make Liszt or Paganini blench and trying to gain entry to the major concert circuits, is an indication, there would appear to be no shortage of musical talent across the concert and operatic world; indeed, the problem seems to be the opposite, that of finding gainful employment for this overabundance of talent and skill.

It is obvious that virtuosi and those who profit from their labors should have an interest in keeping their numbers low; as with diamonds and orchids, it is scarcity that creates their value. In this they are no different from the members of all professions, whose requirements in terms of entry qualifications are designed as much to protect the status of the profession and to maintain the price of their services by restricting numbers as they are to protect the public.

There are plenty of mechanisms for restricting entrance to the big-time concert circuit. Competitions are one; although they purport to function as devices for the discovery and nurture of talent, they in fact operate in the precisely opposite direction; no young artist these days can hope to gain entry to the big time without having been taken up by a major agency, and no major agency will touch a young artist who has not gained at least a second place in a major competition. As the number of competitions is limited, so also is the number of winners; and since competitions are a zero-sum game, for every winner there have to be losers. Those losers, unless they undergo some miraculous stroke of good fortune, are consigned to the minor circuits—although those today are rapidly shrinking because of the dominance of megabuck agencies that are interested only in stars—or to teaching, arts administration, criticism and other such fallback occupations. For every young artist who makes it to the big time there must be dozens at least who are just as good or who, since success breeds success, would be just as good if they were to receive the encouragement and experience that working in the big time brings.

As an aside, we note also that competitions by their nature favor those who are at their best in a highly competitive situation. The reticent pianistic genius Clifford Curzon once remarked in an interview that he would not have got to first base if he had been required to enter a competition; fortunately for us he belonged to the precompetition era. On the other hand, I remember hearing some years ago the winner of a BBC young conductors' competition, when interviewed on TV in the first flush of his success, announcing, rather truculently I thought, "Up to now I've been competing with others. From now on I'm competing with myself." It is in this way that the culture gets the artists it deserves.

There is plenty of evidence of manipulation by major agencies of the market in virtuosi. Over the past few years there has been a series of takeovers of of artists' agencies by megabuck operators, resulting in a small number of superagents who virtually control the market. This has resulted in an outrageous inflation of fees for a few star conductors and soloists while the orchestras they conduct and with which they play frequently teeter on the edge of bankruptcy—a process in which the stars themselves have for the most part cheerfully colluded.

In addition, a conductor's agency will often put pressure on him to employ as soloists artists who are on their books, to the point that those agencies have some of the world's major orchestras and opera houses virtually sewn up, not only for live performance but also for recordings and videos. In view of the fact that these orchestras are generally subsidized by public money, the channeling of so much of that money into the pockets of these stars, and of course of their handlers, might seem morally questionable, but it is no more than normal business practice in the contemporary world of unregulated "market values." It does emphasize the extent to which concert halls partake of the nature of that world and do not exist in isolation from it. Here, as elsewhere in the modern world, it is the passing of money that mediates relationships.

Putting together programs for a concert season is also subject to a number of constraints. The first is that most concert artists today, and to some extent conductors, have at the tips of their fingers, vocal cords or batons, ready to play or sing or even to conduct at any one time, only a relatively small repertory, and they are reluctant to spend time learning anything outside it, especially if it is to be for only one or a few performances. In addition, for many artists the choice of works is to a large extent dictated by their own management, which is naturally interested in having them please as large a public as possible.

The second is that the repertory of works that will today attract a sizable audience virtually froze around the time of the First World War, and little that has appeared since then carries the appeal for the average audience that earlier works do. There is thus only a finite number of pieces to be shared by a large number of virtuosi and orchestras, and the hall's management naturally does not want a series of performers all playing the same works night after night. The number of performances of even, say, Tchaikovsky's First Piano Concerto or Beethoven's Fifth Symphony that can be accommodated in a season is limited.

Third, there is the question of the availability of scores and sets of orchestral parts. With the great warhorses there is no problem; most orchestral managements either have their own or rent them on a permanent loan basis. But with less often played works, publishers are usually prepared to print only a limited number of copies for their hire library; and with symphony concerts an international business extending over every continent no orchestra can afford to program a work from a publisher's hire library without checking well beforehand—and that may mean months or even years ahead—that the score and orchestral parts will be available for rehearsals and performance.

All this means that who plays and what is played at each concert is the result of extensive negotiation, in which those who actually attend the concert and pay for tickets are hardly, if at all, represented. With star performers jet-setting over the face of the globe, computers as well as telephones, faxes, and E-mail are essential management tools.

Then there is the question of publicity. The potential audience has not only to be informed about the concert—about what is to be played and who is playing it—but has to be made to *want* to attend. Concert halls, and orchestras, are businesses like any other, and like all businesses they have a product to sell, namely, performances. The fact that most concert halls and orchestras receive a degree of state, municipal or private subsidy does not alter this fact; what counts is, as they say, bums on seats. Concert halls and orchestras stand in relation to their audiences as producers to consumers, and like all other producers they tailor their products to the assumed preferences of their consumers, while at the same time manipulating those preferences as best they can by deploying techniques of advertising and marketing similar to those that are used for other products.

Concert advertisements in newspapers used to confine themselves to a simple announcement of venue, date, time, performers and works. But as the competition has heated up in recent years (not so much between orchestras, since most cities have only one, but between symphony concerts and other urban entertainments), we find extensive use made of more sophisticated advertising techniques. The style of the advertising is interesting, for it often uses language and images that are similar to those used to sell high-class goods such as expensive perfumes, watches and luxury cars. It is clearly aimed at the same kind of public, or at least at a public that likes to identify itself with the buyers of such items.

I treasure a full-page advertisement that appeared on November 28, 1989 in the *New York Times*, for a series of concerts in which all of the string quartets of Beethoven were to be played. Under a large "artistic" representation of the head of the composer and a facsimile of his signature, both of them familiar icons to classical music lovers, was this text, printed in an elegant Roman typeface: "The greatest music of the greatest composer the world has known, distilled into a rare and unforgettable experience for each privileged listener by the supreme mastery of the world's greatest string quartet . . . the whole-souled dedication and devotion to the master's work of this unique ensemble has earned clamorous ovations and paeans of press praise in performance after performance the world over . . . one of the rare unforgettable experiences of a lifetime, a spiritual renewal for those who return year after year, an indescribable revelation for anyone encountering this marvelous music for the first time." And so on, with at the end the salesman's pitch: "Subscribe now and Save $15 on 6 Concerts."

Such advertisements reinforce the idea that musicians and their performances are as much a part of the modern world and its commerce as is the field of popular music, and indeed as are expensive perfumes and luxury cars and that they are equally governed by its imperatives. What one might find irritating, even a touch hypocritical, is the pretense often encountered, and clearly implied in the above advertisement, that the musicians are doing what they do for pure love of music without a thought for worldly ambition or financial gain—in contrast to rock groups and other popular performers who, of course, are only in it for the money.

Another important functionary of the modern concert world is the critic. The profession of critic developed over the nineteenth century, contemporaneously with the growth of public concerts and concert halls to which one paid for admission, and with the takeover of public performance by professional musicians. As active amateur participation in public music making declined, so did the confidence of many people in their own musical judgment. Today, with so many virtuosi, so many composers and so many orchestras and conductors vying for public attention and offering their performances as commodities for sale, it is not surprising that people should feel the need for a consumer guide, both to tell them what is good and what is bad, what is à la mode and what is passé—in short, what they should and should not buy—and to give them confidence in the rightness of their choice.

Given the mercantile and nonparticipatory nature of today's concert world, criticism is a perfectly honorable profession, but we should remember that wherever people participate fully in musical performance or where musicking is part of a larger social, religious, or political ritual, there is no need for critics. In the medieval and Renaissance church there were no critics, nor were there any in the world of palace or castle or royal or ducal opera house; as like as not it was the archbishop, king, or duke who decided what was good or bad, and everyone else agreed with him. In general the prince's ability to dictate musical taste related to the strength of his political power; Louis XIV of France, in his day the most powerful man in Europe, was also its leading tastemaker. On the other hand, among the egalitarian Ewe of Ghana, John Miller Chernoff (1979) tells us, when he played the drums badly for the dancing, people *danced* their criticism, either by dancing in a listless manner or by simplifying their dancing to help him.

Once people have been attracted to the performance and have ordered, paid for and received their tickets, in itself no mean logistic feat, they have to be brought to and taken home from the hall. Many people will have traveled considerable distances, and few will have come on foot, without relying on some form of public or private mechanized transport. Without a highly developed system of transport extending into a sizable hinterland, none of today's big concert halls would survive. This means that any concert in such a hall depends not only on international managements and advertising agencies, not only on sophisticated means of communication, but also on means of transport: airplanes, buses, trains and automobiles.

Then there is the internal organization of the hall itself. Like any other enterprise in our society, it is organized hierarchically, with its boss and its administrators as well as its proletariat, whose joint task is to keep the place running smoothly and produce concerts throughout the season without the appearance of effort. It needs accountants, lawyers and clerks; secretaries and computer operators; ticket collectors and ushers; program sellers; electricians, sound men, piano tuners, and other technicians; hefty men to shift the piano around and arrange the orchestra seating; and staff for the bars and restaurants, not to mention the cleaners, those Nibelungen of the modern industrial state without whose underpaid services not only concert halls but also school, factories, offices, and airports would quickly choke to death on their own rubbish.

Most of these people are invisible to us or at least taken for granted and unnoticed even when we do glimpse them at work, but all are working to create the illusion of a magical place set aside from everyday life, where we can contemplate, in stillness and in silence, the works of master musicians. All are contributing to the nature of the musicking, and their working relationships, and those between them and the audience, are an essential part of the relationships of the events that take place in the hall and thus of the meanings that the performances generate.

If we imagine a performance in which the members of the orchestra sold the tickets themselves, arranged their own seating and moved the piano around and where everyone, audience as well as conductor, soloist and orchestra members, stayed afterward to clean up, there would be brought into existence another set of human relationships, another kind of society. It would not necessarily be a better society, but we may be sure that those taking part would not remain strangers to one another for very long. Another set of relationships again would be created if one person were to pay the expenses of the performances and if all the audience were to be his guests, as in the old days of aristocratic patronage, or if everyone concerned in the performance were to give their services free and no admission charge were made. It is a matter of choices; there is nothing inevitable about the arrangement that prevails in today's concert halls. It was not ordained by nature but is a social arrangement.

For each concert there are a thousand details to be attended to. Program notes have to be written and edited, the program booklet designed and printed with its photos of conductor and soloist, the piano tuned and its depth of touch adjusted to the exacting demands of the famous pianist, the orchestra's seating placed in the conductor's desired manner and the correct orchestral parts for tonight's works placed on the music racks that stand before each player. The flowers that are presented to an artist with such apparent spontaneity at the end of the performance do not materialize on their own, nor does the bottle of his favorite brand of malt whisky discreetly placed in the famous conductor's dressing room. Even the disembodied hand that pulls aside the curtain or opens the door to admit the conductor to the stage belongs to someone who was told to do it.

Before a note of music has been played, the building and its mode of organization have created among those present a set of relationships, which are a microcosm of those of the larger industrial society outside its walls. As we have already noted, all the relationships of the concert hall are mediated by the passing of money. To put it flatly, those who pay for admission, whoever they may be, are entitled to enter and to take part in an event, while those who do not pay are not. And on the other side, those who get paid will play their part in making the event happen, while those who do not get paid will not. There is in our society nothing very remarkable about that, of course; what is remarkable is the care that is taken to conceal the functions of administration and accounting, to create the illusion in the great building of a magical world where things happen of themselves, where nobody has to work and nobody needs money. It is none of the audience's business how much the performers are paid—and in the case of many conductors and soloists it is remarkably difficult to find out.

If this link between the lofty ceremony of the symphony concert and the down-to-earth values of industrial society as a whole seems farfetched, consider this. In countries outside the older industrial heartland of Europe and the United States of America, an early sign that the conversion to the industrial philosophy and the social relationships that belong to it has taken place and become interiorized is often the takeover of the country's musical culture by Western-style musicking. As the relationships of industrial society take over and a middle class develops that has grown prosperous on the wealth generated by industry, so professional symphony orchestras appear in the major cities, along with opulent centers for the performing arts built to house their performances. Conservatories of Western classical music are opened and infant-prodigy virtuosi, mostly the sons and daughters of the newly wealthy middle class, begin to astonish audiences in the concert halls of the older musical centers, often showing a freshness of approach that must reflect the newness of their encounter with the musical works of the Western tradition.

On the other hand, the Western-style popular music that frequently develops at the same time tends to explore, affirm and celebrate other desired relationships and other identities, in particular that of the industrial proletariat that comes into existence to serve the purposes of the new middle class. As I noted in an earlier book (Small 1987), it tends, as a lower-status music, to be less concerned with notions of correctness and is thus able to absorb into itself elements of traditional ways of musicking, which the middle classes, in their eagerness to align themselves with the international industrial culture, reject, even though at the same time they may pay lip service to them.

It happened in Japan around the end of the nineteenth century; a marker of a kind is that the piano firm of Yamaha is now a little over a hundred years old. It happened in South Korea in the 1960s and is happening today in Indonesia and the People's Republic of China. And if a 1989 article in a London newspaper is to be believed, the wealthier parts of the Arab world are becoming interested (Campbell 1989).

This article tells us, with breathless enthusiasm, of the formation of the Royal Oman Symphony Orchestra in the oil-rich Gulf state of Muscat and Oman, by command of the sultan himself. Teenage boys are being recruited from remote tribal communities and are being trained in the English language and in the disciplines of the symphony orchestra by a former British army musician. This orchestra, if it is anything more than a passing sultanic whim, may well be part of a new phenomenon, for Muscat and Oman is not an industrial state at all in the ordinary sense and has no middle class to speak of; its wealth comes from industry at secondhand, so to speak, through supplying the oil needs of industrial states. But the article speaks clearly of the desire, on the part of the sultan at least, to show that Muscat and Oman is a civilized state. Even the headline, MUSICAL OASIS IN THE DESERT, carries an interesting implication: at last, a *real* musical culture has come to the hitherto deprived Omanis.

This state of affairs has, of course, partly to do with the fact that symphony orchestras and concert halls are expensive and can be afforded only by wealthy societies. Today that means societies that have benefited, whether directly or indirectly, from the wealth generated by industrialization. But for the Western concert tradition to become established, it needs more than the ability to afford it; it needs the desire and the will to spend the wealth on this rather than on other things, including other ways of musicking. That has to do with the acceptance of the philosophy that lies behind industrial development. I discussed this philosophy at length in an earlier book (1977) and shall not reiterate it here, but it concerns the acceptance of the scientific worldview; of Western-style rationality, including the Cartesian split between body and mind; and of the discipline of the clock. Certainly, those values are clearly in evidence in this important ceremony of the industrial middle classes.

A modern symphony concert , then, is a very different kind of event from those at which most of the musical works we hear there today were first performed. It is not unfair to compare the modern concert hall with that other contemporary leisure phenomenon, the theme park, whose archetype is the various Disneylands. There, as here, all the resources of modern technology are put unobtrusively to work to create an artificial environment, where the paying customers are led to believe that what they are experiencing is a re-creation of the world of their ancestors, without the dirt and smells perhaps, but otherwise authentic. It is, of course, nothing of the kind but is a thoroughly contemporary affair that celebrates thoroughly contemporary relationships.

Similarly, in the modern concert hall we hear the ideal relationships of the past re-created, not as they were or in their own terms, which would in any case be impossible, but in contemporary terms, which is to say, in terms of the relationships that those taking part in tonight's performance feel to be ideal. In this the relationships created by modern technology play an important, though largely unacknowledged part. The tension between those two sets of relationships is an interesting matter that I shall be exploring later.

CHAPTER 3

Sharing with Strangers

There is a telling phrase in George Lipsitz's spirited defense of American popular culture, *Time Passages* (1990), in which he speaks of audiences for the performance arts in Western industrial societies coming together to share "intimate and personal cultural moments with strangers." It is an odd thing that Lipsitz reminds us of. Whether it be a play, a film or a musical that we have come to see and hear, an opera, a symphony concert or a pop concert, not to mention a professional wrestling bout, a football game or a tennis match, we accept without thinking about it that not only the performers but also most, if not all, of the audience will be strangers to us. We are prepared to laugh, to weep, to shudder, to be excited, or to be moved to the depth of our being, all in the company of people the majority of whom we have never seen before, to whom we shall probably address not a word or a gesture, and whom we shall in all probability never see again.

What we accept as the norm is, in fact, the exception among the human race as a whole. In the culture of villages, as well as of those quite small cities (by present-day standards), from ancient Athens to eighteenth-century Vienna, which up to the recent past have formed centers of urban culture, performers and audience have known one another as members of the same community. Most of the world's population lived in villages, where if certain members specialized in instrumental music it was in addition to their agricultural activities, as others might specialize in smithing, milling or shoemaking. And if, like the smith and the miller, they were paid for their services in cash or in kind, it was as part of the system of mutually binding obligations that linked the whole community.

Those music specialists were socially necessary for the central part they played in the rituals of the community that celebrated the mythologies of birth, marriage, death, harvest and the other great events of life. Since everyone took part in the singing and the dancing, the distinction between performers and listeners was generally blurred—if indeed anyone could be called a listener pure and simple. Certainly, just sitting and silently contemplating the performance was no part of the experience. The musical performance was part of that larger dramatic enactment which we call ritual, where the members of the community acted out their relationships and their mutual responsibilities and the identity of the community as a whole was affirmed and celebrated.

In a different way, that was true among the aristocracy, for whom musicking also played its part in the social rituals that maintained their conceptual universe. Music was as much for performing as for listening to, and when musicians were employed, they were there as much to help their employers perform as to perform *to* them. The musicians were customarily the patron's servants, and often doubled as gardeners, valets, footmen, and grooms—only the superrich had full-time orchestras—and the listeners were his family, his dependents, and his guests, a tight community. Many of the pieces that the composer–music director composed were not so much for the patron to listen to but for him and members of his household to perform. In addition, the patron himself might well be a composer as well as performer, sometimes of more than amateur competence, as was Henry VIII of England, Frederick the Great of Prussia, and many of the princes of the Hungarian Esterhazy family which in the late eighteenth century was Haydn's employer.

As for the music of the medieval and Renaissance Christian church, it was a communal offering to their God, in which the choir, should there be one, sang not to but on behalf of the congregation, who approved what they sang with their response of "Amen." And of course, as is still true today, congregational singing needed no audience.

In none of these forms of musicking did anybody pay for admission to the performance. You were there by right as part of the community, or you were not there at all. Even the first concert societies, from about 1730 onward, were essentially private affairs, limited to a circle of subscribers, who were strictly vetted for their social suitability before being admitted. The practice of selling tickets, throwing open the event to anyone who had the price of admission, originated in the emerging mercantile society of England in the late seventeenth century, but did not become the rule until well into the nineteenth.

Even in modern industrial societies, sharing with strangers some of one's most profound and personal cultural experiences is not the invariable rule. Not only do there remain smaller communities in which the traditional intimate patterns of performance survive, but even in great cities there are pockets where they remain strong: working-class social clubs;

blues and jazz clubs; local repertory theaters; ethnic communities whose ceremonies of birth, death and especially marriage provide occasions for the affirmation of community; groups of friends who meet to make music together; sports and other activities clubs; and of course churches and other religious groups. But they are islands of community among the great sea of impersonal relations of the modern city.

Those attending tonight's symphony concert come as strangers to one another and seem content to remain so. Even those who have come with friends sit, once the performance begins, still and silent in their seats, each individual alone with his or her own experience, avoiding so much as eye contact with others. Whatever may be the nature of the performance, they experience it, and expect to experience it, in isolation, as solitary individuals.

Strangers they may be to one another, and yet in certain respects not strangers at all. Those taking part in any musical event are to some extent self-selected in terms of their sense of who they are or of who they feel themselves to be, and this event is no exception. Any number of surveys, taken in a number of industrialized countries, confirm that audiences for symphony concerts are overwhelmingly middle and upper class in composition, which is to say, crudely, that they are either members of a group of occupations that includes business, management, the professions and government or are in training for or aspiring to those occupations.

In terms of formal education the well-educated, which is to say those whose schooling was extended beyond adolescence, are in the majority. In terms of income they tend to be above, often well above, the average, and they tend to be older rather than younger. This composition has hardly changed at all over the years since such surveys were taken, despite generations of well-meaning attempts to widen the social base of the audience.

I mention this not to talk about elitism, which is no part of the purpose of this book (the word has in any case become so loaded that it can hardly any longer be used in rational discussion) but to suggest that in the concert hall, as at any other kind of musical event, there is an underlying kinship between the members of the audience. In a certain sense they are at ease with one another, knowing that there are certain kinds of behavior they can expect of one another and other kinds that they need not.

The members of this audience know that they can rely on one another to make the effort to arrive on time and to accept without protest their exclusion if they do not and to keep still and quiet as the musicians play. They expect to be treated with courtesy and respect by the staff of the hall and will complain if they are not so treated. But there is a wider range of behaviors also: not to overdress vulgarly or wear cheap perfume, not to belong to unacceptable racial minorities, not to take too much alcohol or other drugs before the performance or in the interval, not to go to sleep and snore, not to belch or fart or breathe garlic in people's faces, not to make improper sexual advances, not to pick their pockets or mug them.

In a word, a concert hall is a place where middle-class white people can feel safe together. In this respect its relationships resemble those of an ideal city as imagined by the sociologist Jane Jacobs (1961), which, she says, is a place where strangers can encounter one another in safety. But Jacobs envisages the possibility of an infinite variety of human meetings. What takes place in the concert hall is a narrow range of impersonal encounters among people of more or less the same social class, where each goes his or her own private way without being impinged on to any significant extent by others. It is, we might say, an ideal Westchester or Wimbledon rather than the untidy variety of a Brixton or a Lower East Side.

I remember a tiny and seemingly insignificant happening in London's Queen Elizabeth Hall that, for me, illustrates this feeling of safety. It was during the early 1970s, at a concert of avant-garde music, where the audience was mainly student, bohemian, and intellectual. The night was cold, and I was wearing a bulky sheepskin coat. Not wanting to wait in the long line for the cloakroom, I had the momentary thought that I could hang it in the gents' washroom, that with this audience it would be safe there. Then I checked myself, remembering that middle-class intellectuals were just as likely as anyone else to knock off a nice sheepskin coat left hanging in the gents' if they thought they could get away with it. But the thought had come so pat, so unbidden, that it could only have originated in that feeling of being among my own kind, strangers though they may have been to me. In the event I kept the coat on my lap, causing discomfort to myself and annoyance to my neighbors.

Above all, the members of the audience expect one another to respect scrupulously their privacy in the face of the musical experiences they are all undergoing. The aloneness of the individual during the performance is felt not as a deprivation but as the necessary condition for full enjoyment and understanding of the musical works being played. It is not that people do not socialize at a concert; they do, and the socializing is an important part of the event. But we have seen that that takes place in the foyer, before and in the interval of the concert, not in the auditorium. The two halves of the event are physically separated from each other, and the experience of the musical works themselves, the center of the night's event, is a solitary one.

Orchestra and audience, too, are strangers to one another, and there is no opportunity for them to become anything else, for they enter and leave the building by separate doors, occupy separate parts of it, and never meet during the event. This seems to be felt more as a relief than a deprivation by both parties, who apparently treasure their separation and prefer not to enter into a relationship of familiarity with members of the other group. And on the other hand, the audience is expected to sit quietly and accept the orchestra's performance as it plays, the only response open to its members being applause at the end. To boo at the end of a performance one has particularly disliked is possible, though a bit extreme. What is not an option is to make any visible or audible response, of either approval *or* disapproval, during the course of the performance; there is no way in which such a response could be incorporated as an element of the event, in the way that, for example, applause at the end of a solo is incorporated into jazz performance and is a legitimate element of it, or the response of the Jamaican audience I mention below.

The concert hall thus presents us in a clear and unambiguous way with a certain set of relationships, in which the autonomy and privacy of the individual is treasured, a stance of impersonal politeness and good manners is assumed, familiarity is rejected, and the performers and their performance, as long as it is going on, are not subject to the audience's response. Because people who attend symphony concerts mostly go voluntarily, we can assume that they enjoy doing so; therefore, it is not too far-fetched to suggest that those relationships represent some kind of ideal in the minds of those taking part. I shall be discussing later the general proposition that how we relate is who we are. If that is so, then those taking part in this or any other musical event are, at some level of awareness, saying, to themselves, to one another and to anyone who may be taking notice, *This is who we are.*

The silence and apparent passivity of audiences at symphony concerts deserves a little more attention. Historically it is a recent practice. The eighteenth-century scene I described in the Rotunda at Ranelagh was by no means exceptional for the time. Aristocratic listeners of the time felt free to treat the musicians and the performance as background to their other activities, to listen attentively when they felt like it and to talk, eat and drink, and even make love when they did not. Why not? The musicians were their servants. In the Paris Opéra, says the historian James H. Johnson (1995), "gripping moments in the drama or especially renowned airs brought silence and genuine attention, but on the whole the Opéra in 1750 was a public setting for private salons, for which the music, dancers and machines provided an excellent backdrop."

Mozart on his visit to Paris in July 1776, reported in a famous letter to his father his delight when the audience broke into applause during the performance of the symphony he had written for performance there and, perhaps even more significantly, said "Hush!" at the opening of the last movement, which Mozart, cocking a snook at noisy Parisian convention, had written for the violins only, pianissimo. Johnson tells us too that when, in the late 1820s, the symphonies of Beethoven attained a belated recognition with Paris audiences, spectators applauded particularly striking passages and erupted into storms of applause at the end of each movement, sometimes forcing its repetition, while at other times they "bubbled over with happy sighs and murmuring approval." Such noises do not suggest inattention, and certainly not disrespect, but betoken rather an audience that is active rather than passive in its attention, that considers, in fact, that its own audible responses are a legitimate element of the performance.

The silence that will greet tonight's performance while it is in progress suggests a different attitude. Those who wish perfect communion with the composer through the performance can have it, uninterrupted by any noise that may signal the presence of other spectators. On the other hand, while our attention is without doubt active, it is detached; we no longer feel ourselves to be part of the performance but listen to it as it were from the outside. Any noise we might make would not be an element of the performance, as were the sighs and murmurs of the Parisian audience, but an interruption or distraction. I have even known the minute clinks and jingles of a female listener's charm bracelet to put its wearer's neighbor in a rage.

Who we are, then, is spectators rather than participants, and our silence during the performance is a sign of this condition, that we have nothing to contribute but our attention to the spectacle that has been arranged for us. We might go further and say that we are spectators at a spectacle that is not ours, that our relationship with those who are responsible for the production of the spectacle—the composer, the orchestra, the conductor, and those who make the arrangements for tonight's concert—is that of consumers to producers, and our only power is that of consumers in general, to buy or not to buy.

Other kinds of performance conjure up other kinds of behavior, other kinds of relationships. Many reveal a complex ambivalence about their ideal relationships that can tell us much about the nature of musical performances and about the function that they serve in human life.

The differences between the various kinds of performance are not clearcut, of course. It is easy, for example, too easy in fact, to set up a simple antithesis between the relationships of a symphony concert, as a representation of the values of the contemporary industrial world, of the scientific worldview, of the bourgeoisie, or whatever, and those of other ways of musicking—rock for example, or reggae—as representing various degrees of rejection of (or as some would have it, liberation from) those relationships. That kind of neat antithesis has been the basis of a great deal of pop sociology of music, often bringing with it a cargo of unwarranted judgment, either covert or overt. Unfortunately, although there may be some truth in the antithesis, it hardly matches the untidy reality of musicking in the real world.

It is true that there is a good deal of the values of the contemporary industrial world or the scientific worldview built into the symphony concert, including, of course, the musical works that are played there; I suggested that in my first book (Small 1977), and I have seen no reason since to change my mind. But those values permeate as well, to a greater or lesser extent, all the large-scale public musicking that takes place in the Western industrial world.

All public performances, for example, are open to anyone who has the price of admission, which means that the passing of money is an important factor in whatever values are established there. In all of them the experience is shared with strangers, although the degree of intimacy that can be attained during the performance may be different, and in all of them the audience is kept apart from the performers and is to a greater or lesser extent dominated by them. All maintain a network of stars and superstars whose glamour and inaccessibility is part of the deal, and all rely for their very existence, if not as forms of artistic activity then at least as social institutions, on a highly developed technology. The existence of these and other factors in all these kinds of performances makes for a complex ambivalence to which no simple antithesis can do justice.

The great rock festivals of the 1960s and early 1970s, for example, were famous as events where strangers came together for a few days in tens and even hundreds of thousands to share not just a musical but a total social experience. They were experienced by those who took part in them as a liberation from the day-to-day social constraints of their lives, where strangers were free to encounter one another, even perhaps to become lovers, where no style of dress (including none at all) or behavior was too outrageous to be tolerated so long as it did not interfere with the enjoyment of others. The musical performances came in an endless stream, sometimes in the foreground and sometimes in the background (whether foreground or background at any moment was an individual matter), but always a magical presence acting as catalyst for whatever human encounters were desired. The sociability was not separate from the performances but an important element of the total musical experience.

During those two or three days it was as if a new society had been brought into existence—loose, tolerant, intimate, unconstrained, and loving—the Age of Aquarius it was called. It was, of course, to a large extent a cleverly stage-managed illusion. But even to the extent that it was genuine, it was not just, as many commentators hastened to point out, that it depended on the very technological culture from which the participants thought themselves to be escaping; it was also, as was pointed out by only a few crotchety critics, that no society, no sociability, not even in the Age of Aquarius, can exist without constraints on behavior.

At rock festivals, as at any other kind of musical event, there were, and are, right and wrong ways to behave, right and wrong ways to dress, to speak and to respond, both to one another and of course to the musical performances. To dress or behave there in ways that come naturally in Symphony Hall would be to invite ridicule, if not downright hostility. There are even right and wrong drugs to get high on; I remember some hash-smoking friends at one rock festival registering fierce disapproval of a nearby group who were drinking alcohol—cider, for god's sake!

What was extraordinary was the speed with which these norms of behavior became established. Virtually nonexistent at the beginning of the 1960s, they were firmly in place, and even too conventional for some, by the end of that decade. A whole generation of young people was aware of them, even those who did not subscribe to them.

That they were felt by those present not as constraints but as liberation only goes to show how lightly norms fall on those for whom they represent ideal social relationships. But then, that is true of behavior, including dress, at all musical performances, symphony concerts not excepted. The fact that those who enjoy the event do not feel constrained but feel rather that they are behaving in a way that is natural and normal suggests once again that a musical performance, while it lasts, brings into existence relationships that model in metaphoric form those which they would like to see in the wider society of their everyday lives.

It looks as if the relationships that are established in a symphony concert mirror those which we might call the official relationships of our society. At any rate, to take part in a symphony concert, as in other classical music performances, is an activity that earns complete approval from those authorities who provide and attempt to enforce the norms of our social and political lives. As I have already suggested, we behave there according to the canons of middle-class good manners, and we police ourselves for signs of deviance from them. No policemen or security guards are needed to enforce them, no one searches us for weapons or drugs, and we expect to be treated by the hall staff with courtesy and respect.

The further performance behavior deviates from these middle-class norms, the heavier becomes the enforcing presence; even today it is quite common to see security guards patrolling rock concerts. I remember, too, a performance in a London cinema in the late 1970s by a group of Jamaican actors and musicians headed by the distinguished vernacular poet Louise Bennett. Naturally, Jamaicans came in hundreds to see and hear them. It was a happy crowd, mainly middle-aged, with a strong residual sense of their Jamaican roots; there were a few whites, and we all waited good-naturedly in the cold outside the cinema until we were admitted, only a few minutes before the performance was due to start. Finally, we were admitted in single file through the only one of the half dozen entrance doors that was open. Each face was scanned, as its owner passed, by tense and anxious uniformed staff clearly expecting trouble.

As one of the few whites present, I found their attitude offensive, but my black friends shrugged it off, not wanting to spoil their evening by showing resentment too overtly and being refused admittance. During the performance the audience was hardly ever quiet; the buzz of comment and laughter rose and fell with the music, the jokes, the sketches in Jamaican patois, the recitations by Miss Bennett herself, who would probably have wondered what she was doing wrong had this audible reaction not come back to her. It was an essential element of the performance, the audience's contribution, and without it the performance would have been a sad affair indeed.

At an even further remove from the norms of and the social approval accorded to the symphony concert, there is a description in Tricia Rose's book on rap, *Black Noise* (1994), of the indignities that thousands of young black Americans had to endure before being admitted to a rap performance in a big New York stadium. She describes how the initially very good-humored crowd was divided by aggressive security guards into male and female lines, how each individual was separated from others and subjected to a humiliating body pat-down and scan with a metal detector and even a search through handbags and pocketbooks, and how the cheerful, expectant atmosphere rapidly soured. Such procedures not only serve to exacerbate the very attitudes that they purport to control, but they also indicate how heavily the enforcing presence falls upon those whose style of musicking does not fit the approved social norms.

It is not, of course, just the behavior itself that produces anxiety in the authorities—that is for them merely the sign and signal of the identity of those taking part—it is the identity itself that is disturbing. The mere presence of a few hundred middle-aged Jamaicans at a London cinema was enough to inspire fear in the staff and that of thousands of young African Americans coming to enjoy a performance in a New York stadium seems to have caused something approaching panic.

This leads us to an idea that I shall be developing later: that the way people relate to one another as they music is linked not only with the sound re-

lationships that are created by the performers, not only with the participants' relation to one another, but also with the participants' relationships
to the world outside the performance space, in a complex spiral of relationships, and it is those relationships, and the relationships between relationships, that are the meaning of the performance.

An unsympathetic observer might even find a certain hypocrisy in some
popular music situations. Consider, for example, the relation of performers to audience. Many popular artists make a great show of their unity and
their solidarity with their listeners; I remember an aging and justly famous
star of country music sitting on the edge of the stage with his feet dangling
over, thus symbolically breaking through the barrier between himself and
the audience, and announcing, "We're gonna be here all night!" We all
cheered, even though we knew no such thing was gonna happen; neither
the theater management nor the star's own handlers would allow the performance to run much over its allotted two hours or so. But we appreciated the gesture, and—who knows?—perhaps he was wishing as sincerely
as ourselves that it might be true. I doubt if sensitive artists enjoy the conditions under which they have to perform any more than do sensitive
members of the audience.

Again, some popular artists go the the point of behavior onstage that
under other circumstances could be interpreted as an invitation to sex. But
woe betide any deluded member of the audience who takes the invitation
seriously and tries to join the performer onstage. There will be a team of
heavies, hired for the purpose, waiting to bundle him or her off, and not
too gently either. The nearest anyone not in the performers' charmed circle
will get to them will be in the line for an autograph at the end of the show.

Such pretenses are, of course, absent from symphony concerts. Performers, however glamorous, do not issue sexual invitations, not onstage
at any rate, and so do not need a team of heavies to keep people off the
platform, and no one feels the need to pretend that the performance is
going to go on all night. No hypocrisy there, if hypocrisy it is. But
hypocrisy has been called the tribute that vice pays to virtue, and the pretenses that are made in these situations show what it is that those taking
part, performers perhaps as well as audience, are looking for in the performance. We might read it as the quest for an ideal of community and con-
viviality as an antidote for the loneliness of our age.

A festival of folk music shows a similar quest more coherently, through a
deliberate informality of presentation that goes beyond that of the usual
rock concert. There is a studious avoidance of glamour. Stages are generally
small and unpretentious, and amplification, if it is used at all (some folk
artists righteously eschew amplification altogether) is discreet. Performers

are expected to avoid the kind of forceful self-presentation and domination of the audience that characterizes the rock star and, in a different way, the concert soloist, and to fraternize with the audience when not performing.

This is of course as carefully cultivated a set of behaviors as that which is exhibited in any other musicking. Stars remain stars, even if they shine less ostentatiously than some of their pop or classical colleagues, and a paying public remains a paying public. That the experience is more of the desire for than of the actuality of community is part of my point; the relationships created during a musical performance of any kind are more the ideal, as imagined by the participants, than the present reality.

So if the community of the rock or even the folk concert *is* nothing more than a carefully orchestrated set of theatrical tricks played in collusion by performers, their handlers and the audience together, we cannot blame them if the participants feel that counterfeit community is better than none at all. In any case, people are on the whole not so silly as not to recognize the gap between desire and reality. What we need to keep in mind is that those taking part in performances of different kinds are looking for different kinds of relationships, and we should not project the ideals of one kind of performance onto another. Any performance, and that includes a symphony concert, should be judged finally on its success in bringing into existence for as long as it lasts a set of relationships that those taking part feel to be ideal and in enabling those taking part to explore, affirm, and celebrate those relationships. Only those taking part will know for sure what is their nature.

Interlude 1
The Language of Gesture

*

Before we go further into this description of the musical ceremony called a symphony concert, I need to make the first of my digressions in order to establish a simple theoretical foundation for understanding what is going on there.

If, as I have suggested, musicking is an activity by means of which we bring into existence a set of relationships that model the relationships of our world, not as they are but as we would wish them to be, and if through musicking we learn about and explore those relationships, we affirm them to ourselves and anyone else who may be paying attention, and we celebrate them, then musicking is in fact a way of knowing our world—not that pre-given physical world, divorced from human experience, that modern science claims to know but the experiential world of relationships in all its complexity—and in knowing it, we learn how to live well in it.

The first clues I received to this way of thinking came in the 1970s from reading the works of the English anthropologist Gregory Bateson, whose death in 1980 at the age of seventy ended a life given over to evolving a way of knowing that would unite the scientists' impersonal way of knowing the world with the human knowledge of ethics, values and the sacred. The purpose of this way of knowing is not to dominate the world, as is that of scientific knowledge, but to live well in it. My own subsequent readings in neurobiology and the study of mind have made me realize that a great leap in knowledge in these fields has been made in the years since Bateson's death, but nonetheless I still feel the power of his ideas; those later writers have served to confirm for me the essential rightness of his intuitions and of his enterprise.

One of Bateson's recurring themes is the double nature of all philosophical questions. He takes Warren McCulloch's (1965) version of the psalmist's question, "Lord, what is man that thou shouldst be mindful of him?" and extends it into his own investigations. McCulloch asks not only "What is a number that a man may know it?" but also the reciprocal question, "What is a man that he may know a number?" and he points out that the answer to one depends on the answer to the other. Bateson returns repeatedly to this form of double reciprocal questioning, pointing out that to ask questions in this way is a little like binocular vision, in that it gives a greater depth than either question asked individually. He says that "two descriptions are better than one," and I have found, similarly, that if I would ask the question *What is musicking that human beings should like to practice it?* I need also to ask the complementary question, *What are human beings that they should like to practice musicking?* It is in order to propose an answer to the latter that I need to make what appears like a long detour before I can propose an answer to the former; and in the course of my doing so, the discussion of musicking itself will necessarily recede into the background. I can only ask the reader to trust me eventually to make its relevance plain.

One of Bateson's fundamental intuitions is a denial of what is known as Cartesian dualism, the idea that the world is made up of two different and even incompatible kinds of substance: *matter*, which is divisible, has mass, dimensions, and a location in space; and *mind*, which is indivisible, has no mass or dimensions and is located nowhere and everywhere. This mode of thought is very old in Western thinking and in fact, in the form of the concept of an immortal soul that is distinct from the body and survives its death, is part of our society's religious orthodoxy.

It was first made explicit in a systematic way in the seventeenth century by the French philosopher and mathematician René Descartes. Through Descartes it has not only come to form one of the foundations of modern science but has also become so ingrained in the thinking of members of modern scientific-industrial societies (by that I mean not just scientists but everyone, whether trained or not in the practice of science) that it hardly seems like a mode of thinking at all but more like simple commonsensical reality.

How, in this divided Cartesian universe, matter and mind can act on each other is a seemingly insoluble problem that Descartes bequeathed to succeeding generations. In particular, it makes a human being a divided creature, consisting of a corporeal body that is extended in space and subject to the laws of physics and chemistry and an incorporeal mind that in some mysterious way is lodged within it, yet is not part of it, and appears not to be subject to any discoverable scientific laws. Even some of the great neurophysiologists of the twentieth century have been so defeated by this problem that they have found themselves postulating a "suprabiological" mind, a "ghost in the machine," that in some mysterious way that is inaccessible to the methods of science watches over the chemical and physiological workings of the body, including the nervous system. The nervous system, with the brain at the center, appears to be the site of the mind, but what might be the nature of that mind they could only speculate. Others, the so-called behaviorists, tried to solve the problem by denying that mind exists at all; they said it was only an epiphenomenon, the illusion of a phenomenon, whose apparent existence is the outcome of a hugely complex system of automatic actions of the body, like a shadow cast on a wall.

Part of the Cartesian legacy to Western thinking is the assumption that the body plays no part in such operations of the mind, apart perhaps from presenting through the senses the material on which the mind operates (and in some of the weirder manifestations of the mind-body split even that has been called into question). Knowledge exists "out there," independently of who knows it, preexisting any possible knower of it, and continuing after any knower has ceased to exist. Similarly with reasoning; premises lead inexorably to conclusions, regardless of who, if anyone, is doing the reasoning. This idea, that the operations of the mind work independently of the body, is all the more pervasive for being unrecognized for what it is: an assumption, by no means to be accepted without scrutiny.

Bateson has not, of course been the only twentieth-century thinker to call into question these and other assumptions of Cartesian dualism, and over the past two or three decades this questioning has found ample experimental support in the works of neurologists and neurobiologists such as Oliver Sacks, Gerald Edelman, and Francis Crick. It is becoming clearer and clearer that mind is not substance at all but process, one of the processes of life, which is explicable by the organization and working of the brain and the rest of the nervous system, with their billions of intricately interconnected and reinterconnected nerve cells (Edelman [1992] calls the human brain "the most complex object in the entire universe"), and is thus inseparable from the living matter of whose operation it is the outcome. That may sound like the behaviorists' position, but in fact it differs from it fundamentally, since the behaviorist, even as he or she denies the existence of the substance mind, remains caught in the absurdity of the Cartesian split, whereas to understand that mind is part of the functioning of living matter, as much as, say, digestion and reproduction, makes it unnecessary either to affirm or deny its existence as substance. Once that is understood, the Cartesian split between body and mind ceases to exist.

Bateson goes further, and holds that mind in some form is part of the functioning of all living creatures. He defines *mind* very simply, as the ability to give and to respond to information, and maintains that it is a characteristic of matter wherever and whenever it is organized into those patterns we call living. The world of living beings, he says, is suffused with the processes of mind; wherever there is life there is mind.

The neurobiologist may find this definition somewhat too wide and all-encompassing, but it does have a use in our context; anyone who cultivates a garden must constantly be astounded by the way in which plants not only respond to information, such as changes in the intensity and duration of light, changes in temperature, and even the presence of other plants nearby, in ways that are appropriate to them and to their mode of being, but also give information, through their color, their mode of growth and their flowering, and modify their environment in order to make it more favorable to their growth and reproduction. Further, the seemingly infinitely complex interaction between plants, microorganisms, insects, other animals and human beings suggests that the biosphere, the world of living creatures, is indeed a vast and intricate network of what by Bateson's definition we can call mind, all giving and responding to information. The mind relates to the environment outside the creature not by mere passive reception of what is "out there" but by an active process of engagement with it. We could say that creatures shape their environment as much as they are shaped by it.

Not all the information, of course, comes from other creatures, since much also comes from the nonliving environment—changes in temperature, atmospheric constitution, saltiness of water, the lengthening and shortening of days, and so on. Living creatures in turn have their effect on the nonliving environment; the very constitution of the earth's atmosphere, and its maintenance, against all the strictly physical probabilities, at a roughly uniform level over eons is due to the activities of life, so that the entire earth sometimes appears as if it were a single great organism—the point of origin of James Lovelock's (1979) Gaia hypothesis.

Each individual mind, each set of processes of giving and receiving information as it goes on within each individual living creature, may in itself be simple or complex, but it is at the same time a component of the larger and more complex network. Bateson calls this vast network "the pattern which connects" because it unites every living creature with every other, some intimately, some remotely, but not one excluded from the pattern. What holds the pattern together, what puts the world that exists within the boundaries of the organism in continuous interaction with the world that is outside it, is the passing of information. The mind has its external no less than its internal pathways.

The question that then presents itself is: What form does the information take that ties together the living world? The answer Bateson offers is that the information that is given and received by living beings is always what he calls "news of difference," whether it be a static difference between figure and ground as the creature scans it or a dynamic change over time. What is registered may be a shape or color that is distinct from a background, a combination of colors, a movement or way of moving, a posture, a chemical secretion, or changes in the pressure of air or water that, if sufficiently rapid, form patterns of shock waves that are perceived as sounds; it may be a change in temperature or in the intensity or duration of light and other electromagnetic vibrations, even perhaps a change of orientation toward the earth's magnetic field. But it may also be an absence of difference when difference is to be expected, since an event that does not take place when it is expected can be a source of information—in human life, for example, a letter that does not arrive, a phone that does not ring, or as Sherlock Holmes noted, a dog that does not bark.

Those differences that are picked up by the sense organs cannot yet be called sense experiences. They can have no meaning for the receiver until they are processed in the nervous system. How that processing takes place is mysterious; neurobiologists call it the "binding problem," the problem of how multiple stimuli, possibly in different sensory modes, are bound together to create a single image or sense experience—for example that of perceiving that a cat has climbed onto one's lap. In any case, the effect of the differences—what we actually *experience* as perception—is a transform, or coded version, of the physical differences that engendered it.

For our purposes what is important is this: whatever the mechanism may be that binds the various sensory stimuli into a single unified experience, image formation is an active and creative process, not mere passive reception of whatever stimuli are being presented. This is probably true, in one way or another, throughout the living world. The creature, however simple or complex it may be, works on the stimulus, the news of difference, and creates meaning from it. Even an ameba needs to find something analogous to what we call meaning in, say, the presence of certain substances in the drop of water in which it lives in order to move toward the creature that is their source and engulf it. No information can be received unless the creature is ready to receive the raw stimuli and transform them. The receiver creates the context in which the message has meaning, and without that context there can be no communication and no meaning.

The way in which the information is processed is affected both by the inherited dispositions and by the previous experience of the knower. In simpler creatures previous experience plays little part in information processing;

they are, to use the current computer-based metaphor, "hard-wired" to respond to specific information in certain specific ways. We can predict how a fly will respond to a rapidly approaching flyswatter, or an ant to the discovery of a crumb of bread, for all flies and ants respond in the same way (though even there, we note that we cannot predict in which direction the fly will fly off or where the ant will take its treasure trove; I have oversimplified more than a little).

The farther we go up the scale of complexity, previous experience enters more and more into the processing; and since each individual has experiences that differ from its fellows, so different individuals of the same species may well react differently to the same stimuli and take different kinds of action in response. Also, the same individual may respond differently at different times to the same stimulus, as do dogs and human beings. Periodic changes in the way information is processed we call moods, but there are also longer-term and generally irreversible changes that are due to growth of experience and knowledge.

If knowledge of the world outside is the result of an active process of transformation of stimuli, then it must derive not only from the nature of the thing outside that is being known but also from the way in which the stimuli are transformed by the knower. Knowledge is thus as much a product of the knower as of the thing known and can in fact be best thought of as a relationship between knower and known. There can therefore be no such thing as completely objective knowledge, knowledge of the external world exactly as it is, since everything we can possibly know about it is mediated by the way in which we, the knowers, work on the information about it that we receive and convert it into usable knowledge. Probably the nearest we human beings can come to "objective" knowledge lies in meanings that are connected to those bodily experiences that are shared by us all.

Here we find what looks at first like common ground with a long line of European philosophers, including Descartes himself, for whom the irreducible element of subjectivity in human knowledge of the world has been the cause of something like despair. But Bateson (1972) points out that a creature that did perceive everything outside itself exactly as it was would be an automaton, without freedom or power of choice—a "feather blown by the winds of external reality," to use his phrase. Human beings are not completely *objective* in their knowledge of the world, but we need not conclude from that that we are completely *subjective* and can know nothing for certain about it. There is a broad gap between "purely objective" and "purely subjective," and it is in that gap that human freedom and creativity live.

In any case, no living creature, not even a human being, is under any obligation to try to know everything. Those who want to live well in the world, as opposed to those who want to dominate it, can be content with the idea that there are things we cannot and do not need to know. It could even be argued that a creature who knew everything there was to know (assuming that such a creature could possibly exist) would be so completely imprisoned by its knowledge that it would find no room left for creative action, not to mention a sense of humor.

We should note also that there is in the means of communication that unites the living world nothing of the supernatural or the metaphysical. The information that holds together the pattern that connects is physical in nature, and we do not need to appeal to extrasensory perception or to telepathy, to any postulated thought waves or the intervention of higher-order beings or indeed to any nonphysical mode of communication. We are talking about sensory receptors, physical sense organs, and the processing of the information they receive by the creature's processing apparatus. Just as contemporary neurology is beginning to make it clear that the internal pathways of the mind are physical in nature and located in physical structures (even if those structures are marvelously flexible and adaptable in their nature), so it is with the mind's external pathways. The channels of communication between living beings and the processing of them into images are *physical* processes, and they require a physical sense organ, of however rudimentary a nature, to receive the news of difference.

The next question that presents itself is, what kind of information is it that all living creatures need to be able to give and to respond to, and what does it concern? Bateson's answer is that although the means of communication are extremely varied, what is necessary for an organism to know always concerns a relationship: how the perceiving creature relates to the outside entity that is being perceived, and vice versa. Is it predator, for example, is it prey, is it offspring or a potential mate? And thus should I flee it, or attack it, or nurture it, or mate with it? It is clearly of vital importance for the creature to have the right answer to these questions.

But the answers are not absolute. What is offspring to one creature may be prey to another and predator to a third and may even differ for the same individual at different times, as in the celebrated example of the female spider that eats the male after mating with him, making mate into meal. The terms "offspring," "prey," and "predator" denote not essential qualities of a creature but qualities in relation to others; one can be offspring only in relation to a parent, prey in relation to a predator, and predator to prey. This is generally true even when the perceiver is dealing with the inanimate world; qualities such as temperature, weight, saltiness and acidity are perceived in terms of how the creature relates to them. "Too hot," for example, "just hot enough," and "not hot enough" are the vital perceptions, and the point where "just hot enough" becomes "too hot" is different for different creatures; for a humming bird "just hot enough" is doubtless "too hot" for a penguin or a seal.

For living creatures, then, the most important information they receive from the outside world concerns relationships. For simpler creatures, those relationships may concern only the immediate environment, and they do not need to understand the entire pattern. For an ameba, those of its drop of water are enough. More complex creatures will be more complex in their understanding, and the range of their relationships will be wider and more comprehensive. The human mind *appears*, at least to human beings, to have the power to encompass the relationships of the entire cosmos, to conceive it in fact as the pattern which connects. Bateson even suggests in passing that human consciousness may be, at least potentially, the organ of self-knowledge of the entire system.

This may well be an illusion, since human minds also are limited in their compass, however we might like to think otherwise. Who knows but that the ameba thinks the drop of water in which it lives is the entire cosmos and that its understanding encompasses all of it, no less than does a human being? Perhaps the best we find to say about that is that the cosmos is as big as our minds can conceive it as being. There does not seem to be much point in worrying about it further than that because that is all our minds can use, and knowledge about relationships is either usable knowledge or it is not worth knowing.

Once again, as we ascend the scale of complexity, both the gestures of relationship and the possibilities of response become more varied and complex. Bodily posture and movement, facial expression, and vocal intonation provide in the more complex animals a wide repertory of gestures and responses by means of which information about relationships is given and received. In complex and contradictory creatures like human beings these gestures can deal with a number of complex and even contradictory relationships, all at once. Gestures from me may indicate to you at one and the same time that I love, and hate, and fear, and am dominated by you, that I should like to strike you but intend to nurture you. Such complexities of relationship are not unknown in human life, as any watcher of soap opera will testify.

Whatever form the gestures of relationship may take, they have one feature in common: they do not state who or what are the entities that are relating. What the ends of the relationship, the so-called relata, are is taken for granted. Thus, if I make a gesture indicating that I love, or hate, or fear, or submit to, or respect, or dominate, you, or any of these in combination, the "I" and the "you" are not stated, and there is no way in which they can be stated. Only the relationship that unites us is stated. We might say that there are no nouns or pronouns in this language of biological communication. Nor is there any way of saying "no" or "not," no past or future tense, nor any way of dealing with entities that are not actually present. It is an affirmative and a here-and-now communication.

Bateson (1979) points out, however, that it is not enough to send and receive messages about relationships. For the receiving creature to understand fully the message, it needs to know something about the context of that message. A dog will snarl and bare its teeth, for example, in a variety of circumstances, not only when it wants to convey menace but also when playing, even perhaps when greeting its master or mistress. We recognize the correct context from other signals that the animal sends with the rest of its body. Bateson calls these messages about messages *metamessages*, and these are important in the understanding of activities such as art and games, which seem on the one hand to be lacking in survival values yet are practiced with the utmost seriousness by all members of the human race. We are all used to sending and receiving these metamessages and learn to read them ("only kidding," "this is play," "I am serious," "this is for you only"), but there are also other ways of indicating contexts and thus of interpreting behaviors. Certain types of buildings, for example, also act as context markers; the fact that certain behaviors take place in a church, a football stadium, a theater, or a concert hall will make it possible to interpret those behaviors correctly when they might otherwise be inexplicable.

In contrast, verbal languages as they have developed, uniquely among human beings, have equipped us to deal with and communicate about things and persons that are both present and absent, as well as with past and future and even hypothetical or imagined events and relationships, to discuss the contexts in which these occur, or occurred, or may occur, or fail to occur. But unlike the gestural language of biological communication, words deal with matters in sequential order and only one at a time.

This is both a strength and a weakness. It is a strength in that verbal language has made it possible to develop those analytic capacities, that step-by-step logic, that ability to compute about things, that have proved such powerful tools in gaining what mastery we have over the material world. But it is also a weakness, in that verbal languages have proved on the whole less than adequate in articulating and dealing with our highly complex relationships with one another and with the rest of the world.

A second limitation of verbal language is that it leaves gaps when we try to describe some aspect of the world as it appears to us. It is not just that the simplest object—a pebble, for example—contains complexities, down to its subatomic structure, that a lifetime of description could not exhaust and that however finely we draw the net of description there will always be details that are finer. But there are, in addition, gaps between modes of description that we cannot close with words. We can say of a pebble that it is round, and rough, and gray, and heavy. These four adjectives deal with aspects of the pebble's reality—its shape, texture, color and weight respectively—that, try as we may, we cannot make meet in our description, even though we know they meet in the object itself. Verbal language is discontinuous, whereas the world is continuous.

Relationships also are continuous and do not lend themselves to one-thing-at-a-time description. We have to take them all in one piece in all their complexity, and it is here that verbal languages really show their limitations. One thing at a time is just too slow and cumbersome to deal with their many-layered quicksilver nature, and when we try to articulate them in words we keep falling into the gap between description and reality.

The gestural language of biological communication, on the other hand, is continuous, as are relationships themselves, and for this reason it is much better suited to their articulation. It resists all attempts to dissect out, in parallel with verbal language, a specific vocabulary of gestures, whether visible or audible or even smellable, tastable or touchable. It has no vocabulary, no units of meaning. It is seamless, without gaps, and depends not on quantity and the amassing of discrete units such as words or numbers but on shapes, forms and textures—patterns, in fact—and patterns, of course, are built of relationships.

This brings us to another difference between verbal and gestural language: the fact that while in the former the relation between the sound of a word and its meaning is arbitrary (apart from occasional onomatopoeia), in the latter it is not—or at any rate, not completely. There is no special reason, for example, other than that of historical development from a common origin, why the words *eau, agua, aigua,* and *aqua* on the one hand and *water* and *Wasser* on the other should all be used to denote the liquid element; any other combinations of vocal sounds would have served as well and do so in other languages that are not historically related to Latin or German models.

But the relation between the shape or pattern of a gesture and its meaning is not arbitrary. Many gestures are fully iconic and carry within themselves the picture of their meaning: the baring of teeth, for example, to signify aggression has an obvious basis in the attack and defense ways of animals (it has been suggested that the baring of teeth that takes place when we smile reflects the element of aggression that is present in all humor) and the holding out of the empty right hand to show we are not carrying a weapon. This means not only that when we use this kind of communication we are using one set of relationships, one pattern, to signify another (the process that we call metaphor) but also that gesture and meaning are, at least to some degree, analogues one of the other.

To some degree only, however. There is an element of arbitrariness, or at least of choice between alternative representations, in gestural language also. If there were not, if all gestures were exact analogues of the relationship they articulate, those gestures would all be identical for all members of the same species; every gesture would have its significance, and that would be that. Nor would any change or development be possible.

But we know that this is not so, at least in the more complex creatures. The same gesture can be used to mean a variety of relationships, and conversely, the same relationship can be articulated by a variety of gestures. Human beings are constantly devising new meanings for existing gestures and new gestures for existing meanings, and it is this element of indeterminacy, of choice, even of a degree of arbitrariness, that leaves room for creative development and elaboration. In fact, in neither verbal nor gestural languages is there a complete one-to-one relationship between signifier and signified; meanings are constantly slipping and sliding into new meanings, mainly, as we shall see in a moment, through the power of metaphor. Attempts to create a stable one-to-one relationship in either mode seem to remain doomed to failure, and we should be glad of it.

Human beings are, on the whole, more alert to pattern than they are to number, more alert, that is, to relationships than to quantities, which may be why we tend to think in metaphors. This is understandable, since relationships are the most important concerns in human life, as they are in the lives of all living beings. Bateson even goes so far as to suggest that, if the genetic code is ever finally cracked, it will be found to concern relationships rather than things, for example the four relationships of a human hand rather than the five fingers. We even define ourselves by how we relate to others; who we are is how we relate. No one has an identity except in relation to others, and an entirely solitary person, a person with no relationships whatever, if we can so much as imagine such a creature, can have no identity. It must have been one of Robinson Crusoe's greatest problems, in his years of solitude on the desert island, to maintain a belief in who he was, even perhaps in his very existence, because without an identity, who exists?

For most purposes in human life the gaps in verbal modes of description do not matter too much, since human beings have enough experience in common to be able to fill them in, if in a rough-and-ready way. The word *pebble* is enough to summon up an image of the object, and even if we do not all summon up the same pebble image when the word is uttered, there is enough overlap in our bodily experience of that category of object to make communication possible between us. Categories, of course, do not come ready-made but are constructions of the human mind, so that where we draw the line between a grain of sand, a pebble, a stone and a boulder, for example, is a matter of negotiation and agreement. The overlap between the bodily experience of one person and another, as each of us creates it from the perceptions of our senses, is one source of reassurance that what we perceive has some relation to what is actually out there—another reason, I suppose, why human beings like company.

There is another problem with verbal languages. The convenience of having nouns that enable us to name and talk about things inclines us to think of every idea, every relationship, as if it were a thing. We take from the action of loving, for example, or hating, or performing good and evil acts, or telling the truth, or worshiping, or musicking, the abstractions we call love, hate, good and evil, truth, God and music, and if we are not careful we find ourselves coming to treat the abstractions as if they were more real than the actions. This is the trap of reification, or thing-making; we noted earlier that it has been a besetting vice of Western thinking since at least the time of Plato. We saw in the Prologue how the reification of *musicking* into *music* and of making the latter more real than the former has been a major obstacle to our understanding the nature of the act.

But we have not lost the older gestural language of biological communication. It remains with us, today called paralanguage—and the use of the prefix *para*, signifying something subsidiary, something to one side or altered, even improper or wrong, suggests the extent to which this older mode of communication has been devalued in today's highly verbal societies. The languages of bodily posture, movement and gesture, of facial expression and of vocal intonation continue to perform functions in human life that words cannot, and where they function most specifically is in the articulation and exploration of relationships.

While among simpler creatures the conventions of paralanguage are determined entirely or mainly by instinct—which is to say, they come with the genes, hard-wired—the greater degree of flexibility that we have already noted among more complex animals, most especially the primates, means that the conventions have to be learned, not just once and for all but throughout the life of each individual. That in turn means that among our own species we should expect to find a great deal of variation between individuals and even more between those who have grown up in one physical and social environment and those who have grown up in another—in other words, between members of different social and cultural groups. We all know this is so; anyone who has spent any time in a foreign country or even some times with members of different social groups in their own country will be aware of the rich potential for misunderstanding that lies in the interpretation of one another's paralanguage.

To observe paralanguage in action one need only watch as well as listen to a conversation between two or more people. To do so is to see as well as hear a dialogue being conducted in gesture that is complementary to the one being carried on in words. It is likely, in fact, that the gestural dialogue, including the audible gestures of vocal intonation, will have more to tell us about the actual relationships between the conversers—and thus, quite possibly, about the real meaning of the encounter—than do the words that are being uttered.

Anglo-Saxon people, who tend to be more restrained in their gestural language than, say, Latins, need not for that reason think that it is less significant in their lives. The English, with their unique flair for placing people in terms of social class, rely to a great extent on the often very subtle clues (often given and received equally unawares) of paralanguage, especially vocal gesture, for the carrying out of that social placement. But it is Africans and people of African descent who, perhaps of all the world's peoples, possess the most exuberant and at the same time most subtle virtuosity in this field; the African cultural propensity to value and to cultivate the language of gesture was, if anything, strengthened over the generations of slavery, when survival itself might depend on rightly receiving and giving paralinguistic messages. I remember as a schoolteacher in London being driven half mad by the casual virtuosity with which twelve-year-old black girls were able to express their contempt for my rebukes without needing to utter a word.

The fact that we expect to understand at all gestural language across cultures suggests that the intercultural differences in this respect are not as great as those between verbal languages. We know that a dialogue of gestures is possible. We could say perhaps that the different cultural conventions of gesture are more like dialects of a common language than they are like different languages. Many of the conventions even hold *between* species as well as within them, as anyone who has kept a pet can testify. It is not surprising that these conventions should concern especially points of interspecies interaction such as attack and nonattack, edibility, defense, alarm, and so on, suggesting that the kingdom of the wild is a much more cooperative, or at least ordered, realm than some would have us believe.

It is surprisingly difficult to lie in paralanguage, though it is possible, at least for short periods. To a limited degree it is part of everyday social skills: the concealment of boredom, for example, or the sometimes necessary simulation of pleasure at the arrival of an unwelcome visitor. It is also one of the essential skills of actors and politicians. On the other hand, playing with paralanguage is an ancient and important occupation among young animals and among humans of all ages. To play is to change the context of the communication, to lift it temporarily from the context of the everyday in order to explore the implications of a relationship or set of relationships without needing to commit oneself to it.

The capacity for play can be seen at least in all mammals, although it is most highly developed and persistent among human beings. It survives throughout adult life, whereas in other mammals it weakens and may even disappear as the animal matures. The communicative gesture, freed from the immediate and possibly life-or-death situation under the privileged conditions of play, has acquired a perhaps less urgent, but no less important, role as discourse, as a way of articulating and exploring relationships, of trying them on to see how they fit, not only among humans but also between humans and the larger pattern that connects. The function of the discourse is the same as it has always been, but the ancient gestures of relationship have been elaborated over the million-year history of the human race into the complex patterns of communicative gesture that we call ritual.

CHAPTER 4

A Separate World

As we watch, the musicians file onto the stage. All are wearing black, the men in tuxedos with white shirts and bow ties and the women in black ankle- or floor-length dresses. Those whose instruments are portable are carrying them, in the way musicians do the world over, as if they were extensions of themselves and of their bodies. Their demeanor is restrained but casual, and they talk together as they enter and move to their allotted seats. Their entry is understated, quiet; there is none of the razzmatazz, the explosion of flashpots and the flashing of colored lights, the expansive gestures, the display of outrageous clothing, that marks the arrival on stage of many popular artists. Nor does the audience react to their arrival. Not even a round of applause greets their appearance, while they in turn behave as if unaware that some two thousand people are watching them. They seem in fact to inhabit a separate world from the audience, which watches them as from a distance and will in a few minutes listen to them as if through a visually and acoustically transparent but socially opaque screen at the edge of the platform.

Once seated, they talk to colleagues, fine-tune their instruments, play scales and little snatches of melody, perhaps practicing a difficult passage in one of tonight's pieces or just amusing themselves. For a few brief moments before the appearance of the conductor, the stage is the orchestral musicians' territory and their playground, and they seem to enjoy their possession of it. The overall sound, though uncoordinated, is playful and pleasant to hear, but it is for themselves, not the audience, that they are playing. The playground is private, and what they are playing is none of the audience's business.

All public behavior sends a message about the relationship of those who are exhibiting it to those who watch it. It seems to me that the message of these musicians' onstage behavior is that of their professional exclusivity, of their belonging to a world that the nonmusicians who sit beyond the edge of the stage cannot enter. Their exclusivity is heightened by the fact that they have entered the building through their own entrance and have remained in their own backstage accommodation, to which the audience has no access, until the time comes to play. They will address not a single word to the listeners in the course of the performance; we shall not hear their natural voices but only the ritual voices of their instruments as they play.

The separation of performers from audience is, of course, not unique to symphony concerts; theaters, sporting events and popular concerts all keep the performers out of the spectators' sight until the time comes for them to perform. The custom seems to stem from a desire to protect the mysterious power of the performers, a mystery that refers perhaps to the very fountainhead of the performance arts, the healing performances of the shaman. But in few other kinds of event do the performers make it quite so clear that they live in a different world from the audience as in a symphony concert.

We note, too, another aspect of their behavior that sets them apart from the audience: their uniform mode of dress. A uniform diminishes the individuality of those who wear it, subordinating individuals to the collective identity. People in uniform are behaving not as themselves but as representatives of the organization whose uniform it is, and it is to the organization, not to themselves, that the responsibility for their actions belongs. This is seen very clearly in warfare, where soldiers captured in civilian clothes are treated very differently from those taken in uniform; they are felt to be somehow cheating the rules.

The nature of the uniform says something about the nature of that collective identity. For the professional soldier it bestows status, with a hint of sexual power, while for the policeman it is an emblem of state authority. In the case of those musicians of earlier times who were in the service of great families, their uniform emphasized their low status, for it was the livery of the servants, which we have seen that most of them were. In the mid-eighteenth century, Josef Haydn, director of music to the Esterhazy family of princes and famous across the whole of Europe, wore servant's livery and was relieved to find that he had been seated at table (the servants' table, of course) above the cook.

The uniform that tonight's musicians wear is ambiguous in its nature and its meaning. Outside the concert hall, evening dress of this kind is seen much less frequently than in former years, and tends to be worn today by high-status males at formal functions, to emphasize that status. At the same time it is the working garb of their senior house servants, like Hudson in the endless TV series *Upstairs, Downstairs*. It thus locates the musicians in a social between-stairs, on the one hand proclaiming their social equality with the members of the audience and on the other suggesting their continuing status as providers of services for the upper classes. In the United States, that continuing bastion of upper-class privilege, where orchestras are often the private fiefdoms of the very wealthy families that bankroll them, it might signify as much the latter as the former.

Here tonight it reminds us that these virtuosi, all of them masters of their instruments and possessed of a will and an individuality of their own, are expected to submerge those skills and that individuality in the collective performance. And not even to a collective will; it is the will of one man who is set in authority over them.

There is perhaps another message that the formal dress and the stylized behavior send to those who are alert to it. Since professional concert musicians the world over dress and behave in this manner and since male evening dress is a style that has changed remarkably little over the past century or so (women were excluded from professional orchestras until well into the twentieth century; as late as the 1930s the conductor Sir Thomas Beecham was complaining publicly that "women *ruin* music!"), it tells us, as do the dress and stylized gestures of a priest celebrating mass, that musicians, like priests, may come and go, but the music, like the liturgy, goes on forever. The parallel with priests is not accidental. Musicians of the Western classical tradition often perceive themselves, and are perceived, as having a kind of priestly function, as the bearers of something sacred and eternal, something that transcends time and human life. I remember, for example, a celebrated American pianist who used to be billed, without apparent irony, as "The High Priestess of Bach."

Then again, if we look at nineteenth-century pictures of performances in concert halls, one sees that all the men, both musicians and audience, are portrayed as wearing full evening dress. Over the years since then it seems that the dress of audiences has become less formal while that of the orchestral musicians has not, suggesting perhaps that the modern division of the participants in a symphony concert into two societies may be more recent in origin than we think.

Some performing groups, especially those specializing in contemporary avant-garde music, have affected a uniform that is a stylized version of everyday dress, appearing maybe in colored open-necked shirts or roll-necked sweaters with black trousers, apparently to convey the message that the musicians have shucked off the formality and the distancing of the conventional symphony concert and have entered into a new and revolutionary relationship with their audience, in parallel with the technical revolution wrought by the composers whose works they are playing. But in fact, as with the musical works themselves, nothing of importance has changed; one set of conventions has been replaced by another. The concert pieces remain concert pieces, and the uniform remains a uniform, which continues to set the musicians apart from the listeners.

The musicians live in a paradoxical world. On the one hand they are, every one of them, highly tuned virtuosi, many of whom, but for luck or temperament or simply because of playing the wrong kind of instrument (the number of trombonists or tuba players who have succeeded in making a solo career is tiny compared to that of pianists or violinists), could have themselves made solo careers. They work very hard and are rightly proud of their skills and of the way in which they deploy them. They are generally well paid, even if less so in recent years, and their profession enjoys a social status that is respectable and even considered glamorous. And although any glamour they themselves might initially have felt the job to have quickly wears off under everyday work pressures, they do feel themselves generally to be heirs and guardians of a great tradition.

But most orchestral musicians do not investigate their feelings about this very deeply. In my experience it is difficult to get them to talk about the art they practice with such skill. They will talk about the virtues and failings of conductors and colleagues and about which member of the orchestra is sleeping with which. They will complain about the impossible bowings the composer has asked of them and of his apparent ignorance of the most elementary aspects of fiddle technique; even those who are regarded as The Great Composers are not immune to such criticism. They will talk about the latest round of pay talks, about the scandalous contrast between what they are being paid and what conductors and soloists receive, and about the often desperate measures that are being taken to keep the orchestra alive in the face of inflated star fees and the drying up of subsidies. They resemble, in fact, the members of any other occupational group in that they will engage in any amount of shop talk, gossip, and locker-room humor.

But rarely do they question the nature of the relationships within which they work. That certain kinds of relationships within the band are necessary for the performance of the music is an article of faith and scarcely discussed. This is due not to any deficiency in intelligence but to the fact that the training they received in music college or conservatory, like all professional training whether medical, legal, academic, military, or whatever, has been directed as much toward the acceptance of the profession's assumptions and the maintenance of its esprit de corps as it has been toward the acquisition of the skills that are necessary to practice it; and like most professionals in any field whatsoever, most orchestral musicians have come to accept those assumptions unquestioningly.

In general their attitude is more that of the craftsman than that of the autonomous artist. They accept without question whatever is given them to play, provided that it is competently enough written, leaving others, the composer and the conductor, to take responsibility for the performance as a whole. Their responsibility is to their own instrumental part, which they will play as well as they are capable. That is their job, to play what composers have provided for them to play, and the composer's job is to provide it. It seems a fair division of labor, and they are inclined to resent those contemporary composers who require them to invent material for themselves to play—generally within limits that he determines, of course. They reason, not without justice, that if he gets the critical acclaim for the piece—and collects the performing rights fees—then he should not leave creative tasks to them. It is a strange reversal of the situation that existed in the improvising orchestras of the seventeenth century, whose members would have felt their skills were being insulted if a composer were to write out everything they were to play.

Similarly, they feel it is the conductor's job to mediate between them and the score which they never see as they play, to show them how to relate musically, on the one hand, to the composer and the material he has provided and, on the other, to one another as they play. If he does this well they will respect him, and if he does it badly they will despise him; but rarely if ever do they question the nature of those relationships or ask if they really need constantly to play someone else's notes, whether they really need someone to mediate their relationships with one another, with the composer or with his works. They may grumble and smolder under the conductor's authority and constantly test it and his knowledge of the score, in large and petty ways, even sometimes engaging in a kind of guerrilla warfare with him, and they may criticize the way the composer writes for their instrument, but seldom if ever will they seriously question the right of one to tell them what to play or of the other to tell them how to play it.

Also accepted more or less without question is that these relationships should be authoritarian and hierarchical. Under the conductor is the leader, or concertmaster, who acts as mediator between the players and the conductor; below him are the various leaders and subleaders of the sections, and below them are the "rank-and-file" players. It is of interest that it should be a term borrowed from that most hierarchical of organizations, the military, that is used of those orchestral players who are not section leaders or subleaders and never play a part on their own.

The modern professional symphony orchestra is in fact the very model of an industrial enterprise, permeated through and through with the industrial philosophy, and directed like all industrial enterprises toward the making of a product, in this case a performance. Its social relations are those of the industrial workplace, being entirely functional and depending only on the job to be done; members may know and care nothing of colleagues' lives apart from the job, and if, as in other jobs, friendships do develop, they are irrelevant to the task to be performed. The written notes and the conductor's gestures control the actions of the players as they play and mediate their relationships. If the second horn likes the phrase the first oboe has just played, he or she cannot play it unless the composer has authorized it.

As in other jobs, too, the rank and file are rarely consulted about the nature of the product to be made (which is to say, the pieces that are to be played) but are required simply to play the notes that are set before them, under the direction of as dynamic a managerial type as it is possible to engage. Time is money; they are generally unwilling to work extra time without extra pay (though the desperate straits in which some orchestras find themselves today sometimes oblige the players to do so just to keep the orchestra alive), while the foreman (known as the leader, or concertmaster) acts as middleman between rank and file and higher management.

There is a rigid division of labor within the organization, with each player highly skilled on a single instrument or a few related instruments. This again is in the interest of efficient production of a performance, but it is by no means a necessary condition of highly developed concerted music making, as can be seen in the Balinese gamelan orchestra, where each player expects, and is expected, to take a turn on each instrument. There is also a distinct social hierarchy, with the string players accorded the highest status (white-collar, one might say), the brass and percussion having on the other hand a distinct blue-collar image, being generally regarded as jolly fellows, not oversensitive, and given to the consumption of large quantities of beer. The leader, or concertmaster, is always a violinist, a relic perhaps of the days when the leader of the first violins gave the beat and generally controlled the performance (Johann Strauss Jr. was leading his Viennese dance orchestra in this way as late as the 1880s), showing the continuing force of the tradition.

The musical skills that are required of a professional orchestral musician are without question of a high order; in a good orchestra substantial mistakes in the notes are rare and breakdowns almost unknown. At the same time those skills are very specialized and fall within a limited range, consisting of technical dexterity, the ability to sight-read and to respond rapidly to the notations and to the conductor's gestures, as well as those of attuning one's playing to that of the ensemble. Skills that are prized in other traditions, such as those of improvising and memorizing, are of little use to orchestral musicians and tend to atrophy; naturally they form no part of their training. Even longer-term musical thinking is left to the conductor; I remember my astonishment at being told by a respected orchestral double-bass player that when he played a concert he read his part measure by measure and often could not remember the measure that he had just played.

The appearance of an undifferentiated collectivity that is presented by the orchestra on the platform is no illusion. The players, however individualistic and idiosyncratic their personalities may be off the platform, have to submerge themselves in the collective performance as if they themselves were mere instruments on which the conductor plays. Although those with inside knowledge about the orchestra may know that the first flute is Mr. X and the first oboe Señor Y, both marvelous virtuosi, to the average listener they are just sounds that emerge from the ensemble (it occurs to me as I write that my saying "first flute" and not "first flutist" in itself suggests the extent to which players become nonpersons on the orchestral platform, as if the instruments were playing themselves). They receive from the audience little individual acknowledgment of their superb finger technique, breath control, bowing, or exquisite phrasing (the esteem of colleagues is of course another matter). And even less notice is taken of those who play in, for example, the second violins; they are anonymous entities who, as long as they measure up to a certain level of competence and experience, are to all practical purposes interchangeable. Indeed they sometimes are, as shown by allegations a few years back that in some performances by one of the major London orchestras as many as 40 percent of the players were substitutes engaged by regular players while they themselves undertook more lucrative commercial work.

It is small wonder, then, that frustration should be a common occupational disease of symphony orchestra players and boredom another or that a third should be symptoms of stress, relieved often enough by beta-blockers or a couple of gins before the performance (a fourth, revealed by a 1992 survey, is hearing loss, apparently worse among orchestral violinists than that suffered even by musicians in heavy-metal bands). The stress has undoubtedly become exacerbated in recent years by the desperate competition for work among musicians and the remorseless demand for technical perfection in the CD era, where a split note can cost a job. It is no wonder that players are not inclined to take those risks that can lead to exciting and exhilarating performances. No wonder, either, that the number of conductors who can rouse the players from that boredom and feeling of routine as they play Beethoven's Fifth Symphony or Tchaikovsky's First Piano Concerto for the two-dozenth time this season, is small indeed.

For the modern musical profession to emerge and with it the institution of the modern concert, several ideas had to come together. All these ideas are taken for granted today, but none of them is in fact an essential or universal element of musical performance.

The first is the idea that music is for listening to rather than performing, and linked with that is the second idea, that public music making is the sphere of professionals. Amateurs may perform in the home and in certain other limited fields—for example, choirs—but in the public domain the dominance of professionals is virtually complete. The third idea is that of a formal and independent setting where people come together solely for the purpose of performing and listening to music, and the fourth is that of each individual listener's paying for admission to the place where the performance is taking place, with the ticket of admission as the sign of having paid.

These factors are interrelated and interdependent, and it was not until well into the nineteenth century that all four were in place in Western musical culture and giving birth to the modern musical profession. The axis of change seems to have been around the year 1600. It was then that the first operas, the first dramatic musical presentations indubitably intended for an audience of spectator-listeners, were created and with them the art of musical representation and tonal harmony. Those are matters that I shall discuss later.

The first independent settings for the public performance of music, to which admission was gained by the passing of money, were opera houses, the earliest of which opened in Venice in 1637. Concert halls, as we have seen, were a later invention. Once the buildings were built, then the economics of their running and maintenance led inexorably to the admission of more people. With more and more people attending, it became customary for people to accept the company of strangers in their most intimate musical moments; we are told that in 1749 some twelve thousand people attended a rehearsal of Handel's *Royal Fireworks Music* in Vauxhall Gardens in London, causing a traffic jam on London Bridge that lasted several hours. The company of connoisseurs and friends that attended the aristocratic performances was, in the emerging mercantile society of England, already becoming the anonymous public.

The takeover by professionals, on the other hand, appears not to have taken place until the first half of the nineteenth century. Until then members of the European aristocracy thought it a perfectly normal pursuit for a gentleman or a gentlewoman to engage in musical performance, and the task of professional musicians was to assist them in that pursuit. Outside of the opera house, full-time professional orchestras were virtually unknown in Europe and America until well into the nineteenth century; amateurs and professionals playing alongside one another was the rule. The orchestras that gave the early performances of the symphonies of Beethoven were a mixture of amateurs and professionals, and even many of the pianists for whom Mozart wrote his concertos were what we would call amateurs. Naturally so; an important function of orchestras was to give people the chance to play together, and it was the job of composers to give them something to play.

When Weber compiled his guide to Germany for itinerant musicians in 1820, many of the best musicians he listed were amateurs. Only in opera houses were there anything like fully professional full-time orchestras, and even there, in all but the largest houses, local artisans and tradesmen formed a substantial part of orchestras as well as choruses until well into the nineteenth century. Those orchestras did give occasional concerts when the opera house was not functioning—during Lent, for example—but mostly on an ad hoc basis.

The coming of the traveling virtuoso-entrepreneur ended that situation. It was not just that Liszt, Paganini, and a host of others pushed amateurs, who could not hope to match their spectacular technical achievements, off the stage, nor was it just that composers, beginning possibly with the later Beethoven, were beginning to make demands on orchestral musicians that amateurs could not meet. It was that the virtuosi, recognizing the enormous commercial potential of the new middle class, eager to display its wealth and power but individually unable to afford a musical establishment of their own as had the older aristocracy, used their powers of display to seize control of public musical life. Those wealthy middle-class males who took over leadership in musical matters from the aristocracy had less leisure than the aristocrats to develop their musical skills, and middle-class women were not encouraged to appear in public at all; the home was expected to be their sphere of activity. In any case women were not encouraged to learn orchestral instruments; for them the piano and their own voices were generally the only instruments that were considered appropriate.

The first full-time professional symphony orchestras were the Vienna Philharmonic and, surprisingly, the New York Philharmonic, both founded in 1842; by around 1850 amateurs had more or less disappeared from the public stages of the great musical centers of Europe and, a little later, of the United States of America. They appear today only in corners of their own, where allowances can be made for their lack of professional polish. Professionals may earn pocket money by providing a "stiffening" to amateur orchestral performances or by playing offbeat instruments like contrabassoon or bass tuba when the score calls for them, generally with a slight air of condescension.

The elimination of the amateur performer—and with even more force, of the amateur composer—from the public platform speaks of a profound change of attitude. Musical works were made for playing, and now they are for listening to, and we employ professionals to do our composing and playing for us. A piece of music is written not to give performers something to play but in order to make an impact on a listener, who is its target. The greater the impact on the listener, the better the composition.

What the piece's impact may be on the performer is largely incidental, and seldom if ever discussed in the literature, though in fact some pieces that are favorites among concert audiences are loathed by the orchestra musicians who play them. I remember my own composition teacher, whom I had asked whether a passage in an orchestral piece I was writing would be grateful to play, telling me, "Don't worry about that. You write it: they'll play it." Perfectly reasonable, of course; the musicians are being paid and if they don't like it they can get another job, just as in any other occupation in the modern world. (But after the piece had its first and only performance some of my carefully copied orchestral parts came back to me with some very unflattering comments scribbled across them.)

This change in attitude follows logically when we accept the idea that musical meaning is enshrined uniquely in musical works. That being so, we shall want to hear them played as perfectly as possible. But we should realize that the price we pay for that perfection is high.

The price is that the majority of people are considered not to have the ability to take an active part in a musical performance. They are excluded from the magic world of the musicians, whose separateness is symbolized so lucidly here by the division of the concert hall into two. They are fated to be no more than consumers of the music that is produced for them by professionals. They pay for the commodity, music, but they have no more say in what is produced than do consumers of any other commodity; they have only the choice of either buying or not buying.

As they wait for the conductor's arrival, the musicians of the orchestra eye the audience warily and covertly across the barrier of the platform edge. To them it is collectively a fickle creature that changes its nature every night. They have to please it in order to make a living, but they privately despise it for its ignorance of the musical skills and mysteries to which they themselves are privy and for the unreliability of its judgment, especially in regard to conductors. They do not want their world to be too close to that of the audience; and individually and collectively, they guard jealously their privacy and their distance from the public.

It appears that the event may well mean different things for the inhabitants of the two worlds, even perhaps that the interests of the two are different and in some respects opposed. What for members of the audience may at its best be a transcendental experience of communication with a great musical mind, for the orchestra members may be just another evening's work and even, for some, a time of boredom and frustration.

Whatever the event may be celebrating, it does not seem to be unity, unanimity or intimacy but rather the separation of those who produce from those who consume and the impersonal relationships of a society whose dominant mode of relating is through the passing of money. I have to emphasize once again that I do not believe that to be the whole meaning of the event. But it is another strand that has to be taken into account when we try to assess the rich texture of human relationships that are being generated by a symphony concert as a whole.

CHAPTER 5

A Humble Bow

*

Now with the actors, all except one, on the stage, the visual image is almost complete: a symphony of architectural forms and muted but rich color. The hall lights reflect warmly off the polished wood of the stringed instruments, the silver keys of the woodwind and the golden glow of the big brass, set off by the intense black and white of the musicians' costumes, all of them complemented by the harmonious colors of the auditorium. We are now seeing the picture that the architect planned — elegant, discreetly opulent, rich and understated; here we can feel ourselves to be members of a culture that is self-confident, mature, and securely grounded in history.

As well as music, all the major arts are being deployed in this big space, to bring into existence a *Gesamtkunstwerk*, the total work of art that incorporates all the arts, which Richard Wagner dreamed of but was never able to realize. He imagined that it would take place on a stage, but it is here, brought into existence every concert night, and we ourselves are part of it. If we do not perceive it, it is not only because we have been taught to concentrate our attention on the sounds that emanate from the platform and to ignore the rich texture of other meanings that surrounds us, but also because in this total artwork the various arts have blended so seamlessly as to make them almost invisible. Once we are alerted to it, however, we see how total an artwork is created every time an orchestra and an audience assemble in a concert hall to present a program of symphonic works under the direction of a conductor. The experience of the work of art begins from the moment of entering the building.

Or even perhaps before. We might say that it begins from the moment the architect begins to plan the building and elaborates its spaces to make a suitable setting for the events that are to take place within it, when the orchestra first begins to rehearse the pieces that are to be played, or when a manager is appointed to the hall and begins to assemble his staff, from executives to cleaners, or when the composer first sketches his ideas for his symphony or concerto. We could go back to the moment when the performers are first selected as talented and enter music college, or when tailors and dressmakers begin to make the evening dress they will wear on the platform. We could even go back through the centuries and watch the evolution of the instruments that are played and their incorporation, one by one, into the group sound. This *Gesamtkunstwerk* is a complex affair with a complex history, an even more interesting and significant synthesis of the arts than that which Wagner imagined. Its real name, of course, is ritual.

Although the performance of the musical works is clearly at the center of the event, nonetheless nothing that happens in this vast space is insignificant, not even such apparently trivial elements as the buying and giving up of tickets, the arrangement of the seating, the demeanor of orchestra and audience, the taking of drinks in the foyer, the purchase of a program booklet. All are essential features of the event and go toward giving it its character. If this were not so, if the events were concerned with the musical works and those alone, people would long since have ceased to go to concerts and would be happier to sit at home and listen to the works on records or radio.

Many people, of course, *are* happier to do just that. There is no doubt that listening to records at home has some real advantages over listening in a concert hall. Like the audiences who responded so enthusiastically to performances of Beethoven's symphonies in Paris in the 1820s, the listeners can talk, make comments and expressive noises, and repeat at will those movements that give them particular pleasure. Listening to records and radio at home or watching on TV or video is an event of a different kind, with its own meanings, and is not a mere surrogate concert. The participants are in fact free to create their own sonic space, their own ambience, and thus their own ritual, centered on the recorded sounds, in a way that is not possible in the highly mediated space of the concert hall.

I cannot agree, however, with those who claim to hear better *sound* on record than in the concert hall or with those who find themselves disappointed with the concert hall sound after listening to records. It is true that the brilliant, wide-spectrum sound of modern recorded performances has produced in many listeners a taste (one might even call it an addiction) for that kind of highly saturated sound, but for myself—on those rare occasions these days when I do find myself in a concert hall—I am always surprised by the aural pleasure of hearing sounds that do *not* saturate the acoustic space. There is a human scale, a human fragility even, in those less overwhelming, less all-encompassing sounds that I find lacking in any orchestral recording that I have ever heard, however magnificent it might be.

There is in any case nothing in the private ritual of home record-listening that compares in its drama with the carefully staged public event that is taking place in this hall. It seems that the technologies that have made it possible to listen on record have at the same time changed the nature of the symphony concert itself; for if one can hear and these days even see the pieces performed without going to the concert, then the act of going to a concert, *when it is no longer necessary to do so in order to hear the works*, takes on a new and more concentrated ritual significance. Certainly, concertgoing even in our own time remains, for many people, an event of importance, as is shown by the explosion of concert hall building that has taken place over the past fifty years or so.

On the other hand, we need not imagine that the coming of recording has diminished the ritual significance of less formal ways of musicking, such as listening to records or even that of hearing (as opposed to listening to) Muzak in an elevator or a shopping mall. The ready availability these days of musical performances, from any time in history and from anywhere in the world, may appear to have made the act of hearing in itself less special, less ritual; but in fact the significance of the ritual has not diminished even though it may have changed. Jonathan Sterne (1997), in an article on the musical architecture of an American shopping mall, describes the care that is taken in selecting the music to be played in the various spaces and remarks: "If all music is ethnic music, then the ethnicity of programmed music (*or muzak with a small m*) is capitalism." I would gloss that remark as meaning that the performance and hearing of programmed music in those spaces is a ritual by means of which the values of capitalism are affirmed, explored and celebrated in order to induce those who enter the space to stay longer and buy more.

This does not seem to me to differ in essence from those performances in which the values of kings and princes were affirmed in earlier times; one set of values may have been substituted for another, but the call to submission to them is unchanged. Musicking always takes place for a purpose, even in today's world of casual encounters with musical sounds in virtually all public and semipublic places. We can take it for granted that this is so, for if it were not, then nobody would go to the trouble of providing it, either for themselves or for others. The ritual significance of some performances may be hard to divine, especially in these days of the ubiquity of recorded performances, but it will be there for the informed and the inquiring mind. We may be sure that *somebody's* values are being explored, affirmed, and celebrated in every musical performance, at any time, anywhere.

At a signal from the leader of the first violins, who by convention is the orchestra's leader, or concertmaster, the musicians stop their playful playing, and the first oboist gives the A, to which at 440 Hz, orchestras and pianos the world over are tuned. The grand unison swells to fill the hall, then slowly dies away. The musicians hold their instruments in what we might call the standby mode and the subdued buzz of conversation in the hall dies. After a few moments of silent expectancy a curtain at the side of the stage is pulled aside by a disembodied hand, and there comes onto the stage the man for whom we have all been waiting: tonight's conductor.

Every musician who performs before an audience brings his or her own contribution to the public drama that is being played out in the performance space. Not only the sounds he or she makes but every bodily gesture and movement contributes to that drama. Nowhere is this more obvious than in the case of the one musician who makes no sound at all, the conductor of an orchestra.

He—it is almost never she—may appear flamboyant or reticent, dictatorial or amiable, affable or arrogant. He may be young and vigorous, a young lion with symbolic mane of hair approaching the podium almost at a run, making a perfunctory bow to acknowledge the audience's applause and taking up his baton without a moment's delay as if impatient to bring the assembled forces under his control and release their stored energies in sound.

Or he may be an elegant martinet, whose military bearing, steely eye and abrupt movements tell us that for the orchestra this is going to be no pleasure trip but that, love him or hate him, he will wring from them the performance that he desires.

Or he may be an aged maestro, helped by two assistants painfully onto the bench where he is to sit to direct, conveying the impression that every movement is racking his body but that he is fighting the pain and the infirmity of age to bring to those assembled here the benefit of his accumulated musical wisdom and perfection of technique.

Let us say that tonight's conductor is none of these but a man a little past middle age, slim, erect and unhurried, secure in his command of the works to be played and of the musicians who are going to play them. He radiates that air of physical well-being and sexual energy that is often borne by those who are accustomed to command and to being admired for doing so; the stories and hints in the press of his extramarital affairs have done him no harm in this respect. His presence on the platform tonight brings reassurance to musicians and audience alike—and at the same time an excitement, as his charisma hangs in the air like a faint perfume.

His appearance is greeted with a storm of applause from the audience, and he bows low to acknowledge it. The humility of his bow is part of the drama. He is acting the role that is expected of him, that of devoted servant of the public, of the music, and of the great musicians who created it. In fact, he dominates the big space, and as if to emphasize this, the auditorium lights are dimmed as he enters and the stage lights brightened. It is clear that we are expected to give unwavering attention to what is happening on the platform.

Now he turns to face the musicians, his perfectly tailored back to the audience, and opens the large score on the rack before him. All eyes are on him, and he is the focus of all attention. From the strictly utilitarian point of view it is clearly necessary that he turn his back to the audience in order to do the job of directing the musicians, but in this highly charged ceremonial space no gesture is without its ritual significance. Turning one's back is an ambiguous gesture; on the one hand it can signify arrogant authority that cares little for those on whom its back is turned, while on the other it is the gesture of the leader who says "Follow me" as he leads us—to where only he knows. For the audience there is perhaps something of both meanings in the gesture. They know, too, that for the players whom he faces he is the autocrat whose every movement and facial expression controls how they play and mediates their relationships. Love him or hate him, says his gesture, they need him, and their immediate response to his every gesture testifies to their submission.

With casual deliberation he takes up his baton and holds it upraised. The musicians have brought their instruments to the ready, each watching him intently. The silence in the hall is complete, almost tangible, as everyone waits for him to make the gesture that will unleash the forces under his control and release the sounds they have come to hear.

The conductor's appearance on the platform has brought the event into focus. His power over the performance and over the rehearsals that have preceded it appears all but absolute. His authority comes from his control of the score lying open on the desk before him, which he alone among the musicians sees and has the power to interpret. He is a larger-than-life, even heroic figure who, even with his back to the audience, dominates them into stillness while with facial expressions and gestures of his hands he imposes his will on the sophisticated and often bored or stressed professional musicians before him, galvanizing them into life and guiding and shaping their performance.

The players relate to the musical work and to its composer only through him. They see only their own parts, containing the notes they themselves are to play, and they rely on him to coordinate their playing. They relate to one another and to one another's performances only indirectly, through him and through the gestures he makes to them. They do not even look at one another as they play but divide their attention between his gestures and the notes on the written parts they have before them.

He is also the medium through which the orchestra musicians relate to the listeners. From the audience's point of view the orchestra is an undifferentiated collectivity from which only the conductor emerges as an individual. It is he who receives the audience's homage and applause, he who bows on behalf of the orchestra, and if he makes an occasional gesture toward sharing the applause by getting the orchestra to stand, we know it is a courtesy only. The blank expressions on the faces of the musicians as they do so shows that they know where the applause is really directed. It is as if a musician had asked the audience to applaud his instrument.

For the audience, too, the conductor is the visible center of attention, the mediator of their relationships with one another and with the musical works being played as well as with the composer of them. The line of communication from the composer to each member of the audience runs through the conductor; it is he who takes the sounds made by all the individuals in the orchestra, coordinates them into a unity, focuses them and passes them on. The members of the audience, for their part, do not communicate with one another but sit still and silent, each alone with the sounds, receiving them from that other world beyond the barrier that is the edge of the platform.

It seems that any group of people who engage in a common activity requires a leader who will coordinate the activity and be a source of ideas for carrying it out. In general terms there are two different kinds of relationship between the leader and the led: authority may be imposed from without, with the backing of sanctions and even some form of coercion, or from within, with the consent of the group. In the first case the direction does not depend on the consent of the group being directed; in the second the continuance of the director's authority depends on his or her being seen by those directed as valuable to the group.

Each style of direction can be seen in the modern world, but in fact neither style exists in pure form; rather than any absolute antithesis, we see points on a spectrum between one and the other. Even the most powerful external director depends to some degree on the consent, or at least the compliance, of the directed, and even the most laid-back of communal leaders needs to exert some coercive authority from time to time. But the ideal or the tendency is there. Since musicking articulates our ideal of human relationships, we need not be surprised to find these different kinds of relationships in group musical activities.

The great black jazz leaders of this century, such as Jelly Roll Morton, Duke Ellington and Count Basie, belonged mainly to the latter group. Their authority, and the health of their bands, depended less on ways of playing imposed from without than on their ability to coordinate the playing of the very diverse individual musicians in the band while leaving them space to function as creative individuals and to contribute ideas to the performance. They themselves generally played in the band (the three just mentioned were all pianists), often playing a very modest part in the performances as they were finally realized.

The unity of the performance was that of a group of fully realized musicians working together in a state of social harmony, and any social disharmony in the group would soon show itself in musical discord. It is a terribly difficult balancing trick to bring off, and even with those great ensembles it remained for the most part as much an ideal as a reality. This is borne out by Duke Ellington's famous deadpan reply to a journalist who asked him how he kept his band together. "I have a gimmick," he is reported to have said, "I call it money." And Dizzy Gillespie, when asked how often he felt he and his fellow musicians were really in complete harmony, replied, "Once a year" and added, "if I'm lucky."

Nevertheless, the wonder is that these musicians and their sidemen did manage to keep the ideal alive, in many cases over decades. The fact that the leader's authority could never be taken for granted, but was subject to constant examination and negotiation, required of him, in addition to purely musical skills, more than ordinary strength and flexibility of character.

The conductor of a symphony orchestra, on the other hand, imposes his authority from outside the ensemble, backed by all the institutions of concert life and depending on many factors besides his competence at his job. You can even hire an orchestra to conduct if you are rich enough; there is a wealthy American businessman who, being musically nonliterate and having studied the piece by ear, has hired at various times several of the world's major orchestras so that he can conduct them in performances of Mahler's huge choral *Resurrection* symphony. The musicians allow him to do so and pretend to be following his direction. A distinguished college of music I once visited had canceled classes that day in order to allow its students to play extra orchestral parts and sing in the chorus and receive its share of the bonanza. He is only one of several wealthy people who provide a welcome addition to desperately needed orchestral income in return for having their vanity massaged.

The extent to which orchestral musicians despise many conductors, including even certain concert hall and recording favorites, comes to light from time to time in the press; common epithets are "incompetent," "arrogant," and "overpaid." These musicians' strictures often sound like those which are leveled at industrial bosses by those who work under them.

A successful conductor has, in fact, many of the attributes of a business tycoon. It is interesting that, like tycoons, they have increased their earnings enormously over the past few years—tenfold on average over the past two decades according to the critic Norman Lebrecht (1991)—far more than have those who play under them and sometimes even as the orchestras they direct are being forced into bankruptcy. Many conductors, of whom the late Herbert von Karajan was the most famous, or infamous, are in the literal sense tycoons, who spend as much time and energy on power plays and financial wheeling and dealing as on their strictly musical concerns. The pattern is familiar from much of the world of industry today, where bosses' pay skyrockets even, sometimes, as the enterprises in their charge languish and lower-rank jobs disappear.

It is an odd idea, that of a musician who makes no sound himself and who directs the performance of a group from outside it rather than from within, and among the world's musical cultures it seems to be unique to the Western concert and operatic tradition. The role seems to have come into existence in the musicking of the church around the time of the Renaissance, and it came with a new kind of musical ensemble: a unified group that produced a unified, blended sound, whose performances were intended to be listened to from outside rather than to be participated in. The production of such a sound demanded the complete subordination of the individual to the group, a new phenomenon at that time in musical performance.

This kind of unified, blended sound reached its first climax in the works of Palestrina, Byrd, Victoria, and Lassus, masters of Counter Reformation Roman church music at the time of the Council of Trent. It was a unified sound for a unified doctrine, and it was there that conducting technique first developed. There was, however, no separate *profession* of conductor; conducting was only one of the duties of a musician, along with composing, playing instruments and singing, tuning the harpsichord and organ, organizing performances, and teaching the skills of composition and performance.

In the improvising orchestras of the first brilliant explosion of opera in the early seventeenth century, it was leadership rather than conducting that was the keynote. The harpsichordist acted as leader from within the orchestra, confining his direction to keeping time, indicating changes in tempo and dynamic, and seeing to it that the players did not exaggerate the improvised variations that they were expected to invent from the composer's sketchy material—generally only the melody line and a bassline with a numerical shorthand known as *basso continuo* to indicate the harmonies—and that they did not drown the singers.

The demands made on such a leader, as indeed on all the orchestral musicians, were great, for besides his instrumental skills he needed a knowledge of composition to improvise convincingly on the composer's notations while at the same time keeping his ears on what everyone else was doing. We need not imagine that anything was skimped, musically speaking, in those early operatic performances. The orchestras were generally large, up to forty players, and rehearsals were usually thorough. If the composer did not provide a comprehensively notated score such as present-day players have learnt to expect, it was not through ineptitude or laziness. Rather, it was because musicians of the time, both players and singers, were proud of their ability to improvise on the composer's ideas, and would have felt it an insult to their carefully cultivated and highly developed skills to have been told every note they were to play. The modern parallels are closer with jazz leader and sidemen than with orchestral conductor and players.

For the modern conception of conducting to take hold—the conductor in charge of every detail of the performance and the sounds blended into a unified texture that is directed toward outside listeners—it was necessary that the players' musical autonomy and power of independent action be abolished. A musician in his role as conductor cannot exert that kind of control over an orchestra of improvising musicians, nor can he in his role as composer be sure that the sounds that are made by the orchestra are the ones he imagined, as is required by works of music that are intended for listening rather than participating. This meant that absolute faithfulness to the written score was essential; unless, as conductor, he knew exactly what every player was supposed to be doing at any given moment, he had no way of controlling it. This meant, in turn, that as composer he had to notate every note he wanted played, and thus began a long struggle for control of the musical texture in which the two roles of composer and conductor reinforced each other. Many of the great musicians of the eighteenth century were tyrants in their insistence on to-the-letter accuracy; Handel, says Paul Henry Lang (1941), was feared, but Gluck was dreaded by orchestra musicians.

As far as orchestral music was concerned, the struggle had been won by the early years of the eighteenth century, although in smaller groups that did not need an outside leader the older improvisatory practices survived into the nineteenth. In this way three parallel developments in European music making—the rise of the conductor, the growing dependence on fully notated musical scores, and the dominance of those who wrote them—went hand in hand.

Up to the time of Beethoven, composer and conductor were generally one and the same person. The modern professional conductor, who does nothing but direct performances of other people's works, is a nineteenth-century creation; his rise is associated also with the development of the international concert business and the building of big concert halls to house it. Liszt's son-in-law and Wagner's cuckolded friend, Hans von Bülow, was the first to achieve eminence.

Composer-conductors survived into the twentieth century, the last major figures of this kind being Gustav Mahler, who died in 1910, and Richard Strauss, who survived anachronistically until 1946. But unlike their predecessors, they found it necessary to separate the two halves of their work, conducting during the winter concert season and composing during the summer recess. Contemporary or near-contemporary figures like Pierre Boulez and Leonard Bernstein have found even this an almost impossible balancing trick, owing largely to the lucrative temptations of summer festivals. Composers these days occasionally conduct—at least their own works, though the complexity of their scores often defeats their conducting skills—but conductors on the whole do not compose.

The second half of the nineteenth century and the first half of the twentieth was the great age of the conductor. Giants like Gustav Mahler, Wilhelm Fürtwangler, Arturo Toscanini, Leopold Stokowski, and in our own time, Herbert von Karajan were autocrats in their domain, overseeing every detail of the orchestra's work, deciding repertory, hiring and firing players, and imposing their personalities and their ideas on their orchestras and even on their audiences, thus molding the orchestra's composite personality and its sound in their own image, sometimes over decades.

But over the past two decades the real power of conductors has waned considerably, owing partly to the greater independence of orchestras but also largely and paradoxically to the conductors' own worldly success and to the mobility that jet travel has made possible. Following the lead of von Karajan, star conductors appointed to principal conductorships have come to expect (in addition to astronomical fees that in some cases are bringing the organization to the verge of bankruptcy) that they should not be required to spend more than a limited amount of time each year with the orchestra, generally between ten and twenty weeks, leaving them free to accept lucrative engagements elsewhere, perhaps a second principal conductor's post as well as any number of guest engagements. This means that they are frequently absent when important policy matters are debated, appointments made, and decisions taken about repertory.

A new personage has entered the game to fill the power vacuum: the orchestra manager. In the days of the great conductors the manager was simply an unobtrusive administrator who looked after details that were too small for the conductor's attention. But today, with the conductor frequently absent when important decisions are being taken, it has been easy for the manager to assume many of his responsibilities, and with the responsibilities, the power. Choice of repertory, of assistant and guest conductors and orchestral personnel, and of concert and recording dates now frequently fall to the manager rather than the conductor, giving him, or quite frequently, her, a powerful position in the concert world.

The conductor may control the score, may decide how it is interpreted in sound, but the chances are that he has had to cede, at least in part, the choice of what is played to others. With the manager taking most of the substantive decisions, he is left in a position very close to that of mere figurehead, like a head of state whose exalted ceremonial position merely serves to confirm that the realities of power lie elsewhere. On the podium he may act the like the autocrat that his predecessors were, but those in the orchestra often know differently. After this series of concerts with the orchestra he will quite likely fly off at the behest of his agent, perhaps to the other side of the world, leaving little of himself and little imprint of his personality and ideas on the way the orchestra plays. It is no wonder that orchestras the world over are starting to sound the same.

The question is sometimes asked, are conductors necessary? Cannot orchestra musicians just work out their own performances without the imposition of an outside authority? There have been orchestras that have done so, most notably the Moscow Persimfans orchestra, inaugurated in 1922 in the first flush of postrevolutionary egalitarian fervor. It flourished for six years, giving, by all accounts, fine performances of new as well as of old works, even pieces as fiendishly complex as Prokofiev's *Scythian Suite*, until it fell victim to the pressures of having to produce performances in a short enough time to keep itself financially afloat.

There have been others, and where they have failed, as most eventually have, the reasons have usually been, as with the Persimfans, as much financial or political as purely artistic. To make a convincing performance without a conductor, it is necessary that each musician not only know his or her own part, as in a conventional orchestra, but have a concept of the performance as a whole and of his or her place in it. The musicians have to *know* it, by ear and by heart. They have to become self-reliant, and that takes enormous and continuing commitment from each musician, more perhaps than most orchestral players are prepared to give.

It also means that more time is needed to arrive at a performance, and the fact that time is money, in a professional orchestra no less than in any other professional organization, has proved the downfall of conductorless ensembles faced with the pressures of giving enough performances to stay solvent. Often, too, the ensemble gets taken over by an ambitious or power-hungry musician, eager to join the highly paid and envied ranks of conductors and looking for an orchestra to conduct, who converts it into an orthodox orchestral organization.

One criticism that is often made of conductorless ensembles (usually by conductors, who, of course, have a vested interest) is that their interpretations are bland and even boring. It is clear that the interpretation of a symphonic work will be more sharply individualized—by definition, one might say—when arrived at from the viewpoint of an individual than when reached by consensus. Such performances will be likely to emphasize more the dramatic tensions in a symphonic work, whereas a consensual performance will tend to place more weight on resolution, because that is the social nature of the two kinds of performance.

Contemporary concert audiences and critics, and classical-record buyers as well, have learned to prize sharply individualized and dramatized performances; generally speaking, the more dramatic tension there is in a performance, the better they will enjoy it. That is not an absolute or unchanging value but simply a contemporary preference. We can see a similar taste for screwing up the tension to sometimes, for me, intolerable levels in contemporary theater and especially cinema. I am not sure that Mozart, for one, or even perhaps Beethoven would care for the way in which their orchestral works are treated today in this respect, even at times by those who dress up in wigs, knee breeches, and buckled shoes and play "authentic" instruments. It may be that a style of performance that emphasized resolution over conflict would have something new to say about familiar and even over familiar works.

In purely musical terms, then, it does seem possible for an orchestra to work without a conductor and not only in the standard repertory that experienced orchestra musicians can play blindfold. But whether the conductor is *socially* necessary is another matter. He may not be needed for the performance, viewed narrowly as the simple realization of the composer's notations in sound, but he may well be necessary for the social event that is a modern symphony concert when we view it, as I am trying to do, in its entirety.

For in the end the conductor's function is not just the physical coordination of the orchestra and the production of an interpretation. It lies also in his heroic stature as focus for the imagination of those who sit in the audience. His role is that of the powerful and dependable autocrat, who will lead the orchestra and the listeners safely through the tensions and conflicts of the symphonic work, to the final resolution and cadence on the home tonic. His presence gives meaning to those conflicts and to their resolution, in terms that apparently make sense to members of the modern industrial middle classes and in a way in which no orchestra without him could do it. He is the incarnation of power in the modern sense and represents the image of what all of us dream at times of doing and of what many in our time have tried to do in the field of social and political action: to resolve conflicts once and for all through the exercise of unlimited power. It is no wonder that a symphony concert is such a pleasurable ritual, at least for some.

CHAPTER 6

Summoning Up the Dead Composer

*

Isolated within this building—and the isolation, too, is part of the experience—the two thousand or so people assembled here are exploring, affirming, and celebrating ways of relating to one another and to the world. They are not just hearing them in the sounds but perceiving them all around them in the big space. In charge of the ceremony is the conductor; he is the magus, the shaman, who immerses himself in the sacred book and summons up the spirit of the dead composer. He does this in order that those visions of sonic order which the composer imagined may be brought into being and felt by all those present and experienced, not just as abstract sound patterns but as metaphors for patterns of human relationships.

It is not surprising that concertgoers and musicians alike should feel a close, direct and personal relationship with those musicians of the past or that they should have an insatiable curiosity about their lives and personalities sufficient to keep alive a whole industry of composer biographies and critical studies; it is their lives and personalities, as well as their values and their vision of order, that are being summoned up here tonight.

It is curious that all of the musicians whose works are being played here tonight and indeed on most nights are dead, most of them long before anyone present was born. For most people here, a great composer is almost by definition a dead composer, and no musician who is alive today, or who even lived past the first two decades of the twentieth century, has the hold that dead composers have on the imagination of either listeners or performers in concert halls.

There are not in fact many of these Great Composers (one feels obliged to capitalize them, so neatly has the heterogeneous assemblage of personages been tidied up into something resembling an exclusive club), around fifty at most, with a few others who are represented by perhaps one or two often immensely popular works. All belong to the period that began, roughly, with the birth of Antonio Vivaldi in 1678 and J. S. Bach and George Frideric Handel in 1685 and ended with the death of Claude Debussy in 1918. A few stragglers, such as Johann Pachelbel, born in 1653 (of the ubiquitous *Canon*) and occasionally, from further back, Claudio Monteverdi, born 1567, at one end and at the other, from later decades of the twentieth century, Carl Off (*Carmina Burana* of 1936), Joaquim Rodrigo (*Concierto de Aranjuez* of 1939), and Henryk Górecki (Symphony no. 3 of 1977) have attained a place in the repertory, but they are few and their place is modest. Musicians of the twentieth century, even those who critics and historians of music have decided are the Great Composers of our time and fit companions for their illustrious predecessors, generally are rejected by the majority of those who assemble in concert halls to hear orchestral performances. Of the two big names of the first half of the century, Igor Stravinsky and Arnold Schoenberg, only Stravinsky's three pre-1914 ballet scores, *The Firebird, Petrushka,* and occasionally, *The Rite of Spring* are regularly heard, while of Schoenberg's oeuvre nothing at all has become what one might call a repertory piece in concert halls.

For most concertgoers, in fact, The Great Composers fall into an even narrower chronological range, for which cynical managements use the shorthand term "Mozart-to-Mahler." Since Mozart was born in 1756 and Mahler died in 1911, that represents a period of a little more than 150 years, scarcely long enough, one would think, to justify the epithet "immortal" that is often bestowed on the composers and on their works. It seems that, for the majority of those who regard themselves as lovers of classical music, the repertory virtually froze around the time of the First World War.

That an entire musical culture should be based on musical works that have survived from the past is odd, to say the least, the more so in a society like ours that is so powerfully gripped by the concept of inevitable progress and that is inclined to view its ancestors with a mixture of condescension and admiration (how *did* they survive without electricity / transparent tape / scientific medicine / DDT?), and so far as I know it is unique among human musical cultures. If we ask the average concertgoer why this should be so, why he or she prefers the work of long-dead musicians to that of live or even recently deceased ones, we will generally be told something to the effect that modern music is so dissonant, so tuneless, so difficult if not incomprehensible that it repels potential listeners.

There is a certain truth in this, of course, and many composers of the past seventy years or so have even taken a kind of wry pride in the fact (Schoenberg once remarked that when a piece of his was well received he wondered what he had done wrong), but there is on the other hand a repertory of concert works from the present century that are no more or less difficult for modern audiences to follow than those of previous centuries, among them the three I listed above. Yet there is not a single piece from the twentieth-century concert repertory that comes near the regularity of performance that is attained by the symphonies and concertos of Beethoven, for example, or Brahms or Tchaikovsky. Whatever the contemporary concertgoer is in search of, it does not seem to be new musical experiences. There must be another reason.

The Great Composers who are summoned up by the conductor's gestures are not flesh-and-blood people, not the historical Beethoven or Brahms or Tchaikovsky who lived his life and died in his own time. They have gone forever, and no amount of carefully detailed biography will bring them back to life for even the duration of a performance. It is abstractions of these men who are present, mythological culture heroes who, like mythological heroes from Achilles to Abraham Lincoln, from Moses to Che Guevara, have been constructed to serve the needs of present-day people from shards and fragments of biography, and by a kind of backformation of a personality from the gestural language in which they encoded their vision of human relationships and social order.

These figures belong not to secular history at all, not to calendar time, but to myth, to that past that exists in our minds outside of historical time, which is populated by heroes and their adversaries (Mozart and his rival Salieri, Wagner and the critic Hanslick), divinely appointed tasks to be accomplished (Beethoven overcoming his deafness and writing symphonies to the magical number of nine), and destinies to be fulfilled (the intimations of death that many hear in the last works of the prematurely dying Mozart and Schubert). Like all myth, its function is to provide present-day people with models and paradigms for values and behavior—for relationships, in fact.

In that they handed down to us scores whose content is stable and unchanging, those mythological creatures themselves appear stable and unchanging. They cannot be alive in the present. They *have* to be dead in order to be immortal, and they have to be immortal to be mythic heroes.

I intend no sarcasm when I characterize the composer as a kind of prophet, the score as his sacred text, and the conductor as his priest. Like priests generally, the conductor claims the right to interpret the sacred text and to impose his interpretation on others. And if, like many priests, he is sometimes liable to the sin of hubris, to thinking himself above, or at least equal to, the prophet, he may find himself duly chastised for it by those who know the score, especially by those professional curators and expounders of the text who are known as critics and musicologists. But such things happen also in the best-regulated religions.

I repeat, I intend no sarcasm. Nonetheless, the extraordinary veneration accorded in our time to those dead musicians, and to the scores they created, suggests that something more than ordinary secular admiration is at work. As I have already suggested, there is more than a hint of sacred space about this building, and those who come here are, I believe, looking for more than beautiful patterns of sounds to please their ears. It seems to me that they have come to take part in a ritual, and what that ritual enacts is, in a word, stability, certainty. The dead culture heroes are summoned up in order to give reassurance that the relationships they encoded in musical sounds are abiding and permanent, that things are as they have been and will not change.

The movement toward what is known by its advocates as "authenticity" that has characterized the performance of music from the past (to call it "early" music, as many do, speaks to me of a certain shortness of historical perspective) over the last couple of decades must be accounted for by this quest for certainty and security in a world that is changing too fast. The musicologists, as they assiduously seek out the most "authentic" text of a work (I have to put the word into quotes since some of their criteria for authenticity seem to me strange indeed), bring irresistibly to mind talmudic, biblical or koranic scholars with their obsession for documentation, their reverence for any written text and their often centuries-long arguments over the meaning of a single phrase.

Even the musical technologies are held steady. Twentieth-century technology, as we have seen, is used in concert halls, but it is kept out of sight and plays little part in actual performances as opposed to the organizational tasks of concerts. Those technologies which are in evidence in the performances themselves are those of the age of clockwork and the steam engine. The most modern instrument regularly in use in the concert hall is the piano, which in its present form is a product of nineteenth-century technology and production techniques. A piano made in 1996 is in all essentials the same as one made in 1896 or even in 1846, while the mass-production methods used in its manufacture (including farming out the making of specific parts to specialist firms) goes back even further. Improvements made during the twentieth century to it and to other instruments (the key systems of woodwind instruments, for example, and rotary valves in the French horn) have been marginal to their sound and their technique, and in any case have not gone beyond nineteenth-century mechanical technology.

With the repertory held steady and with the authenticity movement thriving, one would think that stasis had been achieved, the flow of time stopped. But of course such a thing is impossible. Each generation of musicians and listeners remakes the culture in ways that will support and sustain their values; hence the revaluation of composers and their works that is constantly going on, with new biographies and critical studies, each author convinced that he or she has finally arrived at the truth about the man and his works. Hence too, the constant rise and fall of posthumous reputations, and constant new revelations of the *only* right way to perform the works which reveal new attitudes toward the patterns of relationships that are modeled by their patterns of sounds.

That means not only new ways of realizing the composer's notations in sound but also new sets of relationships in the performing situation itself. We have seen how today's performing situation may well be very different from that for which the work was intended and in which it was first performed. All these changes are not the outcome of increasing knowledge, an ever closer approach to the "real" musician, but depend rather on a different valuation placed in each generation on already existing knowledge.

Tchaikovsky, for example, was in his own day characterized as a wild and rude semibarbarous Cossack, "without discrimination or taste," according to the famous Viennese critic Eduard Hanslick, quoted in Nicholas Slonimsky's (1953) entertaining anthology of critical assaults on composers. His violin concerto, said Hanslick, "transfers us to the brutal and wretched jollity of a Russian holiday. We see plainly the savage vulgar faces, we hear curses, we smell vodka"; while according to a Boston review of 1892, culled from the same anthology, what we hear in the finale of his Fifth Symphony is "all the untamed fury of the Cossack, whetting itself for deeds of atrocity, against all the sterility of the Russian steppes." "The furious peroration," says the critic, "sounds like nothing so much as a horde of demons struggling in a torrent of brandy, the music growing drunker and drunker."

One wonders how the composer ever managed to set down notes in such an alcoholic frenzy. I quote these opinions not to sneer at them but to show how the picture of a Great Composer (I do not imagine there are any left who would deny Tchaikovsky a place in that august band) and of his works can change over the years, even if national stereotypes do not seem to change much. Tchaikovsky has undergone more than one sea change since then. In my youth in the 1930s and 1940s he was the Sugar Plum Fairy, a sugary, sentimental sissy (his homosexuality was hinted at but not discussed) who just happened to write good tunes. His critical reputation, probably at that time at its lowest, was not helped by the fact that many of those tunes were annexed by Tin Pan Alley for a number of successful songs with titles like "The Story of a Starry Night," "Moon Love" and "Tonight We Love." I remember the American composer and critic Deems

Taylor, sometime in the 1940s, agreeing in an interview that Tchaikovsky's works were overemotional and sentimental and asking "But where did he get those tunes, and where could I get some like them?"

That view of him has given way to the contemporary picture of the agonized homosexual whose end was as melodramatic as his inner life, and whose every work was expressive of a barely controlled hysteria. There is no reason to think of the latter picture as any nearer the final truth about the man than any of the others. What we have arrived at is a myth that suits our time and ourselves, and it tells us as much about ourselves as it does about the man, the meticulous cool-headed craftsman (or am I now making yet another myth?) who lived from 1840 to 1893 and who was able to escape the straitjacket of the choreographer's measure-by-measure instructions (so many measures of this, so many of that, not one more or one less, for each movement) to create the soaring music of *Swan Lake*.

Similarly, the Wolfgang Amadeus Mozart the bicentenary of whose death was so lavishly celebrated in 1991 (a curious event to celebrate when one thinks about it but fully in accord with the myth) is not the Mozart of 1791, or even of 1891. We should not, however, flatter ourselves that we have found the real historical Mozart, let alone the "real" way to perform his works (as if there were such a thing). We have simply demolished one myth in order to erect another. That is understandable enough, since it is the myth, not the actual man, whom we need.

Nineteenth-century mythmakers liked to portray him as a divine child who was too good for this world, while those of our own time show us a dirty-talking street urchin and have him poisoned, in the teeth of readily available medical evidence, by a rival musician who recognized that the Great is the sworn enemy of the merely Good (a modernist creed if ever there was one). But then, myths have always shown themselves to be remarkably resistant to the power of banal historical evidence.

In any case, the helter-skelter of new creation among which Mozart actually lived—and among which popular musicians live today—and the unpredictability of live culture heroes, who are liable to change their minds, backtrack and confound the expectations of their devotees, are too unsettling for audiences in search of reassurance. For this purpose a living artist is surplus to requirements and merely makes a nuisance of himself by demanding that his work be heard.

I shall have more to say about myth in the following interlude. Here let us just note that myths are not just simple untruths but are rather stories we tell ourselves concerning how things came to be and therefore how they are. They thus place the past, whether real or imagined, at the service of the present. Their actual historical accuracy is irrelevant to their value; that lies in the extent to which we are led by them to lead richer or poorer lives.

I shall be suggesting in later chapters that the musical works that are performed in the concert hall are in effect stories that we tell ourselves about ourselves and that they thus partake of the nature of myth. In taking part in their performance in a concert hall we are exploring, affirming and celebrating concepts of relationships that we feel to be desirable. What those relationships are I shall be discussing later in this book. We need now a second interlude to consider the nature of myth and of ritual and their relation to those activities we call the arts.

Interlude 2
The Mother of All the Arts

*

With these words we enter a thicket of related concepts: ritual, myth, metaphor, art—and emotion. They are intimately and intricately linked together, and to speak of one inevitably leads us on to the others. Words being a one-thing-at-a-time affair, I have no option but to talk of them separately, but we shall see that they belong inseparably together. What links them is that they are all concerned with relationships, with the ways in which we relate to one another, to the various social groups to which we belong, to other social groups and to the natural and even the supernatural world. These, of course, are important matters, perhaps the most important in human life.

The word *ritual*, like *myth*, has a bad press these days, being taken in common speech to mean any action that has been repeated so many times that it has lost any meaning it may once have possessed. It is usually used in this sense by those for whom the ritual is unsympathetic: the ceremonies of royalty for republicans, for example, or the ceremonies of the concert hall for those who do not like to music in that way. The word was even used in this way, to my surprise, in the publisher's blurb to my first book, where musicking in the Western concert tradition was characterized unflatteringly as an "artificial ritualized oasis outside normal life."

This interpretation of ritual does little justice to a practice that retains a powerful hold on the human imagination and an important place in human life and looks set to continue doing so for as long as there are human beings—not surprisingly, since it is a consequence of fundamental ways in which the human mind operates. We should note also that ritual is *never* meaningless; even when ritual actions do become "ritualized" in the sense in which my publisher used the word, that "ritualization" is itself full of meaning. The intention behind the phrase I quoted may have been un-flattering, but once the meaning of the word is properly understood, the phrase could stand as a description of any musical performance whatsoever.

Ritual is a form of organized behavior in which humans use the lan-guage of gesture, or paralanguage, to affirm, to explore and to celebrate their ideas of how the relationships of the cosmos (or of a part of it), oper-ate, and thus of how they themselves should relate to it and to one another. Through their gestures, those taking part in the ritual act articulate rela-tionships among themselves that model the relationships of their world as they imagine them to be and as they think (or feel) that they ought to be. As the anthropologist Clifford Geertz (1973) puts it in a resounding for-mulation, when we take part in a ritual act "the lived-in order merges with the dreamed-of order."

Those relationships, and the rituals that celebrate them, may be infor-mal and small-scale, or formal and on the grandest scale, or anything in be-tween. They may involve only one or two people, as in the rituals of courtship and lovemaking; a small and possibly exclusive group, as in ritu-als of family and of clubs and associations; or entire nations and even em-pires and major religious and secular faiths spanning or claiming to span the whole globe.

Coronations, Olympic games, the Roman Catholic mass, symphony concerts, executive lunches, elections, funerals, having oneself tattooed, grand banquets, family dinners and intimate meals à deux, prostrating to-ward Mecca, the "hazing" and bullying of recruits in elite armed corps and exclusive schools, and thousands of other rituals large and small are pat-terns of gesture by means of which people articulate their concepts of how the relationships of their world are structured, and thus of how humans ought to relate to one another. Such ideas held in common about how peo-ple ought to relate to one another, of course, define a community, so ritu-als are used both as an act of affirmation of community ("This is who we are"), as an act of exploration (to try on identities to see who we think we are), and as an act of celebration (to rejoice in the knowledge of an identity not only possessed but also shared with others).

Words may be used, of course, in these patterns of gesture, but they are subsumed into the pattern; their significance lies not so much in their lit-eral meaning as in the gesture of uttering them. One does not, therefore, need to know their literal meaning in order to divine their ritual signifi-cance. The use of Latin in the Roman Mass, abandoned in recent years in favor of national vernaculars, had a meaning over and above the literal meaning of those resonant syllables which the worshipers did not have to understand in order to comprehend the significance of uttering them.

During the enactment of the ritual, time is concentrated in a heightened intensity of experience. During that concentrated time, relationships are brought into existence between the participants that model, in metaphoric form, ideal relationships as they imagine them to be. In this way the participants not only *learn about* those relationships but actually *experience* them in their bodies. They explore the relationships, they affirm and they celebrate them, without having to articulate them in words; indeed, no words can adequately express the relationships as they are felt at that time. Instead, the participants are emotionally involved, often very powerfully indeed, sometimes to the point where the psychic boundary between the mundane and the supernatural worlds breaks down so that they leave behind their everyday identity and become, as we say, possessed.

But the emotion that is aroused is not the reason for taking part in the ritual. Rather, it is a sign that the ritual is doing its work, that it is "taking," that the participant feels at one with the relationships that the ritual has created. And on the other hand, if the ritual articulates relationships with which the participant does not feel at ease, then it will arouse no resonances and may feel as if it is "ritualized," in the sense in which my publisher used the word. So rituals can be used both by communities to exclude those individuals whom they do not want to include and by individuals to distance themselves from communities to which they do not wish to belong.

Of course, there are relationships and relationships, and one's intuitive response to them can often subvert in unexpected ways one's consciously held attitudes. In the little Catalan town where I live, the procession of the town's patron saint every August can move me to tears of joy, not because of the ostensibly Christian connotations of the event (it is in any case at least as much pagan as Christian) but because it affirms, explores and celebrates a centuries-old community's sense of itself and of its social order. It is not, however, a nostalgic celebration of a past order but a thoroughly contemporary affirmation of the community's present-day relationships rooted in its sense of its own history. That sense of its own history does not have to be the history that the history books relate; as long as the history is believed, or half-believed, or even wished to be true, the ritual retains its power. I daresay that if one traced the history of this little town's allegedly ancient Festa Major procession, much of it would prove to be of quite recent origin, but that does not matter as long as one believes the story.

Since a social order is a matter of relationships between human beings, the performance of this or any other ritual act together is a powerful means of ensuring social cohesion and stability. That being so, we need not be surprised to find that it is commonly used, often deliberately and sometimes even cynically, by those who rule to maintain the acquiescence of those over whom they rule. It is obviously appropriate that the rituals used for this purpose should appear ancient, even timeless, for in this way it can be made to seem as if the present social order is legitimated by generations of ancestors, independently of political, economic or social forces and of any trace of historical contingency.

The rituals of the British monarchy are an interesting example of this kind of pseudotimelessness. We are asked to believe that such contemporary royal ceremonies as coronations, weddings, investitures and funerals are survivals from centuries past, in a legitimating line of descent from such mythic figures as Henry V, the victor of Agincourt, or Henry VIII and his daughter Elizabeth I. But a little study of history shows not only that the line of descent from those figures to the present-day royal family is tenuous indeed but also that very few of the "ancient" royal rituals that are celebrated today go back, at least in their present form, farther than the late eighteenth century. Many of them, in fact, including the coronation ceremony itself, were devised by that inventive monarch, Edward VII, in the early years of the twentieth century, with the conscious aim of redefining the monarch's relationship with his subjects in the age of mass industrial society and, especially, of mass communications.

In his enterprise he was aided by a gifted team of artists, architects (many of the great ceremonial streets and buildings of London date from his reign, including Buckingham Palace itself, or at least the part of it that is visible to the common eye) and ritual specialists, including the musician Edward Elgar, who was knighted for his efforts. Those royal rituals are not quaint and harmless relics of a bygone age but are on the contrary thoroughly modern representations, and thus legitimations, of contemporary relationships within British society, including its iniquitous and paralyzing class system.

Ruling classes have their private as well as their public rituals, which are intended to display, more to themselves than to their inferiors, their universe of wealth and power, to affirm their distance from the common people, and also to dramatize the hierarchy that exists within them. Such rituals include hunting and shooting, routs and junkets, balls, salons and dinners, seeking and bestowing membership of exclusive clubs, and musical performances; Marcel Proust's great novel *Remembrance of Things Past* contains brilliantly comic portrayals of such aristocratic rituals. Much of the music we hear today in public concert halls was composed to adorn such events in the past, to which the public was definitely not admitted.

Not all rituals, of course, are intended to legitimate the position of a ruling class. People who live on the margins of society also invent their own, not necessarily consciously, in order to keep alive that precious sense of who they are, where they belong, and what they think the relationships of the world ought to be, without which no human being feels it worth while going on living, and in order to pass on that sense to the new generation. Much "folk" singing and dancing serves this purpose, for example the singing of spirituals by enslaved African Americans and the playing of the *bodhran* drum by oppressed Irish. The young also may well devise their own rituals in opposition to those of their elders, such as hanging out on street corners, taking illegal drugs and dancing in discos.

Some rituals affirm, explore and celebrate the passing of individuals from one social condition, one set of relationships, to another and give them meaning: weddings, funerals, christenings and other naming ceremonies (bestowing a name on an individual is a sign of recognition as a social being), initiations, graduations, and retirement parties. When I was a young man, one's twenty-first birthday was an important event, marking one's arrival at legal maturity, but today, with the greater independence given to teenagers, this rite seems to have become less significant. Such ceremonies as these are known as rites of passage, and they have the function of easing the passage from one social state to another and of giving it social legitimacy.

During such ceremonies the self of the person who is passing is metaphorically dissolved and then reconstituted in the new identity (i.e., set of relationships), with the whole community as witness. Across the human race, ceremonies that mark the passage of adolescents from childhood to adulthood have many features in common, the principal feature being that the initiates undergo a powerful emotional experience. The adolescents are taken from their mothers, who frequently mourn them as if dead, given intensive instruction in the secrets of the community, and finally subjected to a ceremony that generally involves being subjected to pain, being frightened out of their wits, being stimulated with singing and dancing and sometimes with hallucinogenic drugs, and being kept in a state of uncertainty while the society's concepts of relationships are enacted in songs and dances. The instruction is as much gestural and relational as it is verbal, and one mode reinforces the other.

But no matter what form the ritual takes, to take part in it is to take part in an act that uses the language of gesture to explore, affirm, and celebrate one's concepts of ideal relationships.

That is what we might call a "secular" interpretation of ritual. But there is also what we might call a "sacred" interpretation. Neither interpretation excludes the other, for both are valid; they are different ways of looking at the same experience, and each viewpoint—like the differing viewpoints of our two eyes, which give us stereoscopic vision—can deepen our understanding of the other. The secular interpretation emphasizes ritual's links with tradition, which is malleable and negotiable, and emphasizes also its origin in the language of gesture, suggesting that it has survival value. The sacred interpretation, on the other hand, emphasizes its links with the unquestioned and seemingly unchanging values of a society—what is known as the sacred—and with the religious, which is the form of the sacred that comes into existence when the sacred is validated by the supernatural and by deities. This interpretation suggests that to take part in a ritual is to act out a myth.

In ordinary modern usage a myth, as the third edition of the *Shorter Oxford English Dictionary* has it, is a "purely fictitious narrative, embodying some popular idea concerning natural or historical phenomena," or a "fictitious or imaginary person or event." The fact that even reputable dictionaries will furnish us with definitions of this kind is a sign of the low esteem in which the idea of myth, like that of ritual, is held in our time. "It's a myth!" we exclaim, when what we mean is "It's a lie!" or at least, "It's a naive misconception that surely nobody believes any more!" Myth belongs, we are told, to the childhood of mankind, and modern science has enabled modern Westerners, at least, to outgrow such purely fictitious narratives and to see the universe and its origins as they really are.

But mythmaking and mythtelling, like ritual, are deeply embedded and probably ineradicable forms of human behavior, and modern Westerners engage in them no less than anyone else. Myths are stories of how the relationships of our world, or of a part of it, came to be as they are. They deal with exemplary acts of creation and destruction, carried out by exemplary heroes and villains, on a scale that ranges from the cosmic to the intimate and domestic, and those acts provide us with models and paradigms for human experience and behavior and lay the foundation for all social and cultural institutions.

We can put it another way and say that the relationships established in the mythical time ("once upon a time," which is to say, out of historical time altogether) by the mythical characters give us models for how we should relate, to ourselves, to one another, and to the rest of the animate and inanimate world. A myth, in fact, offers an account of how the pattern which connects together the whole cosmos, or at least certain elements of that pattern, originated, and how things came to be is how they ought to be. The myth of the creation, for example, that is related in the first chapters of the Book of Genesis is not just a picturesque story but lays the foundation for rules of human behavior and relationships as well as for an entire theory of human nature, including the powerful concept of original sin.

A myth, therefore, no matter how ancient its origins or its subject matter, is always concerned with contemporary relationships, here and now. Whether or not it is historically true is beside the point; its value lies not in its truth to any actual past whose reality we can establish or disprove but in its present usefulness as guide to values and to conduct.

The confusion that surrounds the word arises partly from the fact that it is perfectly possible, indeed quite common, for historical personages and events, even quite recent ones, to acquire mythic status as paradigms for attitudes and behavior. In the United States of America, for example, certain historical events and personages in the colonization of a large part of its territory during the nineteenth century have become mythologized into a body of stories about the Wild West, and the concepts of human relationships that are embodied in those stories have had important consequences for the internal social order, and sometimes the foreign relationships, of that country. Whether the Wild West mythology was invented to justify those relations or whether the mythology was responsible for their development is an interesting question that need not detain us now (I am inclined to think that both statements are true in different ways; the relation between myth and values is extremely complex). For the English, on the other hand, the historical figure of Winston Churchill has become a mythic character and the Second World War an exemplary event, whose nature defines and justifies many of their present-day attitudes toward the rest of the world.

All these characters and events, and countless others, jostle with stories from the remote past, from sacred texts and from popular folklore, to make a complex, often confused and contradictory pattern of myth whose outlines are shared by members of the same social group, whether large or small; indeed, the sharing of myths is one of the features that defines a social group. What people may think they know about these events and characters may differ considerably from what formal history says about them; myths have indeed shown themselves to be remarkably resistant to the power of historical fact. Richard III of England, Richard Crookback, who limps and snarls through Shakespeare's play of that name has his origin in the writings of the Tudor propagandist Sir Thomas More and is the product of a deliberate piece of mythmaking carried out by those who wished to discredit the deposed Plantagenet dynasty. Historians may know that he bears little resemblance to the historical Richard, but it is of that figure of whom most English people think when his name is mentioned. Separating fact from myth, or rather sifting out the facts that lie enshrined in myth, is one of the most difficult tasks of the historian, a task that is probably ultimately impossible.

But in any case the historical accuracy of a myth is more or less irrelevant to its power as paradigm, as model for thought and action in the here and now. It retains that power for as long as its mythic character remains unperceived. This means that as long as modern Westerners continue to believe themselves to have outgrown the power of myth, so long will they remain in thrall to it.

There is a sense in which all storytelling partakes of the nature of myth. Novels, plays, musicals, films, even at their most frivolous and irresponsible (which is not necessarily to say "bad"), all carry within them paradigms of human behavior and relationships. Even the conventional happy ending implies the question "What makes people happy?" which is not a trivial matter. We learn about ourselves and especially our relationships from the stories we tell one another, as Jane Austen maintained in her celebrated defense of the novel in chapter 5 of *Northanger Abbey*.

But how we tell the stories can be as revealing as their overt content. It is interesting that the novel, a very specific form of storytelling that came to maturity in the late eighteenth century, more or less contemporaneously with symphonic music, typically deals with the development (the "education" as Austen put it) of a protagonist through conflict, climax and final resolution, just as does a symphony. So far as I know, no one in that epoch thought it necessary to defend the performance of symphonies as vigorously as she defended the reading of novels, but it is true that both novel and symphony were then regarded more as light entertainment than as the serious business they were later to become. Myths can be lighthearted as well as solemn.

The making and telling of myths (could we say "mything"?) can function in a society either to give legitimacy and support to an actual social order or to support the beliefs of those who would change it. It can be either confirmatory or subversive of the present social order; some myths, like their associated rituals, will be propagated, often quite sincerely and sometimes not, by those who have an interest in maintaining that order, whereas others will be held, equally sincerely or not, by those with an interest in change. Whose myths and their associated rituals are accepted is a matter of great importance; getting people to accept your myths and your rituals is a key element in the getting and retaining of social and political power, and all politicians, all successful ones at any rate, know this, though they may not articulate it even to themselves.

It is in times of great change or crisis that myth and ritual are most urgently evoked, and the kinds of myth and ritual that are called upon will be closely linked with the ways in which those in power, as well as those who are seeking power, respond to the crisis. Some mythic responses seem to be ways of closing ranks in the (usually eventually futile) attempt to prevent the feared changes from taking place, others seek to ease change by showing it to be a natural outcome of what happened in the past, and still others are representations of total revolutionary change which abolishes all existing institutions.

The shift in economic and political attitudes that took place in Western industrial democracies in the 1980s brought with them many new myths and their associated rituals, most notably the myth of the all-powerful and all-justifying "market" with its mythic heroes Adam Smith and Friedrich von Hayek, not to mention the making over of old ones such as Margaret Thatcher's brazen appropriation of Saint Francis of Assisi and the Good Samaritan and Ronald Reagan's adoption of the football hero he once impersonated in a movie. These were aimed at easing the shift and making it appear inevitable, and hopefully acceptable, even to those whose lives were devastated by it.

Whether we emphasize ritual's secular links with the language of gesture, on the one hand, or with the sacred acting out of myths, on the other, we can say that to engage in ritual is to engage in a form of behavior that we call metaphorical.

Metaphor is much more than the decorative "figure of speech" that we were taught to recognize in school. It is an important means by which we think about and apprehend the world. When we think metaphorically, we project patterns that derive from the concrete experience of our bodies and our senses onto more abstract experiences and concepts. The relations that our senses perceive between the parts of the concrete experience are equated with more abstract sets of relationships such as those of morals, ethics, social relations on both the large and the small scale, and the shapes of political power.

Verbal language itself is shot through with metaphor. We can hardly speak without engaging in it. The very word *metaphor* is itself a metaphor, deriving from two Greek words meaning, roughly, "across" and "bear" or "carry," both of them bodily experiences carried over into abstraction (in modern Greek, the word retains its literal meaning, as "transport," and can be seen on removal vans). The word *abstraction* is another metaphor, coming from two Latin words meaning "carrying away." Such words have metaphor built into them, but practically any word, even the most commonplace, can acquire metaphorical meanings, to the point that we hardly notice what is going on. The often multiple metaphoric meanings that are acquired by words like *high* and *low* (prices are high and morale is low), *hot* and *cold* (the hot line as a medium in the cold war), *weight* and *balance* (the balance of his mind disturbed by the weight of his troubles) and countless other usages show the extent to which we habitually think in metaphors, which is to say we refer to bodily experiences to help us deal with more abstract concepts. All languages seem to have this tendency to drift (another metaphor!) over time toward metaphoric meanings for everyday words. Some words, such as *ruminate* (from a Latin word meaning "to chew") have so completely been taken over by their metaphoric meaning that they have lost their literal meaning, at least in everyday speech.

The American philosopher Mark Johnson (1987) has suggested that these metaphoric associations are not random but are highly structured and depend on the shared bodily experiences of members of the same social group. They cluster around a relatively small number of key sets of meanings, some of which are related to universal human experiences while others are specific to a particular group at a particular point in its history. Such key metaphors as paths, goals, cycles, center and periphery, and movement upward and downward, together and apart, inward and outward, are widely found throughout human speech; but others, such as the clock, the theater or the computer, will naturally be found only among groups where such objects are part of the common experience. The style of our metaphors, in other words, is determined to a large extent by the experience and the assumptions of the social and cultural group to which we belong.

These "image schemata," as Johnson calls them, constrain our understanding of the world and give it structure. Thus it is that the metaphor that underlies much Western thought of the seventeenth and eighteenth centuries—of the universe as a giant clock, and of the creator god as the clockmaker who made it, wound it up, and set it going—could occur only in a society where clocks and clockwork were an advanced and widely diffused technology. Today the computer furnishes a rich source of such schemata, that, sometimes without our even noticing it, influence our way of understanding, for example, human mental processes.

The "pattern which connects" is itself a metaphor, a way of understanding a vast and incomprehensibly complex set of relationships in terms of sense experience; a pattern is a set of visual relationships in which we can perceive repetitions and regularities. Even the deities who are evoked to preside over the pattern, or aspects of it, are the result of metaphoric thinking. The Polynesian god Tane, for example, is—not represents or symbolizes but *is*—the proper relationship between humanity and the life of plants and the forest, and the Yoruba-American goddess Yemayá is that which connects us to the sea and its creatures. To worship Tane or Yemayá is to affirm and to celebrate the pattern of human connectedness to the life of the forest and the sea, and our human tendency to represent the pattern to ourselves as a person results once again from metaphoric thinking.

The multiple responsibilities that are assigned to certain deities also show an awareness of complex relationships that may be different from those connections that modern Westerners recognize; Poseidon, for instance, for the ancient Greeks, presided not only over the sea and its creatures but also over earthquakes, horses, bulls, and the building of cities—to modern minds a curious combination but to them apparently perfectly logical and comprehensible. The great principle of modern scientific thinking known as Occam's Razor, which maintains that entities should not be multiplied unnecessarily—leading to the sensible conclusion that the simplest explanation is likely to be the correct one—does not apply to metaphoric thinking. Entities can be multiplied indefinitely, the more the merrier (and the experientially richer), and if we call those explanatory entities gods and give them names, no harm is done. It seems to me that tendency to reduce the number of deities to the irreducible *one*, who stands outside the pattern and takes responsibility for everything, tends to impoverish our perception of the pattern and leads us away from, rather than toward, a proper understanding of its complexities.

As Bateson points out, a satisfactory image schema must contain within itself a degree of internal complexity if it is to function well as metaphor. The metaphor of the world as theater, for instance, and of human life as performance depends not only on the existence of theaters as part of our experience but also on the fact that a theater is a complex structure. When we elaborate on the idea that "all the world's a stage" or that "life is a cabaret, my friends," we are saying, not that the world is *identical* to a theater or a cabaret but that the relationships between the parts of a theater, which can be grasped as sense experiences, and those of "all the world" or "life," which are too big and complex for us to grasp directly, are in some ways parallel, or analogous, at least in certain respects. Life can also be a battle, a circus, a tale told by an idiot, a bitch, a game or a dream, and the metaphor we choose will reflect the aspects of that infinitely complex process to which we wish to draw attention at that moment.

Metaphor, in fact, like ritual and like myth, is concerned with relationships, and all three are aspects of the same process, in which the physical and sensuous experience of human beings and our bodily experiences of the world are used to understand those often extremely complex and abstract concepts with which we, like all living beings, need to be able to deal. Myth tells us, in extended metaphoric fashion, how the relationships came to be, while ritual can be thought of as metaphor in action.

For metaphor does not have to be verbal. Or rather, what in verbal language we call metaphor has its equivalent in the language of biological communication, where, as we have seen, a physical gesture articulates, or stands for, a relationship. As metaphor is to a verbal concept, so the language of gesture is to a relationship. The elaborated patterns of gesture that we call ritual bring into existence relationships between those taking part, which mimic, or dramatize if you like, that set of ideal human relationships whose origin the myth relates. It allows those taking part to experience those relationships directly and in all their complexity, without needing the mediation of words with their one-thing-at-a-time slowness, and impresses them on their minds, making them appear as natural and inevitable consequences of the way in which the world came into being and thus of how it is.

It is very important to realize that in taking part in ritual we do not only see and hear, listen and watch, or even taste, smell, or touch, but we also act, and it is in the bodily experience of performing the actions in company with others that the meaning of taking part lies. The more actively we participate, the more each one of us is empowered to act, to create, to display, then the more satisfying we shall find the performance of the ritual. This is not surprising, since in acting, creating, and displaying we are bringing into existence for the duration of the ritual a society in which we ourselves are empowered to act, to create and to display. A ritual in which the majority watch and listen in stillness and silence, unable to influence the course of the event, while a minority acts can be a vivid representation of certain types of political relationship; many of the rituals of the modern nation-state are of this kind. Guy Debord (1983) coined the phrase "the society of the spectacle" for such a state and pointed out that in such rituals or spectacles, "one part of the world represents itself to the world and is superior to it"; such rituals emphasize the separation and powerlessness of isolated individuals rather than their unity as an active community. The ultimate passive ritual is, of course, that of watching television, where no active participation is possible, and where viewers are isolated from one another or at most in small groups. It is no wonder that politicians prefer to talk to the voters on TV.

But we can see why it is that to take an active part in a ritual act brings pleasure, even joy, the joy that can sometimes move us to tears. For in doing so we are making our dreams come true.

What has all this to do with musicking? Simply this: ritual is the mother of all the arts.

I do not mean just that in the ritual process we make extensive use of those activities which are known as the arts, though that is clearly true. Not only musicking and dancing, not only drama and movement, but also costume, architecture and visual design, the displaying of images and other precious objects lovingly made, bodily adornment and decoration, cooking and eating and the making and smelling of aromas are brought together in various combinations and as lavishly as can be afforded, to make their contribution to the occasion. None of the rituals of church and state, or the smaller rituals of communities and families or even those of couples and individuals could be thought of as taking place at all without some participation, however slight and however humble, of the arts. This association is not accidental, nor are the arts mere adornments of ritual. Both ritual and the arts are gestural metaphors, in which the language of biological communication is elaborated into ways of exploring, affirming and celebrating our concepts of ideal relationships.

But I believe the association goes deeper than that. Ritual does not just *use* the arts but itself *is* the great unitary performance art in which all of what we today call the arts—and some of the sciences as well—have their origin.

We might almost say—*almost*—that ritual is art and art ritual. Certainly, the idea of art as an autonomous activity is fairly new; as Raymond Williams (1976) points out, if we trace the word back in history, we find that the meaning we give it today is of quite recent provenance, dating back perhaps only to the mid-nineteenth century. Before that the word simply meant "skill" and could be applied to any skilled human activity. If we go a little farther back, as far as the mid-seventeenth century, we even find that the two words *art* and *science* meant practically the same thing, any difference between them lying in the implication in the latter word of a greater degree of theoretical knowledge than in the former. Up to the mid-nineteenth century the word *artist* simply meant someone with a skill, a learned or a practical person; while the word *scientist* did not exist at all in English until around 1840.

The term *scientific music*, meaning a piece or performance that showed a degree of knowledge of the European classical techniques, was in common use well into the nineteenth century. An illuminating example of this usage occurs in a stanza of Thomas Rice's famous, or infamous, blackface minstrel song "Jump Jim Crow" of 1832, poking fun at the aspiration of the ignorant black musician to be taken seriously:

> I'm a rorer on de fiddle
> And down in old Virginny
> I play the skientific
> Like massa Pagganninni.

Today in the West we take pride in the separation of art from ritual, in its "autonomy," its "independence," and especially perhaps its "secularity." We use the arts *in* our rituals, of course, but as independent activities voluntarily contributing their share to the splendor of the occasion, as optional extras, so to speak, rather than as intrinsic and essential elements. You will no doubt realize by now that I believe that separation to be more illusory than real, but in any case it is more recent in origin than we think; it probably did not exist even as recently as the time of Mozart. Like his contemporaries and predecessors, he composed his works, not for the kind of abstract contemplation to which we subject them today but as actively participant elements in the social and religious rituals of his time.

Ritual, of course, is action; it is something that people do. Its meaning lies not in the created objects that are worn, or exhibited, or eaten, or performed, or otherwise used, but in the acts of creating, wearing, exhibiting, eating, performing and using. The crowds who line up in the Tower of London to see the British crown jewels do so not so much for their intrinsic value, great as is the value of the gems and precious metals of which they are made, and certainly not for their beauty (they are mostly rather tasteless pieces of nouveau-riche Victorian goldsmithing) as for their association with the rituals of British royalty—the crowns they believe to have sat on the heads of countless British monarchs and their consorts and the orb and scepter that they have held in their hands. The meaning lies not in the objects themselves but in the viewing of them, and the lining-up and viewing are themselves ritual acts with a wealth of social and political meanings.

All over the world today, in art galleries, palaces and museums as well as in opera houses and concert halls, objects that were originally made for the rituals of the rich and powerful, and occasionally of the poor and humble, are today exhibited out of their original context, their original social function forgotten or obscured. This applies as much to paintings and sculptures, to masses and concertos, as it does to crowns, robes, masks, crucifixes and other, to us, more obviously ritual objects, for paintings, sculptures, masses and concertos too were originally intended for use in the rituals of their time, for display at special events and ceremonies. It is only works created since about the middle of the nineteenth century or perhaps a little earlier (it is difficult to say exactly, because, like so many of the important social facts of any period, nobody talked about it since it seemed to them so obvious), that appear not to possess a ritual function and to have become simply isolated, self-contained works intended as the objects of disinterested contemplation.

Appear not to possess—as I am suggesting in this account of a symphony concert, I believe that to display or perform such works, even those of the most uncompromising twentieth-century modernism, still cannot be separated from its ritual function. The nature of the ritual may have changed, but the essential ritual function remains. That this is so can be seen from the buildings that house the activities of exhibiting and viewing objects of art. Art galleries are ritual buildings as much as are concert halls and theaters and as much as are churches and temples. If I describe in some detail the event that is a symphony concert, it is because it is a ritual in which members of the industrial middle classes are empowered to say, to themselves and to anyone who may be paying attention, *This is who we are.*

But art galleries similarly house the ritual of looking at paintings and sculptures, and the behavior they impose on those within them is very like that which we have noted in the concert hall. This is not the place to discuss the present-day significance of looking at paintings in art galleries (in any case, John Berger and his associates [1972] have already done it brilliantly), but I might suggest that it too has to do with the affirmation and celebration of relationships—especially those of power and, considering the enormous prices that these days are paid for the paintings, money. In any case, just as we ask the question of a musical performance, we may ask, "What is the meaning of looking at this painting / sculpture / photograph / tapestry / collage / installation / anything else labeled 'art' in this place at this time?"

Properly understood, then, all art is performance art, which is to say that it is first and foremost activity. It is the *act* of art, the act of creating, of exhibiting, of performing, of viewing, of dancing, of wearing, of carrying in procession, of eating, of smelling, or of screening that is important, not the created object. Clearly, what we choose to create, to exhibit, to look at and so on is significant, as is what we choose to play and to listen to in a musical performance, but it is the object that exists in order to bring about the action, not the other way around.

In the early phases of human society, as well as in many modern tribal societies, religion, ritual and art were not and are not separate activities. The shaman of the nomadic tribe (the word *priest* is a very rough approximation) uses not only his—or her, for many shamans are women—often virtuoso singing, drumming, and dancing but also the costume, the images displayed, the often amazingly realistic vocal imitations of animals, birds, and spirits, the magic tricks and the displays of strength and balance in order to make a descent into the underworld (a place whose geography they know well through a long and arduous initiation) and assert their control over the underworld spirits that are responsible for sickness, madness, misfortune and social discord so that they will do good and refrain from evil. We could call them universal performance artists who, in their sessions of ecstasy, shared by all the tribe, use all of what we call the arts in the pursuit of their aim, which is to cause all the members of the tribe to experience right, or ideal, relationships and thus to maintain their unity and cure whatever physical, psychic or social ills might have befallen them.

Rogan Taylor (1985) points out that as the centuries of human history have passed, the once unitary healing performance art of the shaman has split into any number of specialisms, each with its own traditions and its own skilled practitioners, who have taken fragments of the universal art and developed them in various ways. And so we have not only musicians, dancers, painters, sculptors, architects and designers, actors, cooks, perfumers, storytellers, costume designers and makers but also conjurers, acrobats, illusionists, ventriloquists and circus artists in general, in fact the whole personnel of what we today call showbiz, as well as healers of the body and the mind, all of whose work is devoted to essentially the same purpose, the maintenance and restoring of relationships, so that humans may learn the shape of the pattern which connects, find their place in it, and be restored to right and harmonious relationship with it if they should lose their place and fall out of balance.

But the separate arts constantly incline toward their former unity. Any "artistic" performance, if one examines it with attention, will show itself to involve more than the art with which it is ostensibly occupied. We have seen how each kind of musical performance, for example, requires of its participants a physical and social setting, a mode of dress and behavior that is not merely specific to itself but is also as appropriate as possible to the occasion and to the felt identity of those taking part. To this purpose all available artistic media are summoned and orchestrated into a total artwork, whose elements are not mere decoration but an essential part of the human encounter that is the performance.

CHAPTER 7

Score and Parts

Unobtrusive, so that we hardly notice them, music racks stand before each player or pair of players on the platform. Without these humble pieces of furniture tonight's concert could not take place, for they bear the orchestral parts, the coded instructions copied from the full score that tell each player what he or she is to play and when to play it. No performance could take place here without each player's ability to understand and obey, in uniform and dependable manner, all the instructions that their parts contain. Each player sees only his or her own part; only the musician who directs the others' performance while making no sound himself has before him the full score, telling him what everyone in the orchestra is to play.

Performance in the modern concert hall always takes place in this literate mode. Its nature and even its very existence depend upon a commonly understood system of written instructions for performance that the composer has set down and the players obey. Nonliterate performance, in which the performers invent some or all of their own material, has no place in tonight's, or any other night's, event in this hall.

The total dependence on notation of performers in the Western concert tradition is a curious and ambiguous practice, unique among the world's musical cultures. On one hand, it is a tremendous enabler, permitting the accurate preservation of musical compositions, perhaps over centuries, and the learning of them quickly and efficiently by a player or group of players. It thus gives them ready access to the musical thought of practically the whole of the Western tradition of composed works. On the other hand, it is a limiter, since it confines what can be played to what has been notated, so the player's power of self-directed performance is liable to atrophy, especially when, as in the modern Western concert tradition, nonliterate performance is judged to be in some way inferior to literate. As a result, performing musicians, even eminent concert and operatic soloists, may go through an entire career without ever making a musical gesture they can call their own.

This situation would strike musicians of the past, including many of those who created the scores on which modern performers depend, as strange indeed. In the first place, it seems unlikely that those musicians would feel much interest in the first of those objectives, having little or no interest in the preservation of musical compositions, not even their own and certainly not over centuries. Dissemination, yes, for which a score is well suited; but preservation, no, and in that respect they have more in common with today's pop musicians making records than with contemporary concert musicians. Nor did they feel any need for access to the whole tradition of Western composed music; their concern was with the immediate situation, with the helter-skelter of today's creation, and they were interested in the past only to the extent that it would serve their creative purposes.

In the second place, neither J. S. Bach, Mozart, Beethoven, nor in fact any of the musicians who are today known as The Great Composers ("Mozart to Mahler"), was totally dependent on notation, either for composition or for performance. All were fluent nonliterate as well as literate composers and performers, who moved easily from one mode to the other according to circumstance. Their frequent nonliterate performances were, to judge from often wildly enthusiastic contemporary accounts, more exciting and moving, even inspired, than any performance could be of those notated works of theirs which have come down to us and which today we treasure. On reading those accounts, one is tempted to wonder whether, when we perform those notated works today, we may not be dealing with only the congealed remains of what was once white-hot inspiration, like those often strangely and beautifully shaped lava rocks which bear witness to the power of past volcanic eruptions.

What those great musicians did in nonliterate performance was only a transcendental version of the improvisation that every musician worthy of the name, down to the late years of the nineteenth century, expected, and was expected, to be able to do. They would no doubt have thought (were they even to consider the possibility of such a thing) that any musician, whatever his level of technical dexterity and powers of interpretation of a notated score, who was unable to improvise was lacking in important skills and, worse, had been deprived of an important aspect of musical experience. One might even argue that a healthy tradition of literate composition and performance depends on the parallel existence of a healthy nonliterate tradition. But in concert musicking today a nonliterate tradition no longer exists. No one improvises any more, at least not in public, and no performance takes place without a score, whether it stands before the performer or has been memorized.

A score, of course, is not a musical work. It is not even the representation of it. It is a set of coded instructions that, when properly carried out, will enable performers not only to make sounds in a specific combination, called a musical work, but also to repeat that combination as many times as they desire. Players and listeners learn to recognize that combination as a unity and to give it a name, which may be Symphony no. 5 in C minor or *Rhapsody on a Theme of Paganini* or *Scheherezade*, but the fact that this title appears on the cover of the score does not mean that the musical work resides in its pages. We find there only a set of instructions for performing.

Nor does the identity of the musical work lie in the sounds of which it is made. Individually, sounds are only sounds; their aural characteristics of timbre, pitch, intensity, duration, and attack and decay may allow us to attribute certain meanings to them, but nothing like the complex meanings that are carried by even the simplest combination of sounds that we call a melody. Until they are placed into relationship with one another, they do not yield even a melody, let alone a whole musical work, whose identity lies in the relationships that exist between the sounds.

We hear the sounds, which means that we perceive the aural images that form in our minds as the result of certain concrete physical events, namely, vibrations of the air as they impinge on our ears, and we perceive their aural characteristics. What we do *not* hear is the relationships between them.

Relationships are mental, not physical, events. They are made in our minds, and it is our minds that place the sounds we hear into those often extremely complex relationships with one another, too complex to be articulated in words, that enable us to create and to perceive patterns—melodies, harmonies, rhythms, repetitions, and variations, as well as larger regularities involving all these over an often extended period of time. It is in our minds also that we learn to attribute meaning to them. It is those relationships that specify the identity and the meaning of the work, whether it be a symphony lasting an hour or more or a simple song lasting no more than a minute or so.

Perceiving relationships and giving them meanings is, as we have seen, an active process. Without a prepared mind, ready and able to create meaning from the sound relations, a musical work cannot exist. That is shown very clearly from the fact that while some hear in a particular set of sonic relationships order, meaning and beauty, others may hear in it only chaos and meaninglessness. There is no way in which a person who hears the first has the right to tell those who hear only the second that they hear wrongly—or vice versa.

If a musical work exists in the relationships between the sounds as performers make them and as hearers hear them (performers, of course, are hearers also), then it exists only in performance. Its identity and whatever meaning it may have are embodied in the act of musicking itself, are inseparable from it, and can be known only in the act of musicking. Once the performance is over, the work "exists," if we can call it that, only in the memory of those who have heard it, again including those who have played it. Only the score, with its written instructions for performance, has a continuous real existence; the rest is memory. If a skilled musician is able, by reference to the score, to hear in his mind how the performance will sound, that does not bring the work into anything more than an imagined existence. In this respect it is like any other imagined or remembered object or event.

I can remember, say, the particular set of sounds brought into particular relationships that is called the Fifth Symphony of Beethoven, and I can run them through in my mind in due succession. But that is memory; if I had not heard the piece brought into existence in performance, I should not be able to do it. My memory no more brings the work into existence than do my memories of my parents bring them back to actual life.

Concert life today, however, is dominated by the idea that musical works have a continuous reality that transcends any possible performance of them, that each musical work we hear has, somewhere Out There, a corresponding Platonic entity that exists prior to, and indeed independent of, all performance, an entity to which all possible performances are only approximations, ephemeral and contingent. This idea stems partly from the undeniable continuous existence of scores as permanent objects, which gives musical works the illusion of solidity, but it stems even more from the tendency in European thought, which we noted earlier, to create abstract entities from actions and then treat them as if they were more real than the real actions to which they refer. It receives support also from publishers' and record companies' need to have something tangible to sell and from scholars' need to have something permanent that will hold still long enough for them to study it—but that is another story.

It is, of course, true that performance is ephemeral, but it is definitely *not* contingent to either the musical process in general nor to the identity of specific works of music. On the contrary, *performance is the primary process of musicking*, from which all other processes follow. It can, and often does, take place without any fixed musical work at all. Composing begins when a performer, liking what he or she has just done, repeats it, perhaps many times, and tries to improve it so that a more or less fixed sequence of sounds, simultaneous perhaps as well as in succession, crystallizes out from the flowing stream. It evolved out of performing and is directed always back toward it. That is its function: to facilitate performing.

Notating comes a long way after composing, and is the exception rather than the rule in human musicking. The function of notation, as we have already noted, has always been twofold: first, to act as a surrogate memory so that the sequence of sounds can be fixed and its integrity preserved over multiple performances, freed from the unreliability of memory, and second, to enable those who may be remote in place or time from its origin to learn the sequence of sounds and perform it. In the Western concert tradition it has acquired a third function as well, which seems to be unique to that tradition: it acts as medium through which the act of composition takes place, not in sounds, not in company, and not in real time as it passes but in silence, solitude and imagined time in the composer's study. The composition is complete before a sound is actually heard. It is this third function, it is claimed, that has made possible the elaboration and complexity of works of music in the Western concert tradition.

But it is perfectly possible for composing to take place without recourse to notation, not only of short simple songs and dances sung or played by one person but even of extended pieces and suites of symphonic length and complexity played by large groups of performers. In an earlier book (Small 1977), I described two such nonliterate ensembles, one from Mozambique and one from Bali, and the manner in which they create and perform.

When there is no written score to refer to, it is probable that the piece will go on changing and developing through successive performances, without anyone caring too much or perhaps even noticing, since there is no stable "authentic" version with which to compare it. As performance circumstances change, the piece will change with them, for no one has any interest in fixing it or in preserving its integrity. It is not the piece that is treasured but the performance, and the aim of performance is not to present the piece but to play in such as manner as will be appropriate to the event at which it takes place, so that it will enhance the human encounter, order it and make it memorable. The piece is valued to the extent that it makes this possible, and when it ceases to do so, it is discarded without qualms. When it falls out of the repertory, it is dead forever, and there is no way in which it can be resuscitated. That is not necessarily to be felt as a loss, since it leaves room for new creative work to take place; and it is the creative work that is to be valued, not the created object.

In these conditions it is virtually impossible to say where composing a piece ends and rehearsing it begins, or when rehearsing ends and performing begins. It really does not matter, for composing, rehearsing and performing are a single process, and piece and performance, composer and performers, are a single group; the musical universe is a unified, seamless whole.

In nonliterate composition and performance the power relationships among those taking part are diffuse, uncentralized; all will have some authority and bear some responsibility. As in all communal enterprises, there will almost certainly be a leader of the ensemble, but his powers are limited and continue to exist only for as long as those working with him feel that he is worth following. He has no monopoly of the creative act, since other performers as well will contribute to the piece. Listeners and bystanders too may well contribute and certainly have a creative role to play through the energy they feed back, selectively and with discrimination (they will most likely have a firm basis for their discrimination, for they too will probably be performers on other occasions), to the musicians as they play, possibly through their dancing and certainly through their visible and audible response as the performance continues.

The moment the musicians feel the need to write down instructions for performance in order to preserve it and hold it steady, a change begins to take place in the nature of the musicking and in the relationships between those taking part. A crack appears in the hitherto unified musical universe; the single process begins to split apart, separating composer from performers, composition from performance, and performers from listeners, centralizing power in the hands of the composer, the person who tells the performers what they are to do, and of the director, the person who tells them how they are to do it.

The score that lies on the conductor's desk tonight is the ultimate center of power in this big space, the symbol of the composer's authority over what is played here and the means by which that authority is exercised. The authority of the conductor, supreme as it appears, is contingent on his obeying, like everyone else on the platform, the coded instructions that the score contains. He can make no gesture that is not inspired by those instructions, make no demands on the players that is not sanctioned by them. He may extend the implications of the instructions to the utmost, but he has, finally, to be able to justify his extension by reference to the authority of the score.

The score was not always so central to performance, nor has it always been the sacred and unalterable text that it is today. We have seen that in the improvising orchestras of the early explosion of opera in the seventeenth century there was not even a full score as we know it, showing the musicians exactly what each one of them was to play, but just a skeleton on which players and singers alike were expected to invent their own parts.

The basso continuo part in orchestral and chamber music of the period also gave ample opportunity for the continuo player to improvise; indeed it demanded of him that he do so.

In eighteenth- and nineteenth-century opera it was commonplace for the performers to make changes in scores, to cut, and to interpolate additional material, even whole scenes, perhaps by another composer. Star singers might arrive at rehearsal with a couple of new arias written for them by Signor So-and-so to be substituted for ones by the original composer. The composer was generally billed beneath the stars, as Hollywood directors used to be until film became Art, and apart from a few star composers such as Gluck and later Rossini, was regarded simply as provider of something for the singers to sing. Nothing about his text was sacred.

As late as the early years of the twentieth century, concert performers treated the scores from which they played in fairly cavalier fashion; old recordings by instrumentalists of the time teem with added ornaments, trills and graces, doublings at the octave and the third, and even interpolated bars and cadenzas, while conductors of the generation of Gustav Mahler and Richard Strauss did not hesitate to reorchestrate even major orchestral works if they thought they could improve the sound, the balance, or the clarity. In the 1920s and 1930s Leopold Stokowski made gorgeously colored orchestral transcriptions of Bach's organ works that were not thought vulgar, as they are today. I have to confess that the first time I heard, at the age of about twenty, the Toccata and Fugue in D minor played on an organ, I thought it very dull indeed.

One could go on. The point is that the anxious insistence on fidelity to the composer's written text that characterizes concert hall and of course recorded performance today is a relatively new phenomenon, one that has emerged only in my own lifetime. The authenticity movement that has emerged in its wake is, of course, a corollary of that insistence, for if we insist on fidelity to the original text, we need to know exactly what that the original text is. The further corollary, that only performance on instruments of the composer's own day will do justice to his text, follows more or less naturally, at least with a gentle push from record companies and concert managements, keen if not desperate to find a new sound to promote, with sources of new musical works more or less closed off. One can sympathize with Nicholas Kenyon (1988) when he says, in his editor's introduction to an influential book on what has become known as authentic performance, that for him these new performing styles for past music had been "perhaps the most stimulating part of concert-going and record-listening over the last couple of decades." Not surprisingly; it is the only new show in town.

The authenticity movement has moved forward in time, from its beginnings in the 1960s with works of the Middle Ages and Renaissance, through the baroque choral, operatic and orchestral repertory in the 1970s. In the 1980s it invaded the regular Mozart-to-Mahler concert repertory with the symphonies and concertos of Mozart, Beethoven and their contemporaries, and is now moving in on the nineteenth-century romantic repertory. Where it will end is hard to guess, but the managements of regular symphony orchestras are starting to show understandable signs of nervousness: if there is another orchestra in town and if it succeeds in making its own the symphonic works of Haydn, Mozart and Beethoven—even Schubert and . . . and . . .—where will that leave us?

I am in no position to comment on the validity of the claims made for the new performing styles. I have to confess to feeling some impatience with the total, even totalitarian, nature of some of the claims: *this* is the only way in which a concerto by Mozart can be performed, *this* is the only performance of the *Saint Matthew Passion* that Bach would recognize, while *that performance* of a piano sonata by Haydn is not to be countenanced because it is played on a modern instrument, and so forth. It seems to me that the proposition implied by the claims—that the way in which the works were performed in their composer's own day, even if it could be ascertained for sure, is the way, the *only way*, in which they ought to be performed in ours—is a big logical jump, which I cannot see as by any means justified.

(Actually, as an amateur pianist I am inclined to tell them to go jump in the lake. Haydn, like Mozart, and Beethoven too, and all the host of nineteenth-century piano composers, wrote his sonatas for people like me to play, and they must have known that we would play them on whatever instruments we had. We were then and we still are their primary market, and they and their publishers knew it, even if today's composers don't, and even if today's professional performers, aided and abetted by concert promoters and record companies, have appropriated the pieces as their own and banished us from public performance.)

I am inclined to agree with the musicologist Richard Taruskin (1995) that the best authenticity that can be claimed for these styles is authenticity to the spirit of twentieth-century modernism, the modernism, that is, of mandarins like Stravinsky, T. S. Eliot, Boulez and the philosopher José Ortega y Gasset, with their mistrust of expressiveness and their insistence on the subjection of personal tastes and desires to the assumed unchanging demands of the impersonal art object itself. Certainly that is in line, as we saw in the Prologue, with the modern philosophy of art generally.

The passion for authenticity has brought onto the scene another, at first sight unlikely, competitor for the power to interpret and establish control over the score. This is the musicologist, whose researches into exactly what the composer wrote and how the work was performed in his time, and thus ought to be performed in our own, are central to authentic performance. The fact that many have themselves taken up conductor's batons and have led orchestras playing instruments of the composer's time in performances of varying degrees of sensitivity lends force to their challenge to the older interpreters. It is a challenging challenge, for it implies not only that the older interpreters have been misinterpreting the sacred text but also that in many cases the text that they have been interpreting is itself corrupt. They claim that only they know what the true text is and how it should be interpreted.

The reverence accorded to the composer's score suggests that it is a sacred object, which is not to be tampered with, whose authority over the actions of all the musicians playing here tonight is absolute, which commands absolute stillness and silence from those devotees who have assembled to hear it performed. The absolute nature of its authority demands that enormous effort be expended in ascertaining exactly what the man who set it down really wrote, or intended to write, since a corrupt text will surely corrupt the ritual of performance. It also demands that the performance reproduce as nearly as possible the sounds that the composer heard when it was first performed so that we can imagine a continuity between his world and our own.

It demands too that the performance be note-perfect, with a perfection of technical precision that would have made the works' composers, those real men who lived in time rather than the mythic figures we have made them into, raise their eyebrows in astonishment, the more so since many of them were content with one rehearsal of their piece or even none at all. And finally, there is an almost total exclusion of the new from the performance. The corps of Great Composers who provided the works that are played here are all dead; living musicians may have their works played here from time to time, as a kind of courtesy, but it is the dead who command the loyalty of audiences, and it is their works that are played here over and over again with loving note-for-note accuracy.

We have seen these works characterized in concert and record advertisements as "immortal masterpieces," as "works that will live forever," and as "the world's greatest music," and we may smile and dismiss such phrases as adman's hype. But adman's hype is generally no more than a vulgarization of beliefs that are commonly held; that is the source of his power. On a profound level these works *are* thought of by those who know and love them as the best the human race has thought and done and as being immune to the passing of time, as somehow, in fact, existing outside time;

"immortal" is not too strong a word for either the works or their creators. Both exist outside time, in a past that is indeterminate and at the same time entirely contemporary. Performers as they play feel the critical presence of the composer beside them and frequently feel a greater responsibility to the works and to their composers than they do to the audience that has paid to hear them.

The magisterial perfection of form and structure that audiences are supposed to hear in these works as they are performed today was certainly not perceived by their initial audiences, who were more inclined to perceive in them dissonance, dislocation and even violence. These qualities were positively valued; it was contemporary excitement rather than timeless perfection of form that was sought. It seems as if we have projected onto these works as they are performed our desires for harmony, structure, comprehensibility and changelessness in what seems to us a time of increasing dissonance, chaos, incomprehensibility of events and uncontrolled change.

The past, it is said, is another country, and through the ritual of the performance of these past works we are enabled to visit it. But it is not the real historical past that we are visiting, with all its turbulence, its dirt and its dislocations that were no less violent than those of our own time. It is a mythical past, a theme park, that we have constructed from the audible features of these works and from selected bits and pieces of their creators' life histories, selected, that is, not necessarily consciously or deliberately but with all the care to which our subconscious needs and desires impel us.

Those works have through familiarity lost whatever power they once had, when performed in their own time, to upset, to excite, to disturb, to disconcert. If one could state in one word the meaning of performing them in our time, that word would be *reassurance*. To perform them no longer disturbs anybody, and the continuing ritual of their performance in concert halls reassures those who attend that things are as they have been and will continue to be so. Like many rituals, it is not itself unchanging; we have seen how it has changed in many ways over the century and a half or so of its existence, and today is continuing to do so at a precipitous rate.

But unchanged and unchanging at the center of the ritual are the musical scores with their instructions for performance; they are the point of intersection between the human relationships among those who assemble here to take part in the performances and the sonic relationships that are the ostensible reason for them to do so. It is no wonder that those who like to take part in the ritual of the symphony concert are those in industrial society who have benefited most from it and have most to lose from its passing.

CHAPTER 8

Harmony, Heavenly Harmony

✱

There is a famous caricature of Richard Wagner conducting, in silhouette according to the fashion of the day. He is seen in profile, his tiny body arched backward with one foot extended behind to balance him, the over-sized head tilted back with its big Roman nose and prominent chin very visible. His arms are at full stretch above his head, one hand holding the baton, and his coattails are flying. He is caught at the moment of maximum potential energy. A fraction of a second later he will bring his arms down in an imperious gesture to release the energy from the hundred or so musicians under his direction. It is clearly going to be something big—the Prelude to his own *Meistersinger* perhaps or those howlingly dissonant opening bars of the last movement of Beethoven's Ninth Symphony.

Tonight's conductor will certainly not engage in such extravagant gestures—in the staid concert world of today the musician who gestures too broadly is considered to have something of the charlatan about him—but the effect produced by his gestures will be very much the same. Let us think a little about the sound that his gesture is to produce before we think about the musical works of which the sound is the raw material.

It will be a brilliant and very dense sound, ranging in pitch across the entire gamut, from the very highest to the very lowest notes of which musical instruments are capable. It will be perfectly coordinated and unified, the sound of a hundred or more musicians all blended into one huge instrument, whose unity is emphasized by the sight of the string players all moving their bows in perfect accord. It will be a powerful sound, whether that power is exerted to the full in great climaxes or held in reserve in quiet moments. Even the sight of a handful of musicians playing while the rest await their next entry can bring home to us the enormous potential energy of this huge musical instrument.

The ensemble's power is exerted without apparent effort. The players' movements are reduced to a minimum, and they conceal the often consid-erable physical exertion that is needed to produce such powerful sounds. The apparent lack of effort is reflected in the suave quality of the sound, which comes in turn from the smoothness of their attack on each note. Nearly all the instruments that have been incorporated into the modern symphony orchestra are capable of a smooth attack and are played in a way that brings out that smoothness. There are few sharp percussive attacks, lit-tle of the sharp "ping" that marks the onset of the sound of a guitar, the "thud" that marks that of the drum, or the "buzz" that African musicians like to hear from their instruments—or even that soft but indescribable sound with which every note from a piano begins (but even with a piano, the gentler the onset of the sound, the better the instrument and the player's "touch" are thought to be).

Such sharp attacks as we do hear come from instruments of more recent arrival in the orchestra—the harp and the glockenspiel, for example—and naturally, various percussion instruments. Because of the nature of their at-tack, these instruments do not blend easily into the unified sonority and are heard sparingly; their individual quality creates touches of what, borrow-ing a term from another sense modality, is called color, rather than forming part of the basic texture of the sound.

It will be a very pure sound, with very little "noise" in it. Noise is a diffi-cult concept to define, since what is noise to me may well be music to you, and vice versa, but we could make a rough definition of noise as unwanted sounds—sounds, that is, whose meaning we either cannot discern or do not like when we do discern it. Noise in a rock band is thus a different thing from noise in a string quartet, and each of those ensembles produces what would be called noise in the other's world of meaningful sounds.

In the sound world of the symphony orchestra, as in fact in European classical music as a whole, we can take it to mean sounds whose pitch either does not stay steady enough to be perceived as a pitch—a bell, for example, or a siren—or cannot be reduced, in the perception of the players and the hearers, to one of the seven tones of the diatonic scale or the five alternative "chromatic" tones that lie between them (that each of these tones may in fact lie somewhere on a narrow spectrum of tones whose deviation, within limits, from the nominal pitch is not merely tolerated but actively sought is a matter with which we need not concern ourselves here). Instruments like drums, gongs and cymbals, whose sound cannot be confined to such tones, are for that reason defined as noisemakers and are heard only occasionally, again as touches of color rather than as part of the basic texture.

It will be an eventful sound. A great deal of change will happen in a short time, so that it carries its listeners along with hardly a pause in which to take breath. It will be as if time were condensed for the duration of the performance, its essence distilled for those who cannot wait for events to unfold at the pace of everyday living. Nothing will stay the same for long. Surprise will follow surprise, with sudden changes and contrasts, between loud and soft sounds, between complex and simple sounds, between slow changes and rapid successions of sounds, between gentle and raucous sounds, between one player or a few playing softly and all the ensemble playing as loud as they can. All this keeps the hearers in a constant state of arousal.

It will be a purposeful sound, carrying its hearers forward through time by creating expectations, moving constantly toward climax, through carefully planned cycles of ever-increasing tensions and relaxations, to final resolution and closure. A sense of struggle, of opposition between forces, is never far away. Even the quietest moments are constantly being swept away by the necessity to progress toward that climax and resolution without which no piece of music in this tradition can be considered complete. To hear a symphony orchestra play, in fact, is to be presented with the very image of power that is under control and harnessed to a purpose.

Here we should stop and think a little, for there is in nature no such thing as a "purposeful" sound. The idea of purpose is a human construct, and the idea of a purposeful sound, one that creates expectations in a listener and carries him or her forward through time, depends on the acceptance by those playing and those listening of a number of conventions, in much the same way as does speaking and understanding a spoken language. We could without too much distortion call those conventions, in parallel with those of spoken languages, a syntax.

All ways of musicking have some kind of syntax, some way of controlling the relationships between the sounds that are made; it is a necessary condition for the creation of shared meanings between those taking part. A necessary condition, we note, but not a sufficient one. Musical meaning is not accounted for by syntax alone. If that were so, there would be no need to perform a piece at all, and we could sit at home and read the score as we do a novel. No meaning is created until a performance takes place; it is the performance that makes the meanings, and the syntax is part of that meaning but is not the whole of it.

It is the use of this syntax that unites nearly all the works that are most commonly heard today in concert halls. It is a complex of procedures called tonal functional harmony, which establishes and governs the relationships, both simultaneous and in succession, between tones, which is to say sounds with determinate pitch, sounds that according to the definition given above, are not noise.

I have written more extensively in an earlier book (1977) about tonal functional harmony. Briefly, it is a technique by means of which simultaneous combinations of tones, or chords, of a very specific type called triads are arranged in succession to create meaning. What that meaning consists of I shall explore a little later, but the relationship that is established between the chords in succession arouses in a listener the expectation that when one chord is sounded another will follow. If the expected chord does not sound, we are left with a feeling of incomplete meaning, as if someone had said, "The cat sat on the." There exists what we might call a normal cycle of chords, in which a constant cyclic movement takes place, starting from a tonic triad that is the center to which all others relate, proceeding through stages of increasing tension to climax and resolution and back to the tonic triad, with what is known as a perfect cadence. We have all been trained from early childhood to recognize this succession and respond to it, and we know what to expect even if we cannot put a name to the successive chords as they are sounded.

But the cycle can be broken at any point so that the expectation is frustrated or teased, and when this happens, further tensions are created that can only be resolved by the final arrival of the expected chord, perhaps in an unexpected way. The ability to play the game of arousing, frustrating or teasing, and finally satisfying the listener's expectation is a major element of the skills of composers in the Western concert tradition. The more the tension can be screwed up before resolving it, the better, it seems, the listener will like it. It is even possible to view the history of composition over the three centuries or more of the dominance of tonal harmony as having been driven by the search for means of screwing up that tension further and further and of delaying its resolution longer and longer. The classic instance of the delaying of the resolution is in Richard Wagner's music drama *Tristan und Isolde* of 1865, in which the erotically charged dissonance sounded at the very beginning of the Prelude remains unresolved until the final measures of the drama, three enormous acts and nearly five hours later.

Those readers for whom that all sounds somewhat like another important human activity, namely, sex, are not necessarily misreading the significance of tonal harmony. It is perfectly possible to consider Western musicking of this period as one expression of a very sexually repressed society finding an acceptable outlet for otherwise dammed-up or at any rate socially disapproved impulses. Wagner in *Tristan* certainly used tonal harmony in this way, stretching not only its resources but also the sexual decorum of his day to the extreme; the teasing dissonance is a quite explicit metaphor for erotic desire, and Wagner allows his pair of doomed lovers to find satisfaction only at the moment of resolution of the dissonance, in the death that is a euphemism for orgasm.

There is nothing "natural" about tonal harmony, however accustomed we may have become to it. The idea of a triad, a specific simultaneous combination of pitches chosen from the almost limitless gamut of possible pitches, does have a certain basis in the physical nature of sound, in that the frequency relationships are in relatively simple mathematical proportion, but there is nothing in either the physical nature of sound or the physiology of hearing to suggest that hearing one chord will make us expect another, let alone suggest that the succession can cause arousal in a listener. Indeed, it seems to be unique to Western musical culture of this four-hundred-year period.

Like all musical systems, the Western system of tonal harmony is a human construct that has been created by many people over a long period of time. Nor does there seem to be anything natural about the pleasure that listeners seem to derive from being aroused in this way. I have sometimes looked around the audience in a concert hall as the orchestra plays and have wondered what strange impulses and desires should lie behind those rows of expressionless listening faces that they should find such disturbance pleasurable.

Because there is no doubt that it *is* pleasurable, at least to those acculturated into the system, and pleasurable from the very start of the performance. Those who believe that musical pleasure comes from contemplating the pure form of a piece and that only when the piece is complete can we perceive that form and receive pleasure from it (they talk about the faculty for "deferred gratification," which seems to be attributed exclusively to the concert-going middle and upper classes) do not understand that, for Westerners at least, the tensions are as pleasurable as the relaxations, the climax as pleasurable as the resolution. Those who talk of delayed gratification ought to be made to sit through all the *Terminator* movies, followed perhaps by the *Die Hard* series. No delayed gratification there either; they grip, as they are meant to grip, from the very first frame.

It is perfectly possible to use the techniques of tonal functional harmony without raising the tension unduly. If the expected chord is always heard when it is expected, then the listener's expectations are not teased or frustrated, and the level of tension does not rise, or it rises very little, especially when the same succession is repeated over and over. This happens in a blues performance, for example, when the same short and quite conventional sequence of chords is repeated ad infinitum, with no variation, no surprises, and no forward motion toward climax and resolution. It happens also, in a more complex way, when a musician improvises jazz variations over a popular tune. In both these highly sophisticated arts, musical form is not an issue, and a performance begins and ends when the performers feel like doing so rather than in response to any sense of completion or closure.

When that happens, it means that the progression of chords has been displaced from the center of interest of the performance and has become simply an underpinning for events whose main interest lies elsewhere. We can say that if the success of a piece of music in performance lies in the balance between the arousal produced by surprise and the security of predictability, then in Western concert music the balance is tipped toward the former, while in popular performance it inclines toward the latter. Its practitioners, we might say, wear the techniques of tonal harmony like a comfortable old suit of clothes while they get on with the real business of the performance.

Even within the concert tradition there are differences in emphasis. Those musicians of the past whose music was once judged to be part of the popular tradition but who have now been absorbed into the concert tradition—Rossini, for instance—inclined toward predictability in their harmonic language; whole stretches of Rossini's operas thrive on the predictable alternation of tonic and dominant harmonies, with only the occasional cunningly placed surprise. At the other extreme, I believe one reason that even the early works of Arnold Schoenberg, in which he was still using tonal-harmonic techniques, will never be popular may be that he does not allow the listeners any moment of relaxation but constantly goads us on, with a surprise in practically every measure. It becomes very wearing after a while. But then, Rossini thought it worthwhile to woo his listeners. Schoenberg, seduced by the cult of genius, disdained them and has paid the price.

Those readers who are not versed in the technical language of Western concert music may think that they do not understand tonal harmony, but in fact everyone understands it as they understand their mother tongue, even if they cannot put names to the chords and their relationships or write them in musical notation. If they did not understand the way harmony operates, they would not feel those tensions and relaxations, those climaxes and resolutions, whether on the grand scale in a symphony or concerto or on the smallest scale in a dance tune or popular song, that have been the essence of Western music for nearly four centuries.

It also, as Susan McClary (1990) points out, forms the basis of the sign language of film and television music, whose composers since the invention of the talkies (and perhaps even earlier, since moviehouse musicians of the silent era drew extensively on the concert repertory for their material) have manipulated, often with enormous skill, the meanings generated by tonal harmony (there is evidence that many of the early producers of sound films deliberately used classically trained musicians to compose the music so as to enhance the social prestige of their product). It is from those sources, in fact, rather than from the concert hall or classical records, that most people learn the meanings of tonal harmony. In any case, in simple or complex form it pervades nearly all Western music making, not only in the concert hall and opera house but throughout much popular and much folk music as well. It is part of our common musical understanding, which we absorb all unawares, in the same way that we learn our mother tongue.

There is a difference, of course. Those who know a mother tongue can speak it as well as understand it. In the case of tonal harmony this is not so; those who understand its meanings when they hear it do not necessarily know how to formulate those meanings themselves, and they imagine that only by prolonged professional training can they learn how to do so. That, however, is partly a result of mystification on the part of professional musicians and academics and partly a result of the way in which harmony is commonly taught to students. It is, in fact, perfectly possible for anyone who can play an instrument or sing to learn the formulations, at least enough to make that "comfortable old suit of clothes" that is necessary for musicking in popular styles, in the same informal way in which we learn our mother tongue. Many musicians in every generation do so and use those formulations successfully and effectively. More complex formulations, such as are found in symphonic works, do of course require conscious study and practice, but only those who want to compose or perhaps to perform such works need to do so.

When the seventeenth-century English poet John Dryden wrote:

> From harmony, heavenly harmony,
> The universal frame began,

he expressed better than he knew the controlling power of the chordal progressions of tonal harmony. That he should have formulated the controlling and creative powers of heaven itself in terms of the relations between groups of simultaneously sounded pitches shows the power that these types of pitch relationship have exerted over the imagination of Westerners.

There is scarcely a piece of music composed during the past four hundred years that does not use those techniques and does not pass the listener through stages of tension and relaxation on the way to final resolution. The sequence of chords controls everything that happens in the piece; every note and every melody is as it is, and every accent falls where it does because the harmony requires it to be so. The composer's skill lies in manipulating the expected and the unexpected, the tensions and relaxations, the surprises and the respites; in planting clues whose significance is to be drawn out at the proper moment; and in placing them all in time. In this respect it is very like the skill of the stage dramatist, and in fact I shall later argue that symphonic works are no less dramatic narratives than are the operas from which they ultimately derive.

Not quite true, of course; readers familiar with the history of concert music will know that during the twentieth century many musicians abandoned the techniques of tonal harmony and that many of them have announced the death of harmony; its possibilities, they say, became exhausted around the turn of the century. That all sounds fine, but we should notice two things: first, that tonal harmony has continued, and still continues, to serve the purposes of many fine musicians, especially but by no means exclusively those who work in popular idioms, and, second, that those who have abandoned tonal harmony often have not abandoned the aim of arousal and relaxation that tonal harmony has served for four hundred years; they have simply changed their techniques of achieving it. A piece by Boulez, Stockhausen or Berio is and is intended to be every bit as arousing as one by Beethoven or Tchaikovsky. The means may have changed but not the ends.

Tonal harmony is a paradoxical technique. On the one hand it is extremely logical and lucidly rational. It is not just that the relationships between the tones that form the basic chordal structure, the triad, can be shown to be based on acoustical logic, but also the relationships between the chords, their progression through gradual accumulation of tension to final relaxation, is governed by rules that are as fully codifiable as the rules of linear perspective in the visual arts, which it much resembles. It is interesting to note that when Europeans thrown into the North American wilderness began, in the seventeenth and eighteenth centuries, to make pictures and to compose music, they first threw overboard perspective, in the first case, and harmony, in the second, and then slowly recuperated them, often in idiosyncratic ways. For those who are interested, my first book (1977) deals with these matters at some length.

There is another aspect to the logic of harmony, and that is that it operates within the closed circle of pitches that is called equal temperament. Every student of elementary acoustics knows that the interval of an octave is the aural experience of doubling the frequency of a tone, while that of a perfect fifth is the experience of multiplying its frequency by one-and-a-half, or three-over-two. Now, no matter how many times we multiply any number (in this case, the frequency of a tone) by three-over-two, it will never come out to a number that is the same as multiplying it by two, so raising the pitch by a sequence of perfect fifths will never come out to an octave or multiple octaves. There is always a small gap, which is called the comma, and the circle remains open.

Try if for yourself on a calculator. Starting from any number, say 27.5, which is the notional frequency of the A at the bottom of the piano keyboard, multiply it by 2 seven times. The answer comes out as 3,520, which is, in fact, the notional frequency of the A at the top, seven octaves higher. Now multiply the same 27.5 by one-and-a-half, or one-point-five, twelve times, and the answer comes out as 3,568.2, which is slightly sharp of the A we reached by simple doubling from 27.5. And 3,568.2 divided by 3,520 is 1.0136, which is the proportional size of the comma.

But the keyboard tells us different. If we start from the bottom A of the piano and go up a fifth, to E, then another, to B, then another, to F-sharp, another to C-sharp/D-flat, and so on, we shall, after twelve such jumps, arrive at top A, an intervallic distance of exactly seven octaves. The comma has been obliterated. This has been achieved by an acoustic sleight of hand called equal temperament, in which each perfect fifth is tuned a tiny and scarcely perceptible amount narrower than the true three-over-two acoustic fifth, tearing up the comma, as the French scholar Alain Daniélou (1943) says, and dividing it between the notes of the scale, changing the infinitely open spiral into a closed circle and "bringing the cycle of sounds within the narrow universe of human logic."

This sleight of hand has made possible total freedom of movement between keys; no matter how flat a key you go into, there is always the possibility of one that is flatter; and no matter how sharp a key, there is always one that is sharper, and they are all equally in tune, or, rather, all equally out of tune. This total freedom of movement makes possible an infinite power of surprise, of interruption of the harmonic cycle, allowing composers to create tonal works of great power. But you cannot leave the system; there is no escape from it. That is the price we pay for those majestic works of symphonic music, especially those created since the mid-nineteenth century that use to the full the potential of the system.

The system is called equal temperament because it makes every one of the twelve half-tone steps that in Western music comprise the octave equal to every other. In the natural acoustic scale, using the natural ratios between the frequencies, this is not so; half-tone steps can vary in size quite audibly according to their position in the scale, so larger intervals such as the fifth can also vary, depending on their position. This in turn means that in the natural scale different keys actually sound different to attuned ears, whereas in equal temperament they all sound the same. The flattening out of the relationships between the tones and the keys is for some an unacceptably high price to pay for the convenience; Daniélou himself (1943) says: "Whatever advantages may be obtained by such an action . . . we expel the heavenly element from music when we obliterate the possibilities of contacts with spiritual forces by disfiguring the intervals. . . . It is not without reason that Plato puts in the mouth of Damo, the last of the great Pythagorean teachers: 'One cannot touch the musical modes without disrupting the constitution of the state.'" Daniélou comments: "He could as well have said: without disrupting universal order."

Cranky that might seem, but it is clear that the way the relationships between the pitches are organized stands behind and governs all the other sound relationships of a musical performance. If, as I believe, the sound relations of a musical performance stand in metaphorical form for ideal human relationships as imagined by the participants, then those pitch relationships must be of central importance to an understanding of all the other relationships of the performance. Equal temperament is a highly abstract and mathematical concept, and the fact that it is in more or less universal use in symphony orchestras as well as keyboards today, regardless of whether the composer heard his work that way (it did not come into universal use until the middle of the nineteenth century), does suggest an attitude toward the "natural" in those Western industrial societies where the works are played and heard that gives credence to Daniélou's remarks.

The logic and the drama are inseparably linked together in the very techniques themselves of tonal harmony, for while a composer may lace his progression of chords with surprises, which may be either dramatic or witty, the only surprises that will please or satisfy an audience will be those that eventually show the surprising chord to stand in a relationship to its predecessors that can be explained by the logic of harmony. Innovative composers over the past four centuries have sought constantly to raise the stakes by making their surprises ever more daring, more outré, their logic being, at least initially, ever harder to comprehend, and they have at times paid for their daring by being rejected by their listeners. But once each generation has become accustomed to those progressions and able to understand their logic, they have lost their power to surprise, and the next generation is forced to find something new. We can never recapture, no matter how we try, the impact on their first hearers of, say, those violent dissonances at the beginning of the last, choral movement of Beethoven's Ninth Symphony or even of the famous repeated dissonant E-flat against F-flat chord in Stravinsky's *Rite of Spring*. Those who ride the tiger can never dismount.

Interlude 3
Socially Constructed Meanings

*

Ritual, then, is a means by which we experience our proper relation with the pattern which connects, the great pattern of mind. We cannot, of course, know the pattern which connects any more "objectively" than we can know anything else outside ourselves. Knowledge of the pattern, as of everything else, is a relation between our internal mental processes and what is outside us. It is the result of an active process of engagement by our mental processes, and those, as we have seen, can vary from individual to individual and between members of different social and cultural groups. To a German businessman the shape of the universe of relationships will not appear the same as it does to a Tibetan monk, and what feels to an Andean peasant like a right relationship according to the pattern of the world may be very different from that which a born-again Christian in Texas feels in her heart to be right. Even parents and children in the same household may feel very differently about their relationships to one another and to the rest of the world.

All of us, in fact, carry around with us our own way of making sense of the world and its relationships. From the moment of birth, and perhaps before, we learn which relationships are of value to us and which are not, what to remember and what to forget, and how to order our experience of the world into categories. None of these are god-given but are the result of an active engagement with the world outside us. They may well change as our experience widens, but the possibility for fundamental change becomes increasingly limited as we become older.

There are good physical reasons for this last commonsensical observation. Recent neurological research has shown that the physical development of the human brain itself and of those neural pathways that embody memory and the formation of categories are profoundly influenced by the personal history of each individual. Even identical twins do not have identical nervous systems. The connections between the billions of nerve cells that constitute our nervous system are selected by experience, by the way in which they are used, in a process very akin to natural selection (Gerald Edelman [1992] in fact calls it "neural Darwinism"). Those neural pathways that are used develop and consolidate, while those which are not used atrophy and die, and once a pathway is lost it is lost forever.

Experiences such as love, hatred, fear, interest, security and reassurance, when undergone in the early years of life when neural development is at its most rapid, determine not just the habitual paths of thought in an individual but the very anatomy of the brain itself. Thus it is that the very way our brains develop physically depends on what we learn to value, and that the way in which they develop is irreversible.

Since how we learn which relationships are of value and which are not is a matter of our experience, it is to be expected that although each person has his or her own ideas of relationships, those held by members of the same social group, whose experiences are broadly similar, will also tend to be broadly similar and in that way serve to reinforce one another. We might say that that is what social groups are for. It is shared assumptions about relationships, with the rest of the world as well as with one another, that holds social and cultural groups together. Further, we might expect that such groups should try to pass on their values to members of succeeding generations, and all social groups do, in fact, have institutions, either formal or informal, for doing just that. In industrial society today all children are required to spend several years incarcerated for several hours each day, under the supervision of specially trained adults, learning those values. This exercise is, on the whole, remarkably successful; by the end of their period of schooling many young people may know little of those "subjects" which the school is ostensibly set up to teach them, but they all know very well indeed what it is that the society values. Whether or not they accept those values is, of course, another matter.

This means that what each of us holds to be reality is not objective or absolute but is, to use the sociologists' term, socially constructed. It is composed of learned sets of assumptions about the relationships of the world, and it is those, overlapping and varying, that constitute the pattern of meanings that holds together groups of human beings, whether large or small, from empires and nations to associations, clubs, families and bonded pairs. How we acquire that sense of what is reality is a dialectical process between, on the one hand, the experience and the inborn temperament of each individual and, on the other, the perceptions of the various social groups to which he or she belongs.

Of course, we all belong at the same time to more than one social group; membership in a nation or empire is not incompatible with membership of a family or, for that matter, with membership of a trade union, a stamp club, a football supporters' club, an occupational group, a political party, a religious organization, an ethnic group and a particular sexual orientation. Our membership of each of these groups shapes our perception of reality, and those perceptions may well change as we pass from one group to another, as we do perhaps several times every day. Our sense of reality and of its relationships is a complex and contradictory affair, as complex and contradictory as our sense of who we are, with which it overlaps in various ways.

The ways in which concepts of reality are acquired and how they operate are mostly outside our scope here. They are dealt with lucidly in Peter Berger and Thomas Luckmann's classic *The Social Construction of Reality* (1967). However, one matter that those authors raise does relate to our present quest. They tell us that the society's concepts of reality and its relationships have to be impressed forcefully on each individual of the new generation, even if the impressing is done in ways that are coercive and unpleasant (I take it they refer not only to such customs as circumcision, clitorectomy, and other tribal passage rites but also to such Western customs as schooling and examinations). And since, they say, humans are often lazy and frequently stupid, these assumptions have to be simplified during transmission into formulas that can be easily learned, in ways that may routinize or even trivialize them—a process that can certainly be seen happening in Western schooling.

There is obviously much truth in this. Words—people telling things to other people—are clearly of capital importance, but we should not allow the verbal bias of our present-day society to make us assume that they are the only means by which concepts of relationships can be passed on. The idea that these concepts have to be simplified, routinized and even trivialized may be due not so much to the presumed stupidity of many human beings (and most of us can remember from our own schooldays people who were dismissed as stupid in school but have functioned very adequately indeed outside it) as it is to the one-thing-at-a-time nature of words and to the limitations they impose upon the articulation of relationships.

As for the idea that concepts of reality, of relationships, need to be impressed on the new generation by means that are coercive and unpleasant, that would seem to be only a special case of the broader idea that, since all knowledge is a relation between the knower and the known, it is principally through the evocation of emotions, which are the representation in consciousness of computations concerning relationships, that learning takes place. The more powerful the emotional experience, the more power-ful the learning will be.

If what Bateson has to say about the language of biological communica-tion—paralanguage—makes sense, then it seems that musicking, dancing, and other facets of the great performance art we call ritual are more potent means of teaching about relationships in all their complexity and of im-pressing them by the emotions they arouse than are words.

In that case simplification and routinization are not necessary. They are taken to be necessary only in societies like ours that have forgotten how the arts function in human life. But the fact that we have forgotten it does not mean that they do not still work that way; if you chase nature out the front door, she comes in again at the back. But it could be that the crudely in-strumental and exploitative relationships that Western societies have adopted toward the rest of the living world have to do with the fragmenta-tion of the great performance art and its relegation to the margins of our lives. Which is cause and which is effect I am not in a position to say.

We can see also why it is that musicking has always functioned so pow-erfully as a means of social definition and self-definition. For if members of different social groups have different values, that is, different concepts of relationships and of the pattern which connects, then the enactment of those relationships that takes place during a musical performance will dif-fer also. Each musical performance articulates the values of a specific social group, large or small, powerful or powerless, rich or poor, at a specific point in its history, and no kind of performance is any more universal or absolute than any other. All are to be judged, if judged at all, on their effi-cacy in articulating those values.

"At a specific point in its history" is important also, for groups change, in both their constitution and their values; and as they change, so do their styles of musicking. We have seen that the style of musicking called a sym-phony concert is a relatively modern phenomenon that has accompanied the rise to power of the Western industrial middle classes and articulates their values. On the other hand, the fact that it has taken into itself many works that were composed at earlier times and for other purposes shows the continuity of certain concepts of relationships, not just those concepts that gave rise to the works themselves but also those which have deter-mined the form and the organization of orchestras that perform them.

Of course, a social group so large and various as the "industrial middle classes" is no more monolithic in its style of musicking than in its other ac-tivities, and within the style known as the symphony concert there are any number of substyles and, especially, subrepertories, some of which are fa-vored by some and some by others. There is also a great deal of internal conflict within the great group, which will be articulated by the performance of differing and often competing subrepertories. Early music, contemporary music, and authentic performance are three significant subgroups, and many members of such groups would not be seen dead at a concert of "routine classics" such as I have been describing, and even less at certain other kinds of events that involve symphony orchestras and their audiences in concert halls: all-Tchaikovsky concerts with cannon and bells for the *1812 Overture* or potpourris under names like "A Night at the Ballet," or "An Evening in Old Vienna."

But that there is an overriding unity within the culture is shown by the fact that the nature of the concert hall ceremony remains the same no matter what the repertory may be. The first seven chapters of this book could equally have been concerned with a performance in any one of the subgroups I have described.

Those taking part in a musical performance are in effect saying—to themselves, to one another, and to anyone else who may be watching or listening—*This is who we are.* If "who we are" should happen to be those who have control of the means of socialization and communication in a society and if the "we," as is probable in that case, believe themselves to be inherently superior to the rest of society, not to mention other societies, then they will have the confidence and the power to impose their forms of musicking as the best and to define all others as inferior or, at best, approximations of their own.

But on the other hand, "who we are" is at the same time composed of any number of individual "who I am's," and as we have already noticed, everyone belongs to a number of social groups simultaneously and has a degree of choice concerning which or whose values they espouse, which relationships they regard as ideal. The "who I am" is not as determinate as one might at first sight expect; in the context of the performance, who an individual is, is to a large extent who he or she chooses to be or imagines him or herself to be. Who we are is how we relate, and the relationships articulated by a musical performance are not so much those that actually exist as they are the relationships that those taking part desire to exist.

It is thus possible to say that those taking part in symphony concerts are generally middle- and upper-class, but it is not possible to say of a middle-class individual that he or she will take part in a symphony concert—or indeed to make anything more than an informed guess about any individual's preferred way of musicking. Reality may be socially constructed, but no individual is bound to accept unquestioningly the way it is constructed. Musicking, being exploration as well as affirmation and celebration, is one way in which the question can be asked.

I have suggested that it is through the emotions they arouse that musicking, dancing, and other facets of the great performance art we call ritual are more potent means of teaching about relationships in all their complexity, and of impressing them, than are words.

There is a cluster of traditional problems grouped around the relation between music and the emotions. Scholars and musicians alike have long worried away at questions such as *What is the place of the emotions in music? Do they have a place at all?* and *Since music appears, at least, to have no reference to anything outside itself, what is it about? Is it about anything at all, other than pleasing combinations of sounds?* There are two apparently opposing points of view on these matters.

The first holds that music is concerned with the "communication" or the "expression" or the "representation" of emotions or groups of emotions, enabling them to be passed from one person, the composer, to another, the listener, through the medium of the performer. This view, at least in its naive forms, is shot through with intellectual holes, with which we need not concern ourselves, resulting in more sophisticated formulations such as that of the philosopher Suzanne Langer, who calls music the "representation of the morphology of the emotions." Those who hold such views are known in the academic world, where such things matter, as expressionists.

The opposing view, known as formalism, denies that emotions have anything to do with the proper appreciation of music (no one, of course, can deny the obvious fact that musicking arouses emotions, but the importance of the arousal is downplayed and its value even derogated as somehow unworthy of music's lofty mission) and maintains that the proper purpose of music is pure, disinterested "aesthetic" experience, with no content whatever beyond the contemplation of the beauty of the tonal patterns and forms and the surprising combinations of sounds that the composer has brought into existence. In its extreme and most puritanical form, this view even denies any value whatsoever to the sensuous enjoyment of musical sound. The nineteenth-century Viennese critic Eduard Hanslick was a leading exponent of such a view, as was the philosopher Immanuel Kant (I have often wondered what would have happened to Kant's idea of the "disinterested contemplation" of music had he ventured out from his musty Königsberg study and gone down the road as far as the nearest tavern).

A third, modern school, led by the American musicologist Leonard Meyer, has tried, without too much success, to reconcile these apparently opposing views.

Whole libraries have been devoted to this problem of emotion and meaning in music; I have always found that neither view had much to do with my own experience of musicking. On the one hand, common sense leads me to ask why people should devote so much of their lives and resources to the communication of emotions as the expressionists suggest and why, for that matter, listeners should be interested in having them communicated to them. After all, we all have plenty of emotions of our own without needing to feel other people's. On the other hand, contemplating the abstract beauty of sound patterns for their own sake would seem to be a very self-centered occupation, if not verging on solipsism (it must be admitted that the conditions of the modern concert hall are very conducive to solipsism), and bearing little relation to the highly social experience that I have always found musicking to be.

The two schools do have more in common than at first appears. In the first place, neither school of thought questions the nature of the emotions or their function in human life. They are simply taken for granted, as autonomous states of mind, some pleasant perhaps and some not so pleasant, but in neither case having any significance beyond themselves.

Second, both schools of thought assume once more the "thingness" of music. If we examine the arguments carefully, we realize that by "music" what is generally meant is a piece, or work, of music. The piece of music is itself taken as given, and the meaning of its being played at the time and place of the performance is not questioned; once again, the fact that the act of performance itself generates meanings is ignored, keeping the cycles and epicycles spinning merrily.

And third, they fail to recognize that the representational style in which virtually all works of the Western concert tradition since the seventeenth century have been written is just that—a style of musicking, one style among many. To generalize from those works to all human musicking is to impose the ideals of that style on ways of musicking with which they have nothing to do. Only by thinking in terms of musicking as being concerned with relationships can we stop the spinning cycles and epicycles.

Once we do this, we find that Bateson, once again, has provided us with a concept that can help us with the problem of the relation between music and the emotions—or rather, it can help us see that there is really no problem. He suggests that emotions, those states of mind to which we give names, such as fear, love, anger, sorrow, happiness, respect and contempt, are not autonomous mental states but are ways in which our computations about relationships—"computations" is the word he uses, suggesting precision and clarity rather than the woolliness and mental confusion that is usually associated with the emotions—resonate in consciousness.

If all living creatures, from viruses to human beings to sequoia trees, need as a condition of survival some means of getting an answer to the question "How do I relate to this entity?" then they need also some way of representing to themselves this relationship. For those creatures at least that are gifted with consciousness, it is through the emotional state that the relationship arouses that it is presented to the conscious mind.

Thus, what we call happiness is the representation in consciousness of the presence of an entity that is loved or desired (those, too, being emotional states that themselves represent relationships—further evidence of the second- and even third-order complexity of everyday relationships), while sorrow is the response to its loss. Fear, on the other hand, is the representation of perceiving the presence of an entity that can threaten survival. How far down the scale of complexity of living things these emotional states may extend is hard to say, but it is difficult, for example, not to perceive as fearful the hasty scurrying of small arthropods when one up-ends an old flowerpot. It could be that such responses are very ancient survival mechanisms that precede by eons the development of consciousness such as we perceive in mammals and even more so that of reflexive or self-consciousness, that consciousness of being conscious, which seems to be the unique property of human beings.

So, if "to music" is not just to take part in a discourse concerning the relationships of our world but is actually to experience those relationships, we need not find it surprising that it should arouse in us a powerful emotional response. The emotional state that is aroused is not, however, the *reason* for the performance but the sign that the performance is doing its job, that it is indeed bringing into existence, for as long as it lasts, relations among the sounds, and among the participants, that they feel to be good or ideal relationships.

It seems to me that to say that a sad piece of music makes one feel sad or a happy piece makes one happy is a crude simplification of the complex of emotional states that is, in fact, evoked by taking part in a good performance (the word *good*, of course, raises all sorts of questions that I shall be discussing later). There is elation there and joy, even occasionally triumph, produced no doubt by having experienced, in our own bodies and senses, relationships that we feel to be right and in accord with our idea of the pattern which connects. This, we feel, is how the pattern of the world *really* is, and this is where we *really* belong in it. This is a cause indeed for elation, and in that it is concerned with our place in the pattern it partakes of the nature of the religious.

But there is also an underlying melancholy, a sign perhaps of recognition that those relationships exist only in the virtual world of the performance and not in that everyday world to which we must return after the performance is over. Jessica's remark in *The Merchant of Venice* that "I am never merry when I hear sweet music" expresses neatly the ambiguity of the emotions. And conversely, if a musical performance arouses in us no emotional response, or a negative one, it is sign that the relationships that it brings into existence are not those which we feel to be desirable. The reality that it constructs is not the reality that we desire.

Actually, the idea that a piece can be sad or happy at all belongs exclusively to the representational style that has been dominant in Western operatic and concert music since the seventeenth century. It depends on a system of musical signs that has been evolved during that period and so can have no claim to a place among the universals of music. The musical act is concerned with relationships, and the emotional state that is aroused is no more than the perception that the musicking is, as it were, doing its work.

Nonetheless, it is perfectly possible to become hooked on the emotional state that is brought into being by taking part in good musical performances. When this happens, one can come to believe that the emotional high is the reason for the performance, but that belief is a symptom of something like addiction. Such addiction appears to be widespread among lovers of classical music. The formalist response to music may have contained something of an intuitive revulsion against the addictive qualities of the emotional high and to that extent could be justified, at least in a society like ours in which pleasure for its own sake is viewed with suspicion.

There is another, related question that has occupied the attention of philosophers of music, which is this: where does the meaning of a musical composition lie? We can look at a picture and recognize, say, the Mona Lisa, Washington crossing the Delaware, or the bridge at Arles; we can look at a sculpture and recognize David, or Abraham Lincoln, or the Thinker; we can watch a play or a movie or read a novel and identify with the characters, who are given local habitations and names. We can even examine a building and perceive that it is "about" its function as office block or cathedral or pigsty. In all these cases there is a recognizable reference to the world outside the work of art that makes the work's subject matter comprehensible.

But a piece of music appears to have no reference to anything outside its own sound world. Apart from a few moments of onomatopoeic reference to natural sounds, like the birdsong and the thunder of Beethoven's *Pastoral* Symphony, it can only be perceived as abstract and nonrepresentational, at least of anything but itself. What then is it about? Is it about anything?

Again, if we think about music primarily as action rather than as thing and about the action as concerned with relationships, then we see that whatever meaning a musical work has lies in the relationships that are brought into existence when the piece is performed.

These relationships are of two kinds: those between the sounds that are made in response to the instructions given in the score and those between the participants in the performance. These two sets of relationships, as we shall see in a moment, are themselves related, in complex and always interesting second-order ways. It is clear, however, that when there is a fixed and stable musical work, the relationships between the sounds will also be stable (or more or less stable, given small differences in instrumental and vocal quality, intonation and suchlike, as well as in the way different performers, perhaps at different times, interpret the notation), while on the other hand the relationships between the participants will be different with each performance and with each different set of participants, each different setting, each different set of expectations that the participants may have of the performance.

The sound relationships thus contribute to the nature and the meaning of the human encounter that is a musical performance, but they do not constitute the whole of it. In the Western classical tradition, those sound-relationships, as we have seen, are dramatic, which is to say, they articulate tensions and relaxations, climaxes and resolutions, developments and variations, in ways which its participants perceive as paralleling the development of human relationships. They can be thought of as stories, or discourses, about relationships, and the nature of the storytelling and the nature of the assumed ideal relationships that lie behind them belong to the Western tradition of thought as surely as does that other major form of storytelling common in our culture, the novel, with which symphonic music is contemporaneous. Novels and works of symphonic music resemble each other also in that, although they are always the same whenever they are read or performed, the *meaning* of the act of reading, or performing, them can change substantially over time. There is thus introduced into the performance process a tension between the two sets of meanings, which increases with the passing of time. Where there is no stable work, this tension does not exist.

But with or without a stable work of music, there is a sense in which all musicking can be thought of as a process of storytelling, in which we tell ourselves a story about our relationships. The storytelling process is carried out by means of the language of gesture, and in the language of gesture there are no nouns, and its tense is always the present. This means, on the one hand, that we cannot tell who or what it is that is relating, but on the other, it means that the universe of relationships is much richer and more complex than anything that can be dealt with in words.

The storytelling is found not only in Western symphonic works. The form of storytelling that takes place when a symphonic work is performed is very specific, with a set trajectory in time and a beginning and a middle and an end, like a novel, and it tells a very specific kind of story, about an individual and his progress through the processes of opposition and struggle. It depends for its meanings on a highly evolved system of musical signs and gestures that represent metaphorically bodily signs and gestures that indicate a certain kind of relationship and its associated emotional state.

But there is also a broader sense in which we can say that all human musicking is a process of telling ourselves stories about ourselves and our relationships. In that all musical performances evolve over time, the relationships the performance brings into being are also evolving. The relationships at the end of the performance are not the same as those of the beginning. Something has changed between the participants through the fact of having undergone the performance together. Who we are has changed, has evolved a little, either through our having been confirmed in our concepts of ideal relationships and of who we are or through having had them challenged. Those relationships are all around us as we music, and we are in the midst of them. We need make no effort of will to enter into the world that the performance creates, for it envelopes us, whether we will it or not.

I believe it to be true of all those activities we call the arts, not just of musicking, that at base they are about human relationships. We shall understand them best if we keep in mind that they all operate within the gestural language that empowers human beings, like all other living creatures, to articulate those relationships. Properly understood, all art is action—performance art, if you like—and its meaning lies not in created objects but in the acts of creating, displaying, and perceiving. It is an activity in which humans take part in order that they may come to understand their relationships—with one another and with the great pattern which connects. In all those activities we call the arts, we think with our bodies. They negate with every gesture the Cartesian split between body and mind.

In putting us in touch in this way with the pattern that connects, musicking is not only grounds for joy but also actually teaches us the shape of the pattern. There is evidence from a number of cultures that musicking does have this educative function. The musicologist William Malm (1967) writes of the Aborigines of Australia that "music is used . . . to teach him about his culture, about his place in it and his place in the world of nature and supernature," while the ethnomusicologist John Blacking (1976) has written that the musicking of the Venda of South Africa "may involve people in a powerful shared experience and thereby make them more aware of themselves and of their responsibilities towards one another."

John Miller Chernoff (1979), who spent some years learning to drum in the Ewe tradition of Ghana, writes, "Africans use music to mediate their involvement in a community, and a good musical performance reveals their orientation towards this crucial concern. As a style of human conduct, participation in an African musical event characterizes a sensibility with which the Africans relate to the world and commit themselves to its affairs. As cultural expression, music is a product of that sensibility, but, more significantly, as a social force, music helps shape that sensibility. The development of musical awareness in Africa constitutes a process of education." And finally, Robert Farris Thompson (1966), in a magisterial formulation: "West African dances [he includes in this the music that is danced] . . . are nonverbal formulations of philosophies of beauty and ethics. . . . The traditional choreographies of tropical Africa constitute, I submit, complex distillations of thinking, comparable to Cartesian philosophy in point of influence and importance."

Expressions like "philosophies of beauty and ethics," "relate to the world and commit themselves to its affairs," "his place in the world of nature and supernature," and "aware of themselves and their responsibilities towards one another" make explicit another dimension of our discussion that has so far only hovered in the background: that of religion and the sacred. To the extent that taking part in a performance puts humans in touch with the pattern which connects, in whatever form it might be imagined to exist, it is an activity that is always to some degree religious in nature.

So we return once more to mythmaking and myth telling, which is the making and telling of stories about how the pattern came to be and thus how it is, and also to ritual, which is the use of the gestural language of biological communication to explore, affirm, and celebrate the relationships whose origin the myth relates. You will believe in the myth only if you enjoy the ritual, and you will enjoy the ritual only if you believe in the myth.

The words "believe in" can be a problem, at least for Westerners. We have been taught, and seem to need, to assert the absolute historical truth of our myths if we are to believe in them, whereas members of most other cultures seem to be able to live with the idea that they are at the same time both true (in the sense of being valid) and untrue (in the historical sense) without feeling any strain. The Western attitude, of course, carries with it the corollary that the myth in which "we" believe, being absolutely historically true, must be the only myth that is valid, whereas members of many other cultures are content to allow the coexistence of any number of myths, all equally true. People do terrible things to one another when they try to impose their version of the pattern which connects as the only right one.

What our long detour has led us to, then, is this: When we take part in a musical performance, any musical performance, when we music, we engage in a process of exploring the nature of the pattern which connects, we are affirming the validity of its nature as we perceive it to be, and we are celebrating our relation to it. Through the relationships that are established in the course of the performance we are empowered not only to *learn about* the pattern and our relation to it but actually to *experience* it in all its complexities, in a way that words never allow us to do, for as long as the performance lasts.

How we relate is who we are. Every way we can think of to specify a human being will involve a relationship with others. Our relationships specify us; they change as we change, and we change as they change. Who we are is how we relate. So it is that to affirm and celebrate our relationships through musicking, especially in company with like-feeling people, is to explore and celebrate our sense of who we are, to make us feel more fully ourselves. In a word, we feel good. We feel that this is how the world *really* is when all the dross is stripped away, and this is where we *really* belong in it. It is as if—no, not *as if* but directly *is* that—we have been allowed to live for a while in the world as it ought to be, in the world of right relationships. The exploration and the affirmation need not be, and in fact usually are not, conscious and certainly cannot be expressed in words, but the celebration can be, and usually is, so expressed, if not during the performance then after it.

The idea that to music is to explore, affirm and celebrate the relationships of the living world brings together also, without metaphysical overtones, many traditional interpretations of musical experience. If what I am suggesting is true, then it is no wonder that so many have spoken of musicking as a kind of communication with the Infinite, or that they should feel in touch with the Music of the Spheres or with the Ancestors. It is no wonder that there is so much talk of the moral and ethical power of music or of finding one's way through music to the elemental psyche. It is no wonder, in particular, that all of humanity uses musicking to call on the presence of the deities and summon them, since deities are the metaphorical embodiment of the pattern which connects, the pattern of proper relationships, and to invoke them is to affirm the pattern's sacred inviolability.

Nor is it any wonder that Plato should have linked the state of the musical modes with the constitution of the state; for the ancient Chinese this was a very practical affair, musicking being for them the link between the cosmic and the human. Thus it was that, when a new dynasty took over, all the royal instruments had to be retuned, since it was clear to them that the old order had fallen because the musicking was out of tune with the state of the cosmos. There is a story also of the sixteenth-century Mogul emperor Akhbar commanding his favorite court musician to play an evening raga at midday; we are told that such was the power of the musicking that darkness promptly descended and remained for as long as he played in all those parts of the royal palace into which the sound penetrated.

Nothing of what I have said is intended to invalidate or to supersede such interpretations of musical experience or relegate them to "mere" metaphor. On the contrary, I am using such widespread understandings to test the rightness of my own musings on the significance of the musical act. Metaphor, in any case, is not a "mere" anything but a principal mode by means of which we come to understand our experience.

The best we can do is to create metaphors that will help us understand rightly our feelings and actions and thus live well in the world. I believe that Bateson, in his image of the pattern that connects, has given us such a metaphor, one that is planted firmly in the observable characteristics of the living world, by means of which we can understand what is happening when we music, free ourselves from the obfuscation that has been placed around the activity, and take back to ourselves the power of musicking that lies within us all.

If the well-known saying that "all the arts aspire to the condition of music" has any meaning, it must be that of all the arts, those splintered shards of the great unitary performance art that is ritual, it is in musicking that we experience most directly and intimately the relationships of the pattern which connects. It is not true, as is often said, that music is the most abstract of the arts. On the contrary, to music is to take part in the most concrete and least mediated of all artistic activities. The relationships we most intimately desire are all around us, brought into existence by all those who are taking part, even if the only person who appears to be taking part is a jogger with a Walkman or a solitary flute player in the African night.

CHAPTER 9

An Art of the Theater

It has been said that all art aspires to the condition of music. That is undoubtedly true, but there is a sense also in which all the arts of the West, including music, at least from the early seventeenth century, aspire to the condition of the theater. It is an art of the dramatist, of the actor, and of the actor's gestures.

All of us obtain much of our information about other people and our relation to them from their patterns of physical gesture. We are so used to interpreting people's patterns and styles of movement, their postures, their facial expressions, their vocal timbres and inflections, that we scarcely notice that we are doing it. We study their patterns of movement and vocal expression and decide whether they are young or old, masculine or feminine, intelligent or stupid, sympathetic or antipathetic, serious or frivolous, sad or happy, pleased or angry, well or ill, solemn or cheerful, dominant or submissive, respectful or arrogant, and so on. Every day we make any number of subtle distinctions and interpret dozens of nuances of relationship from our observations without ever putting them into words. At the same time we ourselves give out signs, sometimes consciously and sometimes unconsciously, that those around us interpret similarly. It is a commonplace of social interaction that it is those gestures that we make without intending them that are often the most significant clues to our real nature and to the ways in which we relate to others.

The actor's art involves study of those patterns of gesture of the body and the voice, which in everyday life are made mostly unawares, making conscious use of them to make others believe, or at least suspend their disbelief, that the actors have personal characteristics that they do not in fact possess, are involved in relationships in which they are not in fact involved, and are feeling emotions that they are not in fact feeling. It is an art of representation—of emotions, of relationships, and/or characteristics—and it is directed outward, toward spectators.

It has been a convention, at least since the time of the ancient Greeks, that there is nothing dishonest in this representation. On the contrary, actors do a service in playing a kind of game with relationships so that the spectators can imagine those relationships and the emotions to which they give rise and even possibly experience them, without having to commit themselves to them. They can learn what are good and what are bad relationships, what are constructive and what are destructive. In this way the actor's, and the playwright's, art contributes to the socialization of the spectators. Of course, whose view of good and bad, of constructive and destructive, is being presented is an important question.

The theater, then, is concerned with human relationships and with how they change and develop over time. We have seen how relationships enter into consciousness through the emotional state that is aroused by them, so fear, for example, is the way in which our relation to an entity that can do us harm enters into consciousness, and anger is the way our relation to an entity that we cannot make behave the way we want it to enters our consciousness. So it is through the emotional states that he or she represents that an actor shows the spectators how those relationships are developing.

If the actor is representing the relationships adequately to the spectators, they will feel emotions in response: pity in response to the protagonist's suffering, pleasure in response to his or her joy, and so on; or if the actor is playing the antagonist or villain, the responses may be reversed. Those emotions are a sign that the representation is working, but they are not in themselves the *reason* for the activity of the theater, which is concerned, as is all artistic activity, with the relationships themselves and with the ways in which they develop.

The conventional gestures that are used for representing emotional states in the theater are not god-given but have to be learned, by both actor and spectators. They do not necessarily correspond to how people in "real life" behave when they feel that way, and they can change over time. What appears today as a natural and effective way of representation may well appear excessive tomorrow, over the top and even ridiculous.

This fact was brought home to me when I recently saw again Lawrence Olivier's 1943 film of Shakespeare's *Henry V*. To those of us who saw it the first time around, it seemed that Olivier had found a way of speaking Shakespeare that flowed and resonated with the sounds and rhythms of everyday speech and of acting with bodily gestures that appeared utterly natural and spontaneous. But on seeing it again fifty years later, it seemed as extravagantly theatrical—as fruity, almost—as those ancient recordings of famous Victorian actors which we in our time found so hilarious. It was not Olivier's fault; it is just that the conventions of representation have changed over the fifty years. There *is* no natural way to speak Shakespeare.

All art is a matter of gestures, whose meanings are determined as much by convention as by nature.

At the same time, there is a constant feedback from theatrical gestures to real life, as people, especially the young and impressionable, who have seen the actor's representations come to behave according to the convention when they feel that way. The streets of any town in the West today are filled with young Bruce Willises, Madonnas and Mickey Rourkes. Oscar Wilde may have had something like that in mind when he said that the best life can do is imitate art, and certainly his remark reminds us that art can mold as well as reflect the ways in which we respond to reality.

This is true of the visual arts as well. The characters in the paintings and sculptures of post-Renaissance Europe are representing relationships in much the same way as actors do. All those ecstatic saints, Ledas beset by swans, jolly peasants, voluptuous lovers (the fact that the female figure is almost always nude while the male is at least partly clothed itself says something about male-female relationships as perceived by the painter and his patron), haughty princes and supercilious landowners surrounded by symbols of their wealth and power, not to mention those exuberantly theatrical painted wooden images of the suffering Christ and the weeping Virgin Mary that are paraded through Spanish streets in Holy Week, are not so much feeling as acting—in other words, representing—for the benefit of the spectators. They are telling us by their gestures that they are experiencing the relationship and feeling the emotions. They are actors caught at crucial moments in their performance, and they use the same conventional gestures as do actors, frozen by the painter's art.

That art consists at least in part in choosing the moment in which to reveal their relationships, which may be to one another inside the frame or to someone outside the frame. Often it is the spectator him or herself to whom the character is relating (definitely *him*self in the case of those numberless female nudes that adorn the walls of every picture gallery in the Western world). Even a portrait can be thought of as being not so much of the subject as of the subject playing for the spectator the role of him or herself: the king playing the king; the university president, the university president; the smiling peasant the smiling peasant, the duchess, the duchess. Like actors, the characters in Western painting are aware that they are being watched.

Western concert music is also an art of representation that aspires to the condition of the theater. The musicians, both composer and performers, are representing to an audience a set of relationships, and the ways in which they represent them and the way they are interpreted by the audience are governed, like the actor's gestures, by conventions that both musicians and audience have to learn. We need not be surprised, then, to learn that it is the theater that has been the source and location of most of the technical innovations in Western concert music ever since the time of the first Italian practitioners of what they called *dramma per musica*—drama not just *with* but *through* music (what we today call opera)—in the early years of the seventeenth century.

It was those musicians—Monteverdi, Caccini, Peri, Cesti, Cavalli and others—who began to develop a systematic vocabulary of musical signs and gestures—relationships between sounds—by means of which could be represented not only human relationships and their associated emotional states but also personal characteristics (what they called temperaments) and to place these gestures together in time in order to represent developing relationships between the characters whom the singers, now become actors as well, were impersonating on the stage.

As the singers became actors, so the composers became dramatists, and they struggled to master those techniques of pacing and timing of events, of controlling tension and relaxation, of working toward a climax and resolution that are the essence of dramatic art. Their musical representation of the relationships and the spectators' understanding of them were assisted by the fact that the representation was at the same time being acted out on the stage, supported by all the visible artifices and devices of the theater; only later, when the significance of the musical gestures became thoroughly understood by audiences, would they be used in the more abstract dramas of concert music.

It is not to be wondered at that the development of tonal harmony began in earnest with the beginnings of opera, for it was tonal harmony, with its ability to create in a listener tensions and frustrations, desire and fulfillment, to delay resolutions and to tease expectations, that served their purposes most fully. The parallel between, on the one hand, the cycle of arousal, climax and resolution that occurs in the tonal-harmonic process and, on the other, the cycle of sexual arousal and satisfaction was not lost on those early masters of opera, or on their audiences, even if later generations have tended to forget or obscure it. They exploited it uninhibitedly. They aimed their music unashamedly, to an extent that we today, with our politer musical manners, find hard to imagine, at their listener-spectators' solar plexus.

In the new art of musical representation the musicians drew upon the ancient association between bodily movement and music, between musical and physical gesture. There was little that in itself was new about that; music for dance has always drawn upon parallels between musical and bodily gestures: at its most elementary, slow music for slow movements and fast for fast, strong accents for stamping, staccato for leaping, legato for glides, rising melodies for upward movement, falling for downward, and so on. Even these parallels are of course not literal; music does not move in the literal sense and so cannot be literally slow or fast, nor are tones literally high or low, melodies rising or falling, in anything but the metaphorical sense. Even in the dance the relationship between physical and musical gesture is always metaphorical and has to be learned.

What was new in the early seventeenth century was, first, that the musical gestures were abstracted from physical movement so that the listeners no longer moved their bodies but sat and watched and listened, and, second, that the musical gestures represented not an emotional state itself nor a temperament but the type of physical gesture, both bodily and vocal, with which the emotional state or the temperament was associated. The musical gesture represented metaphorically the physical gesture that the audience recognized as belonging to that state. It thus had to be constructed at one remove, and the masters of that first brilliant explosion of the new art form worked through conscious striving, exchange of ideas, polemics and a good deal of trial and error, to perfect the representation.

They were very proud of their newly won representational ability. Convinced that they had made a great advance over their sixteenth-century predecessors, they called their art *seconda prattica* (as opposed to the *prima prattica* of sixteenth-century polyphony) and, most revealingly, *stile rappresentativo*. The impulse that gave rise to those innovations was always the same: a desire to represent developing relationships onstage in ways that were ever more dramatic, more explicit, more exciting to the audience.

Susan McClary (1990), in her brief but magisterial book *Feminine Endings*, points out that it was in the field of gender, of what is masculine and what is feminine, that the creators of the early explosion of opera in the seventeenth century needed to work most assiduously to evolve musical representations.

From its beginnings opera has concerned itself primarily with two intertwined themes. The first is that intractable mixture of the sexual and social that today we call the relations of gender, and the second is the fate of heroic and often aberrant individuals who threaten to disrupt the social fabric. These two themes are intertwined, since those who step out of their socially assigned sexual role, whether they be male or female, are always taken to constitute a threat to social order, and they expose themselves to the possibility of destruction or at least containment by coercive means. From Orpheus, and Nero and Poppaea (who, atypically, obtain their antisocial desires), through Don Giovanni and the Queen of the Night, Don Carlos and Otello, Norma and Lucia di Lammermoor, through Siegfried and the lovers Tristan and Isolde, to Tosca, Peter Grimes and Lulu, these disruptive larger-than-life creatures have trodden the operatic stage for getting on for four centuries and do not yet look like losing their fascination for audiences in the opera house (one might add that it is thus not surprising that the art should have attracted to itself, from earliest times down to figures like Norman and Pavarotti in our own day, larger-than-life artists of heroic, not to say aberrant, character).

One's sex, which is to say, whether one is born with a set of male or female reproductive organs, is biologically given and is an individual matter; everyone is either one or the other. But gender, whether one is masculine or feminine or a mixture of both (as are most of us), is a social matter and has wide social implications, not only in that it assigns one to a particular social role or position but also because each word comes trailing a constellation of significations that are in many respects of more consequence than the basic concepts themselves.

"Masculine" trails strength, aggressiveness, rationality, stability, straight-forwardness, transcendence and independence, while "feminine" trails passivity if not weakness, irrationality, instability, deviousness, sensuality and dependence. What we might call the secondary gender characteristics of femininity can cause a great deal of anxiety in men, for they are seen as deeply subversive of the social order, tending at the extreme to insanity and to chaos, and it is this anxiety, all unspoken, that powers much of what is depicted on the opera stage. Like gender itself, none of these characteristics is biologically given, but all are socially assigned; each is a role that we are all called upon to learn to play. Those who do not care to play their assigned role expose themselves to any number of social dangers, and opera has always been a powerful medium through which those dangers have been dramatized.

Generally in opera, the masculine is conventionally represented musically by melodies that stick to the seven tones of the diatonic scale, by stable tonality and harmonies whose logic is clearly perceptible, and by four-square rhythms and deep-toned timbres; the feminine is represented by chromatic melodies that may use all twelve tones of the chromatic scale, by unpredictable harmonies whose logic is difficult to discern, by irregular rhythms and soft-toned timbres. The two contrasting themes that open Rimsky-Korsakov's *Scheherezade*, representing, respectively, the brutal sultan and the voluptuous Scheherezade, are, despite the fact that they come from the symphonic rather than the operatic repertory, textbook examples of this musical dichotomy.

The musical representation of masculinity and femininity soon became consolidated into a complex of highly conventional gestures that still form one of the most powerful of all kinds of representation and are still manipulated by musicians and understood without difficulty by listeners. Without them, the average film or TV score would be unintelligible, as would much of what goes on on the opera stage or, for that matter, on the concert platform.

It is, of course, not a simple antithesis between two mutually exclusive sets of characteristics. There is an infinity of shades of masculinity and femininity, of which we all partake, and skillful musicians have learned to articulate them and put them to dramatic ends, none more skillfully or more subtly than Mozart, whose three great comedies use the conventions to articulate the finest nuances of gender relations. The conventions allow also the delineation of weak or devious men and strong and forthright women—for example, on the one hand, Don José in *Carmen* and Mime in *Siegfried* and, on the other, Amneris in *Aida* and Brangäne in *Tristan*; but even there they hold, for to make the one sound weak and the other strong the characters have been given the musical signs of the opposite gender. It seems that secondary gender characteristics are even more crucial in musical delineation than are primary ones.

Again, baritones and basses are cast as wise men, doughty warriors and cruel villains, all characters who are deemed to be more masculine than young men that show extreme emotions, especially, of course, love (but also mad villains, who tend toward the feminine), who are tenors (it may the slightly androgynous character of their voices that gives tenors the fascination they seem to exert over audiences). On the other hand, young women who suffer the pangs of love (and how they suffer!) are sopranos, more feminine than mature wise women, who are contraltos and are *never* allowed to be heroines.

Since those with real power, the power to define and to delineate in the world of music making, especially opera—composers, conductors and stage directors, not to mention managers and administrators—are and have always been more or less exclusively men, it is inevitable that these characterizations of women are not necessarily what women *are*, or even what they think themselves to be, so much as what men think they are. Susan McClary (1990) remarks dryly that most of the female characters who populate the opera stage are "first and foremost male fantasies of transgression dressed up as women. Real women . . . do not enter the picture at all. We sit on the sidelines and watch as mainstream culture concocts such figures, then envies, fears and finally demolishes and/or contains them." Certainly, it is rare on the opera stage to meet a heroine who is permitted to be strong and independent, which means not depending on male support, and get away with it. Women who transgress their traditional (male-defined) role are contained, tamed, or destroyed.

There is, of course, more than an element of fantasy also in what men think *they themselves* are. The order of "masculine" logic, rationality, stability and so on that is required to triumph in the end is an ideal, not a real order. It does not correspond at all to how men actually are; in real life men can be just as irrational, just as deeply emotional, just as unstable as women, no more and no less, while women can be just as logical, just as rational and stable as men—in many respects more so, for their social position demands it of them even while denying them recognition of the fact. The qualities of both masculinity and femininity as held up in opera and, as we shall see, in its offspring symphonic music also (and, one has to add, in many movies, plays and novels) are chimeras. But the power of the vision is such that it is accepted in our male-dominated society as simply the way things are, and it is reinforced every time an opera or a symphonic work is performed.

It is a dangerous vision, for by denying to themselves—ourselves, I should say, presuming to speak for a moment on behalf of my sex—those qualities that are regarded as feminine, we men induce in ourselves anxieties that frequently manifest themselves as violence, directed often against the most obvious target of our masculine anger, which is women. That violence not only can be read about in the pages of newspapers but is underlined, as we shall see, by what is acted out on the opera stage and even in the concert hall.

The enormous adulation accorded to female operatic divas does not contradict this in the least; indeed, it stands in powerful confirmation of it. The only power those divas have is momentarily to ruffle the rational masculine systems of power in the operatic business; it is expected of them that they be everything that is trailed under the heading "feminine": irrational, unstable, devious, sensuous, and above all passive, for they are also expected to do as the conductor, the stage director and the manager tell them to do. That is their expected role behavior. Maria Callas, arguably the greatest diva of the twentieth century, was all of those things, and she was admired, ridiculed and loved in about equal proportions for it. And if today people are shocked when Jessye Norman demands to occupy the chief conductor's room in London's Barbican Hall and to have the backstage cleared for her or when Kathleen Battle refuses the stretch limo provided to take her to the White House because it is not long enough, those divas are only taking to extreme the behavior that is expected of women and confirming male fantasies of transgression. What they are not doing in the slightest is challenging the male dominance of the concert and operatic world.

Representation did not appear overnight but took a long time to become explicit in Western musicking. Its beginnings can be seen as far back as the love songs of the troubadours, who sang *as if* they were in love and who evolved a sign language of musical sighs and swoonings for their purpose. Its more immediate origins can be heard in those Italian dramatic madrigals of the late sixteenth century out of which opera grew. It was only when the musical representation became associated with action on the stage and singers became actors as well that it became the dominant mode, through the rapid expansion of the new dramatic art form.

Over the nearly four hundred years since that time, the representational style has completely taken over Western musicking, and we can say that all of those works of what today we call classical music are concerned with the representation not of emotions but of the gestures that articulate those relationships that give rise to emotional states. All Western concert music, in fact, composed since about 1600 has been in the *stile rappresentativo*, and our understanding of concert works today owes more than we realize to the semiotics, the system of commonly understood signs, first established on the stage by those early masters and by their successors over nearly four centuries.

Representation has also flowed over into Western popular music, especially in those styles that are "whiter" and in which tonal-harmonic procedures play an important part. It is found less often in "black" styles, which tend to give less importance to harmony and to representation in general; how the tension between the two has proved a powerful creative force in African American music is a fascinating topic that forms the subject of an earlier book of mine (Small 1987).

When Frank Sinatra or Barbra Streisand sings of his or her love, each is acting a part, representing a relationship, and is using the semiotic devices of Western concert music, and ultimately of opera, to assist their representation. We should remember not only that those twentieth-century composers of popular song who are today called the "Broadway Masters"—for example, Jerome Kern, Cole Porter, Richard Rodgers, and George Gershwin—all received classical training in composition but also that up to the early twentieth century the boundaries between popular and concert music were much more permeable than they appear to us today. And, of course, many of the best known of their songs originated on the stage, in musicals, and depend no less than do arias in opera on the musical devices of *dramma per musica*.

By way of contrast, Samuel Charters found among the *jalí*, or praise singers, of West Africa no sign of the techniques of representation. When, for example, he asked one famous *jalí* to sing a love song, the nearest that this fine musician could come to it was a song that told the story of a famous king who loved a beautiful woman—not the same thing at all. He had in his repertory not a single love song, which is to say a song in which the singer impersonated a lover who addressed a beloved, which is surely the dominant genre of all song in Western traditions, whether of concert or popular music.

It is not just the techniques of controlling tension and relaxation, climax and resolution through the progressions of harmony that were learned in the theater. The play of qualities and textures of massed instrumental sound that we call orchestration, the associations we make with the sound of certain instruments—the swordplay of cymbals, the call-to-arms of massed brass instruments, the pastoral strains of the oboe, the anguished heartbeat of plucked double basses, the solemn procession of trombones and horns, the celestial song of violins high up on the E-string, and so on and so on—also originated on the stage.

Just as the operatic repertory teems with funeral processions, triumphal marches and scenes of celebration, mourning and intimate confession, so too concert music is full of such scenes, as well as of the representation of emotional states—fear, rage, joy, sorrow, madness—and of personal characteristics such as youth and age, good and evil, and those which we have learned to recognize as masculine and feminine, in addition to opposition and reconciliation, confrontation, overcoming and triumph.

This suggests that there is no such thing in the Western concert tradition as "absolute music," that is, a musical work that exists purely to be contemplated for the abstract beauty of its patterns of sound. On the contrary, to take part in a performance of a concert work, whether as performer or as listener, is to take part, no less than if one were in a theater, in a dramatic representation of human relationships, which is no less real for giving its characters neither local habitations nor names. Nor are those dramatic meanings which the listener and the performer take from the piece as it is performed "extra-musical." On the contrary, they *are* the musical meaning of the piece. The drama is built into the relationships and is not to be dismissed as external to or imposed upon the real musical meaning.

It is therefore no coincidence that the development of purely instrumental pieces—instrumental pieces, that is, that were aimed at a listener who was supposed to sit and contemplate them—also began only with the inception of the *stile rappresentativo* in the early seventeenth century. Apart from that intended for dancing, there was no purely instrumental music before then; it had no reason to exist. It was only after the representational style became established, also, that abstract dance pieces, dances that were meant not to be danced to but merely contemplated, began to appear, generally in those dance suites that served social purposes of polite entertainment similar to those which were later served by the early symphonies.

Representation requires, of composer, performer and listener alike, a certain detachment from what is being represented, a certain analytical frame of mind, in order to divine the characteristics of what is being represented or embodied in sound. In addition, since there is no point in representing only to oneself, it presupposes the existence of listeners who are not only separate from the musicians but are prepared to maintain an attitude of detachment in order to appreciate the qualities of the representation.

Just as the spectator stands outside the picture, looking into it, so the listener listens to the piece from outside. Unlike most of the world's musicking, including earlier kinds of European musicking, the piece does not draw the listeners in as participants but keeps them at a distance as spectators. It is already complete, and they have nothing to contribute to its nature, nothing to do in fact but contemplate the performance.

People have of course always listened to one another playing and singing, and in most societies there are people who are paid for performing. What is singular about the culture of the modern concert hall is the extent to which listening—detached, contemplative listening—has become the *purpose* of the performance. The act of performance itself is no longer central, no longer even regarded as an activity with its own meanings and satisfactions and has become merely the necessary—even, in the minds of some, the unfortunately necessary—means by which musical works are brought before listeners for them to contemplate. Further, each listener listens on his or her own; how he or she might relate to other listeners is of no significance.

In today's concert hall performances, the musical work is taken to exist for the sake of a "listener," in the singular. It is directed outward, toward that listener, who is outside it, rather than inward toward the performers; and what matters is its effect on the listener, not on the performers, whose response to the work is not taken into account; they are expected to make themselves as transparent as possible and not to interpose themselves and their human personalities between the musical work and the listener.

On the operatic stage, the relationships that are represented are explicit, and the characters whose relationships are being represented are given names, appropriate costumes and a recognizable physical setting. People with physical bodies interact in specific locations, and they relate in visibly recognizable as well as in audible ways so that the two modes of perception reinforce and support each other. In a concert hall, on the other hand, there is nothing to be seen except the performers and their instruments. The piece is an abstract drama of relationships that are not tied to specific physical bodies, and the musical relationships are abstract and generalized. The listener is left to create his or her own spectacle within his mind, and it is therefore not surprising that the devices of representation became meaningful to listeners to concert pieces only after they had become familiar from the operatic stage.

At the same time, one can imagine that once listeners in the concert hall became used to the idea that they were *supposed* to imagine musical meanings in this way, the semiotics of concert music might well have taken on a life of its own. The abstract drama of the concert hall became at least partly independent of the visible drama of the operatic stage probably in the early nineteenth century, when symphony displaced opera as the most prestigious form of musical activity and became an autonomous art form capable of generating its own system of signs. But opera remains always in the background, even if most musicians and listeners alike have forgotten the fact.

The musicians of the concert hall are actors also, no less than the singer-actors of the opera house, and like them are representing relationships that they are not actually experiencing. But the convention of the concert hall denies them any expressive use of bodily gesture, confining them to gestures in sound that are made through their instruments. The art of representation has alienated itself completely from the human body and its gestures, in which it originated.

This is the great paradox of the symphony concert, that such passionate outpourings of sound are being created by staid-looking ladies and gentlemen dressed uniformly in black and white, making the minimal amount of bodily gesture that is needed to produce the sounds, their expressionless faces concentrated on a piece of paper on a stand before them, while their listeners sit motionless and equally expressionless listening to the sounds. Neither group shows any outward sign of the experience they are all presumably undergoing. It is no wonder that members of other musical cultures should find it a curious, if not a downright comical, scene.

How relationships are represented has changed over the four centuries or so of musical representation. In the first phase, coinciding broadly with the period known as the baroque, from roughly 1600 to 1750, the relationship that was represented was static and did not change or develop over the course of a piece. The musical idea was accordingly single and was exposed over time by a process of single-minded expansion that left no room for contrasts or opposites but proceeded on its way until the composer's interest in the material was exhausted. Each piece was the elaboration of a single set of musical relationships, and those relationships neither changed nor developed during its course. That the musical relationships were understood metaphorically at the time as exploring varieties of identity, or temperament, was part of the period's aesthetic theory, the so-called doctrine of the temperaments—and temperaments, it was assumed, do not change.

Typically, a musical statement would be made in full at the beginning of a piece, would reappear in fragmentary form and in different, related keys during the course of the movement, and at the end would be repeated note for note, a procedure that made for an absence of development or change. The uniformity of baroque instrumental sound, with a single texture and instrumental combination established at the beginning and continuing until the end, or at most two alternating textures, speaks not of primitive or undeveloped orchestral technique but of this concentration on a single idea. We hear this static concentration in the orchestral and instrumental works of J. S. Bach, Handel, Vivaldi and a host of contemporaries and predecessors.

But around 1750 (again, the change was gradual and had its roots farther back) a new dynamism appeared in the representational style. The relationships that were represented began to change and develop over the course of a piece. We can illustrate it best by comparing arias from two operas that were composed some forty years apart. Opera, of course, like all drama, is concerned with the change and development of relationships between people, and the early composers of opera quickly evolved a form of musical dialogue, or recitative, in which melodic and rhythmic shapes mimicked the rhythms and the rise of fall of speech. It was recitative that carried forward the dramatic development toward a point of repose. At that point the character would comment on the situation in an aria.

The first of these two arias is the famous "Where'er You Walk," from Handel's "dramatic ode" (an opera in all but name) *Semele*, which was first performed in 1744. The text is very concise, only four lines of verse, and in it the god Jupiter, enamored of the mortal Semele, promises her, in stately eighteenth-century fashion, that:

> Where'er you walk, cool gales shall fan the glade,
> Trees where you sit shall crowd into a shade.
> Where'er you tread, the blushing flowers shall rise,
> And all things flourish where'er you turn your eyes.

Just as the four lines express a single idea, so the musical shape of the aria makes change and development impossible, since nineteen of its twenty-seven measures are taken up with the first two lines (there is of course much verbal repetition), and these nineteen measures, including the orchestral introduction, are repeated note for note at the end. This type of aria, known as a *da capo*, or from-the-top, aria, was typical of its day. It is by no means undramatic, since it serves to clarify and intensify the relationships at that point in the drama, but it is static, and nothing changes during its course. The variations and graces with which the singer was expected to ornament the melody the second time around do not affect this situation.

To hear an aria by Mozart, on the other hand, is to realize how things had changed in forty-odd years. In *The Magic Flute* of 1791, for example, Mozart has the Queen of the Night in her first aria give the hero, Tamino, a graphic and tearful account of the abduction of her daughter by a wicked magician. But she concludes not in that vein but on a note of confident resolution in the certainty that the youth will rescue the girl and all will be well—all in a duration of less than five minutes and through the medium of the highest vocal virtuosity in what sounds like an outburst of spontaneous melody. The static comment has become an active element in the developing dramatic situation, and the character's discourse actually contributes to the process of change and development.

It was this concentrated and economical process of change and development that became also the ideal that was embodied in purely instrumental music from about 1750 onward, and made possible the presentation of an abstract drama of developing relationships without reference to any verbal text.

CHAPTER 10

A Drama of Relationships

✳

The type of dramatic orchestral work that emerged around 1750 was initially strictly for entertainment and was intended as introduction to, or diversion from, the more serious business of the occasion at which it was played. It might function as overture, entr'acte, or afterpiece to an opera, a concert, a play, a ball perhaps or some kind of private celebration, even before and after Mass in the larger churches and cathedrals. The intention was to create something graceful, elegant, and above all entertaining, with just enough dramatic tension to keep the listener intrigued while an enchanting procession of melodies was unfolded—about as serious as, say, an early-twentieth-century musical comedy.

As happens frequently with works of art that are intended strictly for entertainment, a set of narrative conventions was quickly established, and the form crystallized around the middle of the eighteenth century into a sequence of three pieces, in the order fast–slow–fast, with a fourth, a minuet, added later, generally coming after the slow movement. The first of these would create an atmosphere of bustle, movement and strong dynamic and tonal contrast; the second, elegance and grace with perhaps a hint of refined melancholy; and the third, carefree celebration. This was enough to create an element of dramatic progression, however slight, and it was this element of drama that from its beginnings defined the piece.

It was quite usual for the first two movements to be played at the beginning of the occasion and the last one or two at the end. It was as much music for use—for arriving, settling down, and leaving—as it was for listening to; and it had no pretensions to being "art" and certainly none to demanding the undivided attention of an audience. It was at first known by a variety of names: cassation, serenade, divertimento, all signifying something intended for entertainment. But before long the name emerged that had for a long time signified an introduction, or prelude (in some popular music the word is still used in this way): symphony.

The output of symphonies in Europe in the fifty years between 1750 and 1800 was prodigious; it has been estimated that the number was well in excess of twenty thousand. It was customary to order a symphony for a specific occasion, as one might order a new coat or wig; one would no more play an old symphony at a special occasion than one would wear an old suit of clothes. The musicians who composed these pieces to order regarded themselves more as skilled craftsmen producing for a market than as artists in the modern sense.

Symphonies were generally played at sight or after a single rehearsal; typically, they would receive one or at most a handful of performances, and then the score and parts would be put away to gather dust in a cupboard or used to light the fire. The demand for new symphonies was as insatiable as the demand for new pop songs in our own time, and last year's symphonies were as stale as last year's songs.

The great ages of both the novel and the symphony were more or less contemporaneous—the second half of the eighteenth and the nineteenth century. A symphony, like a novel, is first and foremost a dramatic narrative in which a change in relationships occurs. In the novel the developing relationships are those the writer establishes between his characters, and in the symphony they are those the composer establishes between the sounds, the rhythms and the melodies—the musical gestures, in short—that constitute his material. This means that a symphony is experienced in performance, by performers and listeners alike, not as form or structure but as a sequence of significant events in time, a drama of opposition and resolution. What makes this drama possible is the system of conventionally understood musical gestures, which, as we have seen, was developed first on the operatic stage.

Early symphonies were loosely connected sequences of movements, with only a casual narrative connection between them, and they were not expected to be taken too seriously. It was Johann Sebastian Bach's son Carl Philipp Emanuel, followed by Josef Haydn and his younger contemporary, Mozart, who introduced a new complexity, a new seriousness, into the drama, beginning the process of integration of the four movements into a coherent narrative and intensifying the processes of change and development in ways that demanded, and repaid, repeated playings and hearings (it seems that many of Haydn's symphonies were, in fact, composed as incidental music for the theater, a fact that emphasizes not only the essentially dramatic nature of the form but also the permeability in those days of the boundary between symphonies and other kinds of musical works).

Haydn's one-time pupil Ludwig van Beethoven brought the symphony to a pitch of dramatic tension that has not been surpassed since, expanding the scale and scope of the drama in ways that set the tone for symphonic works for the next two hundred years. Johannes Brahms, who perhaps more than any other felt the weight of Beethoven on his shoulders, once remarked that a symphony was no laughing matter; he did not complete the first of his mere four until he was in his forties. It was in Beethoven's symphonies also that there appeared for the first time an explicit narrative progression across the four movements; in this they served as models that were followed, with more or less success, by subsequent composers of symphonic works.

Today the comfortable familiarity of Beethoven's symphonies deafens us to the fact that when first performed they struck their audiences like a fist in the face, confounding their expectations at every turn and dislocating completely their sense of how the narrative should proceed. Any formal perfection that critics may find in them today was certainly not apparent to their contemporaries, who reveled in, or complained of, according to taste, their violence, their dynamic excess, their discontinuities and dislocations, and their brusque dismissal of eighteenth-century narrative conventions.

The integration into a coherent narrative brought new problems for nineteenth- and twentieth-century composers, for if the ending of the first movement was nothing more than a standoff or truce between opposing forces, followed by the relative calm of the slow movement and the relative relaxation of a dancelike movement, how does one finish off the struggle with the desired once-and-for-all triumph? It is like the joke quotation that used to be attributed to Samuel Goldwyn: "I want to make a movie that starts with an earthquake, fire, and tidal wave and goes on to a big climax." Beethoven managed it but only by invoking an unprecedented level of violence, and it remained an insoluble problem for most of his successors.

Behind all Western storytelling for the past three hundred years or more, whether it be novel, play, film or piece of symphonic music, lies a kind of master narrative, a meta-narrative, which not only gives shape to the story and directs the nature of the events portrayed but controls the very manner of the storytelling itself. This meta-narrative can be put in three very short sentences:

Order is established.

Order is disturbed.

Order is reestablished.

The scale of the initial order may be small, maybe only a pair, as in conventional romances (boy meets girl, boy loses girl, boy regains girl) or two sisters, as in Jane Austen's *Sense and Sensibility*. It may be huge, such as the Russian nation in *War and Peace;* it may be a village community as in Chinua Achebe's *Things Fall Apart* or a family as in Eugene O'Neill's *Long*

Day's Journey into Night. It may be a conventional social order or an un-conventional one, like the group of bums in John Steinbeck's *Cannery Row,* or even perhaps scarcely recognizable as order at all, like the strangely devastated city in Samuel Delany's *Dhalgren.* In each case the initial order is introduced as a set of relationships between characters: their affinities, their oppositions, and the tensions between them.

Since a perfect order would contain no tensions to drive the narrative along, the initial order is generally portrayed as only apparently stable, re-quiring only some kind of disturbance to set it in motion. The disturbance may come from the order's own inner tensions, or it may come from with-out, in the form of a new character perhaps, a change of external circum-stance, or perhaps a natural or man-made catastrophe as in the genre of dis-aster novels and movies. It may be the merest rippling of the waters, providing just enough energy to keep the narrative moving, or it may be a huge and devastating upset, or anything between. Typically, the disturbance proceeds through a series of minor climaxes in increasing order of tension, carefully paced by the author to keep the reader/spectator interested, to-ward a climax, a major confrontation, after which order is reestablished.

But it will not be the order of the beginning. Something in the initial order has to have changed; otherwise there would be no point to the narra-tive. Generally speaking, order is reestablished in one of four principal ways: the first is by the protagonist overcoming, containing or eliminating the disturbing element (the struggle to overcome will itself leave the initial order altered); second, by the protagonist accommodating and coming to terms with the disturbing element; third, by the protagonist's reconcilia-tion with the disturbing element; and fourth, by the protagonist's being overcome, the final order then being that of the disturbing element. The fourth is the inversion of the first, for if someone overcomes, then some-one has to be overcome; life, according to that scheme, is a zero-sum game. It is a matter of whom the reader or spectator or listener is expected to identify with, the winner or the loser.

In beginning with one order and ending with another, the narrative pro-gresses from a clear beginning to a clear ending; the final order is closed, complete, and nothing more need be said about the characters or their rela-tionships. The ending is expected to be a development of possibilities that were inherent in the beginning. The characters are expected to interact in ways that are consistent with their personalities as they are exposed to the reader or spectator at the beginning and to develop according to the logic of their own being as it has been invented by the author. The more strictly all the incidents in the story are shown to be related to the main narrative the better the story is thought to be constructed, and certainly an economical and logical use of character and incident does make a narrative more satisfying to many readers or spectators.

It is true that the twentieth century has seen forms of storytelling that do not conform to these canons, for example certain modernist novels and plays (those of Samuel Beckett, for example) in which nothing changes, as well as soap operas, in which each new order sets off a new set of instabilities so that the plot is kept in motion ad infinitum, with no final and conclusive ending (until perhaps the ratings fall to an unacceptable level)—a state of affairs that may resemble the narratives of "real life" more than does that of the novel. But for the ordinary reader of novels the canons of development, climax and closure remain firmly in place, as they do for the ordinary listener to symphonic music, for the scenario fits the symphony as well as it fits the novel.

In their early days novels, like symphonies, were intended, and received, purely as entertainment. Reading novels was even regarded in intellectual circles with some suspicion; as late as 1818, Jane Austen, in her novel *Northanger Abbey,* felt obliged to make her famous and spirited defense of novel-reading. But there is of course no such thing as pure, contentless entertainment. Every narration, from the most serious to the most frivolous, carries within it an implied set of values; after all, even a conventional happy ending implies an idea, however conventional, of what constitutes human happiness, whereas identifying a character as hero, heroine or villain implies concepts of goodness and badness that are not necessarily universally shared.

Even the narrative conventions—the ways in which the narrative is shaped, how it begins, climaxes and ends (indeed, whether it climaxes and ends at all)—imply ideas of what constitutes order, what kind of order is desirable, and what kinds of order deserve, or need, perhaps for their own good, to be disturbed, as well as what kinds of events are important and what oppositions and resolutions are crucial in human life. Values, in fact, are built into the narrative style itself, no less than into the explicit content of the story that is being told.

The parallels with the symphonic narrative are striking. The symphony's drama may be cast in terms of comedy, tragedy, epic, even farce, or any other theatrical genre; it may be grand and public or small-scale and intimate, fast-moving or leisurely, expansive or terse. The formal canons and taxonomy of symphonic form that students of music learn today were not arrived at until much later by study of those works that had proved most effective as dramatic narratives. One does not read a novel in order to admire its formal perfection, nor, one hopes, do novelists write in order to be thus admired. Similarly, no sensible musician will strive to make his work conform to those after-the-event models of "formal perfection" but will look instead for ways in which to make his drama more effective and evoke maximum response from his listeners. What is called formal perfection is the *product* of that dramatic effectiveness, not the *source* of it.

What is today called sonata form is a narrative technique that was developed to allow for effective dramatic representation of conflict and its resolution. The codification of the narrative into "exposition," "development," and "recapitulation," with their "first and second subjects" and all the other analytical apparatus with which students of music are today all too familiar, dates from the late nineteenth century; such terms were unknown to the the great eighteenth- and early nineteenth-century masters of the medium, and many of their finest symphonic dramas can be made to conform to sonata form only by a Procrustes' bed distortion of the real processes at work in them. By the time the codification took place, the way of shaping the narrative that seems to have come so naturally to Mozart, Haydn, and Beethoven had hardened into a mold that many musicians felt had to be broken if their creative powers were to be set free.

The concept and the vocabulary of sonata form that was developed through the study of scores, though perhaps useful in a limited sense, have misled musicians into viewing synoptically, as a structure, all of whose features exist simultaneously, what is actually a series of events in time. Structure is a static concept, carrying an implication of something permanent or at least lasting and, in the case of musical works, of something that transcends the ephemerality of performance and has nothing to do with its dynamics. It thus inclines us to think of performance as at best contingent to the work's nature and meaning and even as irrelevant to it.

If our enjoyment of a work of music depends on our perceiving its structure, as is seriously maintained by many scholars of music, then it is clear that, since we can perceive in its entirety the structure of a work of music only at the last moment of any performance, the work itself can be enjoyed only after the performance has finished. Such a notion is not only absurd but also hopelessly at variance with the way in which we actually perceive a musical performance. Mozart, we recall, was delighted when his Parisian audience showed its appreciation loudly *during,* not after, the performance of his symphony, and there have been times in a concert hall when I should have liked to do the same. If enjoyment is not present from the first moment (and Mozart knew better than anyone how to grip an audience's attention right from the start), then there is not much point in listening. It seems that it is only in the Western concert tradition that that is not fully understood.

We hear sounds in combination, both simultaneous and successive, and in our minds we place them into relationships to create meaning. The dramatic narrative can be directly inferred from the sound relationships themselves. To perceive structure requires a shift in the direction of abstraction, which is, I suppose, a legitimate activity for those who want to understand what lies between the covers of musical scores; but insofar as it requires those who engage in it to ignore the fact of performance, it is also a potential obstruction to the understanding of what goes on when the work in question is actually performed and heard. That is the important question, since without performance there is no music. A score, as we have seen, is not music.

What is at work here is once again reification, the taking of an abstraction to be more real than the reality it represents. The structure of a musical work is an abstraction of the actions of composition and performance. Those who study a score in order to ascertain the way in which a musician went about composing his piece may well find structure there, but it is the consequence, not the cause, of the way the piece was composed.

A more fruitful way of understanding a symphonic work is to think of it in terms of the great meta-narrative: order is established, order is disturbed, and a new order is established that grows out of the old. Typically, in a symphony the initial order is established with a strong, perhaps aggressive, even heroic gesture that establishes strongly the tonic key. It is this order that is disturbed by the establishment of an aberrant key, presented generally in the form of a softer, more lyrical gesture (older analysts often actually called them the masculine and feminine subjects). This section of the movement ends with a cadence in the aberrant key that seems to signal its victory. The movement thus far may then be repeated, making the apparent victory of the aberrant even more emphatic.

There ensues a period of tonal instability, even seeming disorder, during which either or both of the two themes may be developed and transformed in a variety of keys. The climax of the piece comes with a powerful restatement of the initial theme, which restores also the tonic key. The more lyrical theme comes dragged after it, now also in the tonic key. Order is restored, the aberrant safely contained, if not totally vanquished, by the logical.

For the narrative to carry any tension, the appearance of the aberrant key has to be signaled as something desirable, beautiful, even seductive. Thus, we find in many symphonic movements not only that the so-called second subject is "the beautiful tune," the one that we remember most, but also that the moment of its appearance in the aberrant key may be one of great beauty, often an unexpected shift of tonality that places the new melody in an unexpected relationship with what has gone before. At the same time its desirability has finally to be overcome, or a least contained, for the sake of narrative closure, and so at its reappearance it has to be shown this time in a logical rather than a paradoxical relationship. The more beautiful and desirable the aberrant second-subject theme (sometimes a group of themes), the more violent, it seems, needs to be the reaction to it in order to bring it back into line.

Initially, the aberrant key was by convention that of the dominant, or fifth, degree; but as the history of the form progressed, composers raised the dramatic stakes by using increasingly remote keys, keys that were increasingly difficult to justify by the logic of the tonal order. This caused ever greater upset and made necessary ever greater dislocation and even violence in order to bring it back into the orbit of the tonic key at the end.

This drama of abstract relationships bears many parallels to those other dramas that we encounter nightly, our dreams. In a dream, too, the working out of relationships appears to be of more importance than the actual identity of the characters that are relating; they can die and be resurrected, can change their shape, their size, and their appearance, can merge into one another, be turned upside down and inside out, can appear and disappear, all according to no logic that we can perceive.

Similar things happen to the protagonist themes of symphonic works, though such works bear within themselves a tension that does not exist in dreams, between the composer's intuitive sense of the rightness of such transformations and the demand made of him that they conform to a narrative whose logic can be perceived and analyzed. The existence of technical terms, such as inversion, retrogression, diminution and augmentation, for these processes of dream transformation bears witness to the continuing struggle to tame the irrational logic of dream narrative and bring it into the daylit realm of the rational. (But even at the high noon of such rational control, by means of total serial organization, its high priest, Pierre Boulez [1964], found himself writing: "Despairingly one tries to dominate one's material by an arduous, sustained, vigilant effort, and despairingly chance persists, and slips in through a thousand unstoppable loopholes.") Thus it is that the theme of taming the irrational occurs at a level even deeper than that of narrative, in some of the basic techniques themselves of symphonic music.

When I first encountered these symphonic works as a boy, I remember understanding much of this intuitively. I could rehearse in my mind, and even whistle after a fashion, whole symphonic movements—of the Beethoven Fifth, for example, and Dvorak's Ninth, the *New World*, of which my family had recordings (proudly proclaimed as made by the "new electrical process")—and knowing nothing of sonata form, I enjoyed them as narratives, dramatic sequences of musical events, rather than as forms or structures. I heard melodies and motifs placed in certain relationships with one another, and even at that time, when I knew nothing of harmony, I learned in an empirical way, through my ears, which were in paradoxical and which in logical relationships. I learned to hear also that the repetition of a theme was not just a matter of formal convention, of which I knew nothing, but was more like the reappearance of a character in a story and that, as so often in a well-told story, the point of the reappearance was likely to be the changed relationship of the theme to its surroundings.

But when, in my early twenties, I started formal musical studies and learned the conventional terminology of musical form, I learned to forget about drama and concentrate on structure. It took me many years to regain that earlier feeling for narrative progression, which I am certain is the truer meaning that is conveyed when a symphonic work is performed. Today, when I hear what is to me a previously unknown symphonic work (thanks to the joint labors of record companies and classical music radio channels there are not too many of them left), I find that the drama comes across most forcefully in earlier hearings, before the work has become too familiar; when I get to understand the formal aspects of the piece—the exposition, development, recapitulation, and so on, as my training taught me to do, something of its dramatic force is lost. I begin to hear repetition where before I heard narrative flow.

I recount this simply to show what it is that makes me certain that naive, which is to say, musically untrained, listeners to works of symphonic music are not wrong to hear them primarily as dramatic narratives, whatever their musical "betters" may tell them about sonata form and the like. I should go so far as to say that if they are not narratives, if they were not concerned with the development of human relationships, then I cannot imagine what interest they, or indeed anyone, would find in them. I have certainly never listened for "perfection of form" and should almost certainly not recognize it if I were to hear it. It is perhaps interesting in this regard that Mozart, whose works more than any others are cited by academics for their perfection of form, shows in all his letters no awareness whatsoever of something called sonata form, or exposition and development and never uses the terms even when our generation might imagine that in talking about his works such terms would have come in useful.

It makes me wonder if those who are so keen to have listeners understand the structure of sonata form, rondo form, and all the other forms that turn up in textbooks—and in record sleeve notes—are not assiduously destroying for them that very mystery, that very "what comes next?" excitement that is surely at the heart of the symphonic narrative as it is of all narrative—and worse, in doing so, obscuring the fact that, again as in all narrative, important issues concerning human relationships are being articulated as it proceeds.

All narrative arts, of course, have their conventions and their conventional procedures; it is perfectly possible to analyze novels, plays and films and detect what we may call formal features, and sometimes it even seems that the lower the quality of the story, the more rigid the narrative conventions; porno movies, for example, are especially rigid (if I may be pardoned the expression) in their formal structure. But to discover the form it is necessary to paralyze the narrative movement. You cannot have narrative, which is dynamic, and form, which is static, at the same time; it is a little like the uncertainty principle in physics, which states that it is impossible to know both the position and the velocity of a particle at the same time. One or the other but not both.

Physics, of course, unlike storytelling, does not concern itself with human relationships, so there is no problem in switching from one mode of understanding to the other. But to paralyze the act of musicking in order to extract formal principles is an operation that has to be undertaken, if at all, with great care and a clear understanding that in doing so one is switching off meaning. That is not necessarily fatal, as long as one remembers to switch it on again; otherwise formal means take over from narrative ends to become ends in themselves, and the human significance of musicking is lost.

This leads me in turn to wonder whether the multiple playings of symphonic works made possible by recording do not have a hand in the loss of narrative meaning; how many times, one wonders, would Beethoven have imagined that a person might hear his Ninth Symphony in a lifetime? Single figures at the most, one would guess, which, for a non-score-reader, would mean no chance for the piece to attain the comforting analytical familiarity that we have with it today (the Spanish national railway system recently treated me to a complete performance of it at full volume, punctuated by station announcements and the pips that warned when the doors were closing, on a train trip from Madrid to Aranjuez).

There is no doubt that with multiple playings the bones of structure, willy-nilly, do begin to show beneath the flesh of the narrative. One finds the same thing with certain classic films—*Casablanca,* for example, or *The Maltese Falcon*—whose famous complexity, not to say impenetrability, of plot has faded over time to reveal a rather flung-together succession of incidents, leaving the impression of only a few lyrical or dramatic moments and a certain period charm, rather like a run-of-the-mill eighteenth-century symphony or concerto.

The musicologist Hans Keller once defined symphony as "the large-scale integration of opposites." That definition certainly accommodates the narrative element, but it omits a crucial reference to how the integration takes place, which is through a process of struggle and by the overcoming, or at least containment, of one element by another. It is this element of struggle that as much as anything defines symphonic music.

Struggle and conflict are the engines that drive the symphonic drama, and the sense of struggle between opposing forces is never far away, even in the most placid moments. That struggle is not insignificant. In any narration, even the most trivial, important issues are being raised, important values are being asserted and contested. There is no doubt that who wins and who loses in the symphonic drama are important questions.

But perhaps even more important questions concern the narrative style itself: why what is represented should so persistently be stories of opposition, struggle and overcoming or at least containment, why the drama should always end with such finality, why indeed the *stile rappresentativo* should have taken over at all in Western concert music. Perhaps all could finally be subsumed into one great question: *What vision of order is represented in the symphonic drama?*

CHAPTER 11

A Vision of Order

*

We have seen how, starting with the seventeenth-century practitioners of *dramma per musica*, musicians in the Western concert and opera tradition have constructed a vocabulary of musical gestures—melodic shapes, harmonic progressions, rhythms and tempos, timbres, especially orchestral colors, shifts in dynamics, and combinations of these—that could be made to represent, in as near as they could get to one-to-one manner, not relationships themselves but the bodily and vocal gestures that articulate a relationship and its associated emotional state and to combine those gestures in ways that constitute a narrative.

Because the relationship between the gesture and its musical representation is more metaphorical than literal, the attempt, fortunately, has never been more than partially successful, and no musical gesture, or for that matter any other kind of gesture, can be said to have a single, univocal significance (actually and also because of their persistent metaphorical content, not even words exist in a stable one-to-one relation with their meanings—again fortunately for human creativity and freedom). For this reason, we are left not only with a number of possible interpretations for each narrative but also with the possibility that there may be more than one narrative going on at once as a musical composition is performed and heard.

This in turn has brought about a tension between, on the one hand, the intended meaning of that specific sequence of musical gestures that we call a piece or work of music as we hear it performed and, on the other hand, the meaning of the total act of performing it—musicking—on a specific occasion. It has also caused confusion for those who try to frame and to answer questions about the meaning of "music"—by which they generally mean a musical work, since there is no such thing as music.

I have suggested that what is being represented when a work of symphonic music is performed is a narrative of human change and development, in which one kind of order is disturbed and a new one is established. The change takes place through a process of struggle and conflict in which one character—I have searched but I cannot find a better word and must let this stand – is overcome by another.

Each of these narratives has not only a protagonist, with whom the spectators need to be able in some degree to identify if they are to care what happens in the course of the drama, if they are to feel pity at the protagonist's misfortunes and sorrows, pleasure in his victories, sorrow if he should finally be destroyed and joy if he triumphs, but it has also an antagonist whose values, whose identity, are in opposition to his and with whom he will enter into a new relationship by the end of the story, generally through a process of struggle and overcoming.

The victory of the protagonist is signaled in the overwhelming majority of symphonic works by a scene of triumph and celebration that forms the final movement. This is not an abstract celebration (I cannot imagine what such a thing might be like) but is *somebody's* celebration, and if it elates us, it is not because of the symphony's perfection of form or structure (though we may enjoy it also as a story well told) but because we have identified with the protagonist's struggles in the course of the work and now celebrate with him his victory. If we do not to some degree identify in this way, then the triumphant ending is just so much noise and inflated rhetoric (it will indeed sound like that if the importance of the struggle is not commensurate with with the scale of the rhetoric).

I have characterized the protagonist as "he" with good reason. By any reading of the semiotics that have evolved over the past four centuries, the protagonist of a symphonic work, the person with whom the audience is expected to identify in the drama, is masculine. The tonic key is generally established right at the beginning by a theme that, were it to occur in opera, would be associated with a male character, while the aberrant key is established by a theme that would be associated with a female character. The irruption of the feminine into that logically ordered world is the source of the conflict and thus is the mainspring of the drama that ensues.

The outcome of the drama is not necessarily the overcoming, or even the containment, of the aberrant feminine antagonist. As I suggested when discussing the meta-narrative, the outcome might also be accommodation or reconciliation or even, rarely, the overcoming of the protagonist himself, but the point is that none of these outcomes is reached without considerable struggle and conflict, even violence.

It is important to remember also that when I use the words *masculine* and *feminine,* I do not mean just "male" and "female," a man and a woman. Only on the operatic stage is it possible to be so specific; the symphonic drama might specify gender, with all the secondary characteristics that the words *masculine* and *feminine* come trailing behind them, but it does not go so far as to specify sex. It is those secondary characteristics that we are really talking about when we consider what is really going on as a symphonic work is performed. It is not just an acting out of men versus women, which would be a crude conflict indeed, but rather the acting out of all the anxieties and conflicts that are implicit in those two words.

At the same time, we have to acknowledge that all (the word is not too strong) symphonic works are composed from the male point of view. Without any exception that I know of, the symphonic protagonist is male, and the narrative is related from the male point of view, regardless of the outcome of the conflict. This is understandable when we consider that the world of symphonic music, like that of opera, is a men's world; with very few exceptions, men are the composers and the conductors, and women, when they do manage to penetrate that world, generally find themselves bracketed off. I remember the resigned irritation of my own composition teacher at hearing herself described in a BBC broadcast of a program of her works as "one of Britain's finest women composers." What is interesting is that, without this clue, I doubt if anyone among the listeners could have detected that what was being played was the work of a woman, so completely had she assimilated—had been *obliged* to assimilate if she was to get a hearing—to the masculine system of signs of concert music. Indeed, as Susan McClary (1990) remarks, it is difficult even to imagine what a genuinely feminine semiotics of representational music might be like, so completely has it, from its inception in the seventeenth century, been a masculine affair.

To show how the narrative operates, I shall examine briefly two symphonies, both generally regarded as masterworks, one from the beginning of the nineteenth century and one from its end. Both are regularly performed in concert halls, and dozens of recorded versions of both are available in record shops. I shall give as straightforward an account as I can of what seem to me to be the principal incidents of each work as it is heard in performance.

Such descriptions are generally dismissed by the musically knowledgeable as hopelessly naive, fit only for record sleeves; only full-scale analysis, from the score, of harmonic structure, tonality, thematic relationships and the like will do for them. But maybe it is possible to do too much study of scores and not enough listening; a symphony is, after all, primarily an aural experience. To study a score is, of course, a rewarding activity for those who want to know how its effects were achieved, but we should not mistake means for ends. The first and most important thing is to understand what those effects are and what is meant by them.

I am aware that anyone who would venture to put into words the entire content of a musical work is doomed to failure before he starts because of the divergent natures of the two media. Each of those musical gestures which are woven together into a composition is, like all gestures, multivalent, capable of meaning many things, even mutually contradictory things, at once, while words, or at least sentences, can generally mean only one thing at a time. The musician dances through time, throwing out his multiple meanings like multicolored sparks from a fireworks display, while the writer plods after him, trying to reconstruct the significance of the spectacle from the burned-out cases.

If I am rash enough to make the attempt, it is not because I imagine for a moment that I can put into words the entire content of these two major works of the Western tradition but because I believe there are some understandings of them that can be articulated in words, as long as we are clear that our verbal description can give only one dimension at a time of the multidimensional experience. The synopses that I shall give are meant to draw attention to certain meanings, not generally recognized but, I believe, important, that are generated whenever these works are performed. They are not meant to be either categorical or exhaustive.

Some may find objectionable my associating with persons the forces and impulses that drive these works and the struggle that takes place between them, even if the persons' identity is not specified. They may consider that my interpretation compromises the abstract and universal character of these works. My reply would be, first, that if they are able to understand what is going on in these works in purely abstract terms, they are at liberty to do so. I cannot, because I do not believe that it is possible to deal in abstractions like aggression, triumph, struggle, tension and relaxation without attaching them to a human being who is aggressing, triumphing, struggling, and so on.

I would reply also that I do not believe these works to be either abstract or universal. On the contrary, they are each firmly anchored to a specific time, place and cultural situation; they articulate a specific way of viewing the world, especially human relationships; it is that, and not any putative perfection of form, that is the source of whatever interest and value that they have had for generations of performers and listeners alike. If their significance has extended into our own time, it is because our time shares with theirs enough of those assumptions about relationships to make an exchange of meanings possible. But we cannot be sure that that situation will continue indefinitely.

To maintain that abstractions such as those mentioned can exist unattached to human beings is to return to that Platonic notion of ideal essences, which, as I have maintained before, is one of the silliest ideas ever to have befuddled human minds. On the other hand, of course, it may be that only minds that *have* been thus befuddled can contemplate at all the idea of a drama whose characters have no fleshly existence and whose events take place not in terms of the human body and voice but through musical gestures that have been divorced from the bodily gestures that gave them their meaning in the first place. We have to admit that, however great we might consider these and other symphonic works, an abstract drama is a very curious kind of drama indeed.

But abstract or not, I have to insist that these and all other symphonic works are narratives that tell of the development of human relationships, and in telling their stories they explore, affirm, and celebrate certain concepts of what those relationships are and what they ought to be. Those are important matters by any reckoning, and it behooves us to pay attention to how they are discussed and dramatized. I cannot imagine what could be the point of listening to the performance of a symphony—or of performing or composing one, for that matter—if this were not so. This must be why the language of musical signs and gestures was adopted into instrumental works from the opera stage in the first place.

First, then, the Fifth Symphony of Ludwig van Beethoven, in C minor, performed for the first time in Vienna in 1804, when its composer was thirty-six years old. It is perhaps the archetype of the heroic symphony, which, along with his ground-breaking Third (*Eroica*) Symphony and his monumental Ninth, the *Choral Symphony*, helped to set the pattern for most symphonic works composed during the succeeding two centuries, down to our own time.

The work is in the four-movement form that we saw was established in the mid-eighteenth century, but the scale of the drama has been so enlarged, the stakes so raised, that it has become almost another kind of piece. Its opening theme, which serves as protagonist, is a powerful and brusque gesture, hardly a theme at all and certainly not what most people would call a melody that we recognize throughout the movement and indeed throughout the symphony, as much by its rhythmic as by its melodic contours. Its initial *di-di-di-DA* (G-G-G-E-flat)—pause—*di-di-di-DA* (F-F-F-D)—pause, surely one of the most famous openings in the whole of the symphonic repertoire, is played in unison by the whole orchestra, with the exception of certain softer-toned instruments, giving the very sound itself a gruff quality. From the very beginning we are made to understand that this protagonist is masculine and aggressive.

The harmonies in which the protagonist and his order are presented in the opening section are forthright and straightforward, though the prominent presence of the chord known as the diminished seventh, which conventionally signifies disquiet, unease, suggests that although it may be a powerful and logical order, it already contains its own inner tensions. We might also be forgiven for finding this protagonist something of an obsessive, for there is not a single measure in this section in which we do not hear his rhythm.

After a few seconds of onrushing movement he pauses to make a grand gesture (always at this point my corny visual imagination treats me, all unasked, to an image of him seen from below, arms outstretched against a stormy sky, in black cloak and stovepipe hat, like something from an old German expressionist movie), before resuming his progress. Then with a horn fanfare that incorporates a less abrupt version of his rhythm, he stands aside briefly to usher in a new theme, in the aberrant key of E-flat. This theme is much more of a "melody" than the brusque protagonist theme, more conventionally beautiful, more appealing. It is also tonally unstable, and each of its phrases ends on a weak beat, with what musicians call a feminine ending, which is coded as weaker and less decisive—in short, as more feminine—than the strong "masculine" ending that falls on the strong beat.

Its phrase endings are punctuated with mutterings of the opening rhythm in the bass; even when this second theme is supposed to have the stage, the first is still making its presence felt. In any case it does not have the stage for long but is thrust aside after a couple of dozen measures by the aggressive onrush of the opening rhythm.

But brief as its appearance has been, it seems that it has disturbed the protagonist's order, and he retaliates by reiterating his rhythm in an obsessive monologue in a variety of keys, only pausing occasionally to take breath. The monologue climaxes in a powerful assertion of the opening theme once more in the tonic key. This assertion is followed once again by the big "here I am" gesture, which this time, however, trails off in a tiny phrase of appeal from that most plaintive of orchestral instruments, the oboe. It is as if we have been allowed a glimpse of the frightened child behind the protagonist's heroic posture.

But he quickly regains his poise and his momentum and presents once more the second theme, which has not been heard from since its original appearance, this time in the home key of C. The disturbance has been contained, but there is still no peace. The abrupt response that follows the second theme's appearance is expanded into an extended peroration in which the rhythm of the first theme is hammered out with obsessive force. Even the horn fanfare that first introduced the second theme now adds to the violence with which the second theme is being denied. I should go so far as to describe the ending of this first movement as overkill if the word were not anachronistic to Beethoven's world. For me there is more than a hint of insecurity in the intensity with which the hammering chords continue, long after it appears that the argument has been won.

The slow second movement is remarkable for its expansive quality, its tonal stability, its rhythmic foursquareness, its predominance of "masculine" timbres; the protagonist is relaxed, jovial, at ease. In the third movement the struggle resumes. A spooky dance full of jocular menace is opposed to the protagonist rhythm from the first movement—an unmistakable sign that Beethoven intends us to hear these movements as a single narrative—but as if shadowboxing and without reaching any decisive conclusion. Instead, the struggle subsides into a harmonically and rhythmically indeterminate passage, in which we dimly hear it continuing, as if in darkness or fog.

Out of this darkness, in what is undoubtedly one of the most striking and dramatic transformation scenes in all the symphonic repertoire, emerges a triumphal march and a great scene of jubilation. The struggle is over, and the protagonist has triumphed, though the celebration is interrupted by recollections of the struggle that preceded it. The lengthy peroration that ends the movement and the work assures us that the victory is final, that a new order has come into being, that what has been overcome has been overcome once and for all time—though one might wonder once more whether the much-repeated affirmations may not conceal a hint of continuing doubt or insecurity. At any rate we, the listeners, can share the protagonist's triumph and take from it what we want in terms of vicarious glory and exhilaration.

Maybe I read too much into the work. But it seems to me that there *are* three indubitable facts about it that anyone who is acquainted with the traditional semiotics of western operatic and concert music can hear for him or herself whenever it is performed. The first is that it is a drama, representing the struggle to overcome or at least contain something, some element, that disturbs the initial order and concluding with a great scene of celebration signifying that what had to be overcome has been overcome. The second is that the element that overcomes, whether we take him or it to be a person or just an abstract quality, and in whose triumph it is assumed that we share, is represented as aggressive-masculine, while the disturbing, aberrant element is represented as appealing-feminine. The third is that the level of violence in the struggle between the two is extraordinarily high.

As I become older, I find the level of violence that I hear in many symphonic works, including a number of Beethoven's, increasingly disturbing. Especially in some of those that are among his most highly esteemed works—as well as this symphony, the *Eroica*, and the Ninth Symphony and the Third and Fifth Piano Concertos—the violence seems to come from within the protagonist, as if it were a part of himself that he was trying to subdue. Indeed, it seems as if the higher the level of violence reached, the more the work is admired by present-day audiences.

It is here that the parallel between symphonic works and the novel breaks down. The novelist is able to externalize his or her conflicts into characters that, even if we know they all originated in the author's mind, have a seemingly independent existence, expressed in the fact that they are given names and habitations. But in a symphonic work no such externalization takes place or can take place. The only presence we find in the work is that of the composer himself or, rather, that mythical personage that we have made of the flesh-and-blood person who lived in his own time; and all the personages of his drama, not only the protagonist but also whatever antagonists that may be encountered and overcome in the course of the work, are aspects of himself.

It is not the bald fact of the violence that one unmistakably hears in these works that I find disturbing but the fact that the violence is generated from inside the protagonist, that it is presented as an appropriate response to an antagonist, whoever or whatever he or she may be. I do not find it too extreme to link it with that self-righteous brutality which we encounter in many present-day fictions, not to mention in the real-life actions of those who feel themselves justified by being right. The fact that these works are without question works of the highest genius makes them, for me, even more unsettling. Genius is not neutral, and we are entitled to ask, genius for what? Those who find unacceptable the level of violence in Rambo movies might care to listen a little more carefully here.

It is interesting in this regard that those masters of symphonic music who do not engage in such violence are generally regarded as less strong, less powerful, less profound even, than those who do, with Beethoven himself taken as a kind of criterion or standard of judgment. Mozart, who in both his symphonies and his operas was kinder to his heroines and more subtle in his perception of the feminine, and Schubert are both regarded as more "feminine" (the word is often used of them) than the "masculine" Beethoven. I do not think I am wrong in hearing in recent recorded performances of Mozart's symphonic works, especially, interestingly enough, by groups who claim "authenticity," a new abruptness, bigger dynamic contrasts, louder fortissimos and so on than in the performances of my youth, as if they were trying to show us that Mozart was not the sissy earlier generations thought him to be but was really butch all the time.

In Haydn's vision of order, on the other hand, the feminine seems hardly to exist. His works exist in an ideal of masculine order of Enlightenment rationality and possess a curiously sexless quality (it is interesting that in many of his symphonic works the second subject is a mere transformation of the first), which may be one reason why those works occupy an ambiguous position in the symphonic repertoire, being in general more esteemed than loved by audiences.

There is one other symphonic work of the nineteenth century on which I wish to comment, because it is a work of startling originality that stands the symphonic narrative on its head. It is the Sixth Symphony of Tchaikovsky, in B minor, known as the *Pathétique*. It is the only symphonic work with which I am familiar in which the protagonist does not triumph but is unmistakably overcome and destroyed, his order overturned. Further, it is clear that whatever it is that destroys him is not the feminine, which in this work is associated not with anxiety but with reassurance and consolation.

In view of Tchaikovsky's well-known homosexuality, we cannot help linking this fact with his sexual nature; it could be that gay men, whatever guilt they may be led to feel over their sexual preferences (and the record shows that Tchaikovsky felt such guilt powerfully), do not in general feel that anxiety when confronted with the feminine, whether in themselves or in actual women, which straight men tend to do. The protagonist of this work is, of course, still masculine and uses the conventional masculine-oriented semiotics of the symphonic genre, even though Tchaikovsky has inverted many of its meanings.

The piece opens with a brief prelude, as erotically charged as the prelude to *Tristan und Isolde*, in which fragments of the protagonist theme slowly emerge from the darkness. That theme, when it arrives, is not powerful or aggressive but hesitant and nervous, even perhaps "feminine" in its flutteriness and hesitancies as well as its orchestral timbre (the "feminine" flute, excluded from Beethoven's initial presentation of his protagonist, is prominent here). The second theme, by contrast, is calm, relaxed, and sensuous, tonally stable and harmonically transparent, one of this great melodist's most memorable melodies (it was taken over in the 1940s for a successful popular song called "The Story of a Starry Night"). It is no antagonist but the image of security and comfort, complementing rather than conflicting with the protagonist theme. Tchaikovsky allows his great melody, with its playful tag theme, to extend itself expansively (in a recording I have been listening to, for an astonishing five minutes of the movement's eighteen-minute duration), to reach its climax and its natural ending—an unusual procedure in a symphonic work.

The real conflict of the movement begins with a fortissimo chord, which abruptly shatters the apparent peace. The struggle is violent, but the violence is external, as if the protagonist were being battered by outside forces as fragments of melody appear from nowhere to collide with him. It climaxes with the return of the protagonist theme, now forceful and assertive on the big brass instruments. Some hear this return as hysterical rather than as truly strong (but then, some hear everything Tchaikovsky composed as hysterical); either way it leads into one of the most astonishing dramatic strokes in the whole repertory of symphonic drama. The struggle subsides incoherently into throbbing chords, out of which emerge those fragments of melody which comprised the prelude, now transformed into a powerful melody, the very representation of desire, naked, shuddering desire of an intensity that even Richard Wagner never managed to portray. The desire is fulfilled by the return of the great melody, strong now and passionate and without its playful tag, serene and sensuously beautiful and followed by a peaceful coda, which might even sound like a brief lullaby for the tortured spirit, that ends the movement. In this movement, it seems to me, we have the representation of struggle followed not by overcoming but by reconciliation (in Walt Whitman's words the "word over all, beautiful as the sky") and the attainment of peace.

But it seems that the tortured spirit cannot rest there. There follows what sounds at first like a waltz as graceful and elegant as any by this master of the waltz, except that it is not exactly a waltz for it is in lopsided five-four time and it cannot fly. The dancer is crippled, his happiness illusory. A middle section with pathetic falling apoggiaturas—feminine endings again!—over a throbbing static bass seems to confirm this. It is this falling melody that has the last word in the movement, an omen of what is to come.

The third movement displays a ferocious energy, a throw-another-peasant-on-the-fire abandon. Hearers, in my experience, respond to it in various ways, some perceiving it as bursting with vitality and others hearing it as grotesque, even demonic, a kind of march to the scaffold. Still others just hear it as hysterical. Whatever its real meaning (if indeed it has a single "real" meaning), it leaves the resolution of the struggle to the final movement.

In place of the expansive celebratory fast movement that conventionally provides a happy ending to a symphonic work, the final movement enacts the destruction of the protagonist. There is no mistaking it. Its opening theme is a cry of anguish (the program booklet for tonight's concert tells us that it is marked to be played *adagio lamentoso*) that is pitted against a beautiful second theme whose name must surely be consolation. A terrible struggle ensues, and then there occurs an event that resembles the *peripetía*, or turning point, of ancient Greek tragedy—a moment of revelation up to which a happy outcome appears possible but after which catastrophe is inevitable. The *peripetía* in this case is a hushed, hymnlike melody played by brass instruments, which reintroduces the consolation theme for the last time, now transformed, not only into the minor key but in the very texture of its sound, into a song of utter desolation beyond the possibility of consolation. The hero disappears into the depths and the darkness from which he emerged, and the symphony not so much ends as dies.

What I have given is the merest sketch of what seem to me to be the most salient features of the two great dramas. But there is not a single gesture—that is, sound relationship—however minute, in these works as they are performed or indeed in any musical performance whatsoever, whether literate or nonliterate, composed or improvised, that is without significance, whether or not it is consciously made or consciously perceived. As social beings (and musical composition and performance are above all social acts) we give and receive gestural signals all the time, using bodily postures and movements as well as vocal intonations, and it is the giving and receiving of these signals, many of them minute, that is an important, if not *the* most important, means by which we establish and perceive our relationships with others. While we may achieve partial control over those gestures (actors are best at it, and politicians), nobody's control is complete; however we may try to regulate them, there are always some that slip out unnoticed or are noticed only after they have been made and cannot be recalled. Indeed, it is arguable that it is in the gestures that escape our conscious control that we reveal ourselves most clearly.

We cannot, of course, know for sure how conscious are the gestures that a musician makes, whether composing or improvising. Improvising musicians accept the fact of the impossibility of total conscious control over their every gesture and when they perform, are content to let go and let the subconscious guide their performance—always, of course, within the strict order of tradition and of their carefully cultivated technique. Indeed, such letting go is one of the pleasures of improvisation.

But the musician who works with notation is aiming—has to aim—to achieve total conscious control of the material. Working with notation gives the illusion that such a thing is possible, and we have in the surviving notebooks of Beethoven evidence of the furious struggle that he waged to bring everything under control. But however passionately they may have struggled to achieve it, we may be sure that no musician, not even such consummate craftsmen as Beethoven, Tchaikovsky, or as we have seen, Pierre Boulez, have ever had complete control over every musical gesture they make or have completely understood the significance of what they were doing.

I do not imagine, for example, that either Beethoven or Tchaikovsky consciously intended the two main themes of their first movement to represent the masculine and the feminine or intended his treatment of the relationship between them to represent ideal relationships. Perhaps it would be better to say that they did not *verbalize* such intentions; they did not say even to themselves that *this* theme was masculine and *that* feminine or that the relation between them represented ideal relationships. But they did *musicalize* them; in other words, they selected from that enormous repertory of melodic and rhythmic ideas that any musician carries in his or her head a pair of themes that, by all of the traditional semiotics of Western concert and operatic music, represent those qualities and their relationships. They were thinking not in the language of words but in that of gesture, and they made their artistic choices in that language without the intervention of words.

It seems to me, too, that behind the heroic struggles followed by, in the first case, triumph, and in the second, disaster, which are represented in these two works and which we cannot doubt that their composers intended to represent, there is going on another, less conscious struggle that is concerned with the anxieties not just of individuals, of Ludwig van Beethoven the man or of Pyotr Ilich Tchaikovsky the man, but of a whole culture.

It is not too much to say that every time these symphonies are performed, the whole of European culture and social order is metaphorically put at risk. To hear them performed is to hear articulated its fears and anxieties, its struggle to maintain order and to keep chaos at bay. Beethoven was composing at the beginning of the nineteenth century, with a newly powerful middle class, with the French Revolution under its belt and armed, as Theodore Roszak (1972) puts it, "with a bold liberal ideology, a weapon with which they might intimidate the parasitic clergy and aristocracy who had for so long smugly thwarted the bourgeois desire for full citizenly dignity," and was able to offer reassurance that its masculine (rational, stable, strong, aggressive) order would prevail, that subversive forces would finally be overcome.

Tchaikovsky, on the other hand, writing at the end of the century and beset by personal doubts and anxieties, summoned up the power to descend like a shaman into the underworld and return with a terrible and wonderful vision, that faced squarely the possibility of despair and disintegration and that by articulating it in sound he was able to share. The shaman descends to the underworld to find a cure, not just for his or her own psychic wounds but for those of all the community. In this tour de force of the musical and dramatic imagination alike, Tchaikovsky has used the conventional masculine semiotics of symphonic music to subvert its meanings, converting it into an honest exploration of defeat that is to me more moving, more *usable*, than all the manly heroics and victorious rhetoric of most symphonic works since the time of Beethoven.

The great meta-narrative, of order established, order disturbed, and order reestablished, dominates the concert hall just as it dominates all other forms of storytelling that our society offers us. The struggle that is represented by every piece that goes by the name of concerto is that which in Western society is assumed to take place between the individual, with his or her need for freedom and mobility, and the need to preserve the integrity of the social fabric. There is a paradoxical relationship between soloist and orchestra, for the soloist, who represents freedom and mobility, appears to be set in opposition to the orchestra, representing the social order. The sharply defined individual is set against the large and anonymous group, and his energy and powerful transgressive individuality threatens to tear apart the social fabric.

It is, of course, all play, all representation. Nobody is going to get hurt. They are both taking part in the same performance, under the same rules, sharing the same harmonies under the direction of a single conductor. We know that the soloist's energy and individuality will always be contained by the orchestral texture and that it will not be overwhelmed by the orchestra. Much of the time, in fact, the orchestra acts in a subordinate role to the soloist's virtuoso figurations, providing support and harmonic context for them. It is the way in which containment, on the one hand, and individual survival on the other, are achieved; how near the situation can come to tearing apart the fabric without actually doing so, provides much of the excitement of listening to a concerto being performed.

In the classical concerto-drama, the soloist, like Hamlet in the play (another disturber of the social order, who is finally destroyed by it), does not appear until well into the piece. The orchestra establishes its own order with a procession of melodies, all in the tonic key, stable and solid, though seeming to be awaiting the subversive energies of the soloist. In the concert hall, the sight of the soloist, still and silent, sitting at the piano or holding his or her fiddle, waiting for the moment of entry, warns the audience of the potential for disturbance that exists behind the bland surface of the opening *tutti*. His or her absence of movement brings a rare visual element to the symphonic drama. The drama begins in earnest only after the solo instrument starts to play, for not only does it bring a new energy and individuality, but it further upsets the stable and solid tonal structure with melodies of its own in new keys.

The concerto is one of the few instrumental forms popular in the seventeenth century that has survived into the present. The representation of conflict between unequal forces, of the struggle of the heroic individual to keep from being overwhelmed and of the society to contain the individual's energy, which threatens to tear it apart, seems to be a perennially exciting drama for concert audiences.

As in a symphony, the level of disturbance can vary greatly. Some concertos, notably those dating from the later years of the eighteenth century, give the impression that what is being represented is more a polite dialogue, more an exchange of views, than a struggle—though in many of the piano concertos of Mozart one can hear powerful tensions beneath the politesse of the dialogue—while in others it seems that the soloist's heroic, even manic virtuosity, pitted in opposition to the containing powers of the orchestra, is going to tear the whole thing apart; Tchaikovsky described his First Piano Concerto as "a duel rather than a duet." The more explosive the soloist's energies, the more forceful, even violent, will be the orchestra's gestures of containment.

Those who are assembled here in this hall have come to take part in the performance of these symphonic dramas. It is time now to stand back a little and try to discover what an event such as this, taking place in this hall, with these participants, might mean in the closing years of the twentieth century. In the following chapter I shall frame as clearly as I can the questions that one might ask of the event and of those who take part.

CHAPTER 12

What's Really Going On Here?

What is going on in this concert hall is essentially the same as that which goes on during any musical performance. Members of a certain social group at a particular point in its history are using sounds that have been brought into certain kinds of relationships with one another as the focus for a ceremony in which the values—which is to say, the concepts of what constitute right relationships—of that group are explored, affirmed, and celebrated.

Since I use those three words a lot, perhaps I should briefly explain why I do so. Musicking is about relationships, not so much about those which actually exist in our lives as about those that we desire to exist and long to experience: relationships among people, as well as those between people and the rest of the cosmos, and also perhaps with ourselves and with our bodies and even with the supernatural, if our conceptual world has room for the supernatural. During a musical performance, any musical performance anywhere and at any time, desired relationships are brought into virtual existence so that those taking part are enabled to experience them as if they really did exist.

By bringing into existence relationships that are thought of as desirable, a musical performance not only reflects those relationships but also shapes them. It teaches and inculcates the concept of those ideal relationships, or values, and allows those taking part to try them on, to see how they fit, to experience them without having to commit themselves to them, at least for more than the duration of the performance. It is thus an instrument of *exploration*.

In articulating those values it allows those taking part to say, to themselves, to one another and to anyone else who may be paying attention: these are our values, these are our concepts of ideal relationships, and consequently, this is who we are. It is thus an instrument of *affirmation*.

And third, in empowering those taking part to explore and to affirm their values, it leaves them with a feeling of being more completely themselves, more in tune with the world and with their fellows. After taking part in a good and satisfying musical performance, one is able to feel that this is how the world *really* is, and this is how I *really* relate to it. In short, it leaves the participants feeling good about themselves and about their values. It is thus an instrument of *celebration*.

The relationships that are created in a musical performance are of two kinds: first, those among the sounds that the musicians are making, whether on their own initiative or following directions, and second, those among the people who are taking part. As we shall see, these two sets of relationships themselves relate in an ever more complex spiral of relationships, which become too complex for words to articulate but which the musical performance itself is able to articulate clearly and precisely. It is for this reason that I have been looking in this book at the total experience of a symphony concert and at the kinds of relationship that are being generated there.

Although the sounds that the musicians are making do not constitute the whole of the experience, they are nonetheless the catalyst that makes the experience take place, and their nature and their relationships are therefore a crucial part of the nature of the experience as a whole. Therefore, in the first chapters I looked at some of the relationships that are brought into being between those who have assembled within the great building where the concert is to take place, many of them before a note has been sounded; in the chapters that followed I discussed the nature of the sounds, of the relationships between them, and of the works of music commonly played and heard in symphony concerts, which they comprise.

Whatever the nature may be of those relationships and those works, they are clearly not trivial, since our society, like all human societies, devotes so much energy and resources to their creation and performance, some people even giving over their entire lives to bringing them into existence. If it is true that they articulate in some way desired human relationships, perhaps a desired social order, then we ought to be able to divine, however dimly, and to articulate in words, however inadequately, what those relationships might be.

Inadequately, yes, for when we talk *about* musicking we are using a different mode of articulation from that which the participants are using *in* the musicking itself. The language of musicking is the language of gesture that unites the entire living world, and unlike verbal languages it has no set vocabulary or units of meaning. Being gesture-based, it can deal with many concerns, even apparently contradictory ones, all at the same time, while words can deal with matters only one at a time. Words are literal and propositional where musicking is metaphorical and allusive, and they insist on a single meaning where musicking has many meanings, all at once. The writer plods behind the performers as they shower their multiple meanings over the listeners, describing and explaining their gestures one after the other, reducing the many-layered, multidimensional experience to a one-dimensional discursive stream. The best one can hope to do with words is suggest ways in which we might begin to understand the experience. The understanding itself can come only from the musicking itself.

So how *do* we begin to draw out the meaning of the experience we call a symphony concert? How *do* we begin to understand what's really going on here?

The conventional conception of a symphony concert is that it takes place in order to present works of symphonic music to a public, which is to say, to anyone who is prepared to pay the price of admission. Those works are thought to have been bequeathed to our time by great musicians of the past and to have a permanent existence and a meaning and value over and above any possible performance of them. It is in order to play and to hear these works that musicians and audience come together in this great hall. The performance, in other words, is assumed to take place so that the audience may enjoy the works, which in some not-understood way provide them with refreshment and spiritual nourishment.

But this is a very impoverished way of understanding the rich and complex texture of relationships and thus meanings that is brought into existence when a symphony concert takes place in a concert hall, or indeed when any musical performance takes place anywhere and at any time. What I am suggesting instead is that these people have come together here—players, listeners, and hall staff alike—to take part in a ceremony in which their values, which is to say, their feelings about what are right and proper relationships, are affirmed, explored, and celebrated.

At the center of the ceremony is the performance of pieces from a certain repertory, often known as the canon of great works. But they do not constitute the whole of the ceremony; everything that takes place, every gesture that is made, contributes its meaning to the event. Even so banal an act as the passing of money is more than mere payment for service and takes on a metaphoric meaning as well. It is not so much that the event takes place in order to present the works but rather that the works exist in order to make possible the performance that forms the center of the event. That it should be these works, chosen from a certain repertory, and not others, that the musicians choose to perform and the audience to hear is, of course, highly significant, but the central element of the ceremony is the act of performance, not the works themselves.

I can perhaps elucidate what I mean by reference to another kind of ritual performance, one that is just as important to its participants as are symphony concerts to theirs: reading stories to children at bedtime. This act in itself—we can quite properly call it a ritual since it, too, explores, affirms and celebrates a set of values—carries a meaning in the lives of both parents and children that may almost be said to be independent of the actual story that is read and of its content.

Almost but not quite. In the first place, only stories from a particular repertory are thought suitable for the bedtime ritual; certain types of story (not to mention whole libraries on psychology, nuclear physics, philology, history and plate tectonics) are thought of as unsuitable and indeed are so. It would be a strange parent who read to their child from the works of Geoffrey Archer, Michelle Steel, James Joyce or the Marquis de Sade.

And second, we know that even within the repertory of suitable stories both readers and read-to do have their preferences, reflecting deep-seated individual desires, concerns, or needs. Some stories are liked and stay in the repertory, some are disliked and disappear after maybe only a single reading, and some are loved and are read and listened to over and over again. A story that arouses a positive response in one child may arouse a negative one in another; one that is funny for one may inspire terror in another, and one that appears fantastical and farfetched to one will be everyday and commonsensical to another, and so on.

This, of course, has to do with the kinds of human relationships that are represented in those stories, those that are displayed as good, sensible, and desirable and those that are displayed as absurd, undesirable, or even wicked—in other words the kind of order that is established, disturbed and reestablished—and with the ways in which those relationships are represented. Not all people, not even children with their limited life experience, respond in the same way to the same vision of order. And, further, even though some stories may initially be exciting, disturbing or downright terrifying, all these characteristics can be annulled and turned to reassurance by the comfortable repetitiousness of the nightly ritual reading, allowing the child to go quite peacefully to sleep after their recitation.

Children's stories display the formal features of the great meta-narrative as clearly as does any other kind of narrative in modern Western society. Order is established—"once upon a time"; order is disturbed and order reestablished—"they lived happily ever after." The old formulas may have been dropped from modern stories, but the formal features they represent have not. Those features reflect values and concepts of order, of disorder, and of happiness and unhappiness that have a powerful influence in the socialization of young children.

But it could still be that the central socializing function of the little ritual lies not so much in the content of the stories themselves as, first, in the fact that it takes place at all and, second, in that it places the child for that period of heightened ritual time at the center of a world that may well have marginalized him or her during the day, empowering him or her to control certain features of it—which story is read, even perhaps who reads it, how many times it is read, and often, in the case of well-loved and often-repeated stories, the word-perfect correctness of the reading. The ritual, as we know, is helping the child to build a sense of security, which, it is hoped, will empower him or her in later years to go out to meet life and to take risks, and lucky indeed is the child in whose life it is a regular feature.

Even luckier perhaps is the child whose parent is able to improvise stories on the spot, who within the safe regularity and predictability of the ritual itself is able to produce not only constant surprise and novelty but also to allow, even encourage, a certain active degree of control by the child over the course of the narrative—"And what do you think happened next?"—and to help develop an ear for absurdities, contradictions, non sequiturs and cheating. In strongly oral societies, many of the stories will be memories of those that the parent him or herself was told, permutated and adapted perhaps but carrying within them the weight of the society's traditional values and ideal relationships which are being passed on by this means to the child.

I intend no insult to either the ceremony of the symphony concert or to the works that are played there when I characterize them, at least in part, as bedtime stories told to adults. The two ceremonies have features in common. The first is that what is going on in both is telling of a story and that the story partakes of the nature of the great meta-narrative. The second is that the stories have become so familiar through repetition that they have lost whatever power they might once have had to disturb. The third is that in both there is an insistence on perfect repetition of a series of actions that are prompted by a text, which in one case is the reading of words that comprise a story and in the other is the performance of sequences of musical sounds that comprise musical works.

Let us think a little about these features of a symphony concert and see if we can use the parallels with the other ceremony to understand a little better what is going on there.

A work in the Western concert tradition is a pattern of sounds that is always performed in the same combinations, both simultaneous and successive. Those sound combinations are metaphorically invested with meaning through the operation of a semiology of sound relationships that has been developed over the past four centuries or so, and the way in which they are put together tells a story that presents us with certain paradigms and models of human relationships.

The narrative tells of the establishment of an order, of the disturbance of that order by an element that may be attractive, even seductive, but that threatens its existence, and of the struggle to reestablish order, to contain or overcome the disturbing element. The order may itself be small-scale and even trivial or on the largest scale, involving whole cultures, as in the major symphonic works of Beethoven, for example. He was one of the few musicians whose musical vision was large enough to create sound patterns of an amplitude and a complexity that was equal to the telling of such a story. The fact that, as I have suggested, his vision of order was of a rather special kind that might not be everyone's idea of an ideal order, that the sound relationships he created are not everyone's idea of ideal relationships, or that the level of violence resorted to in bringing those relationships into being is high does not lessen the force of his achievement.

At the same time, it is curious that the ideal of heroic individualism that he outlined should be that which appeals so strongly to members of the Western industrial bourgeoisie. At this point I can see some readers pulling a face and hear them saying, "Here we go again," but the fact is—and it is confirmed by social surveys of audiences taken over and over again in a number of countries—that those who like to take part in the ceremonies of the concert hall belong in the overwhelming majority to the industrial middle classes. That is not a judgment, just a fact, and like all facts about this fascinating ceremony it needs explaining.

The stories that are told, however well they may be told, will arouse no response unless they resonate, or can be made to resonate, with the desires and values, spoken or unspoken, conscious or unconscious, of those at whom they are aimed. Those desires and values may well change over the life span of an artwork like a symphony so that those who hear it performed at different times may well hear in it different satisfactions for different desires.

One possible way of understanding the resonance that these works continue to find among contemporary middle- and upper-class people in Western-style industrial societies lies not merely in the fact that they represent struggle, the overcoming of one force by another, and the celebration of that victory but also in the fact that the force that overcomes is that of logic, clarity, rationality—all those values of Enlightenment Europe that were contemporary both with the development of the symphony and with the coming to power of the bourgeoisie and that come trailed behind the concept of masculinity that is the central propulsive force of symphonic works.

Nor are the formulas "once upon a time" and "lived happily ever after" irrelevant to the performance of symphonic works. The first takes us out of historical time, the time of everyday, into the time of myth, which is where, or when, the events of the symphonic narrative also take place. The events of the narrative are not simple tales but myths, involving the activities of heroic individuals, and demonstrating in their conflict and their resolution exemplary struggles and exemplary resolutions. These can be socializing agents that are just as powerful as are fairy stories told at bedtime.

The second formula, "they lived happily ever after," reminds us of one of the central characteristics of the meta-narrative—that it is closed. It has a beginning and ending, and both are clear and unequivocal. The order that is brought into existence at the end is indeed final; the grand cadence that invariably concludes the work tell us that he, the protagonist, lived happily ever after, and nothing could be more final than that (it is interesting that Tchaikovsky's narrative of the destruction of a soul ends with no such grand cadence but simply trails off into silence).

We should understand that despite the prevalence of the meta-narrative in Western storytelling today—by which I mean not only novels but also films, plays and any other narrative medium—it is not the only way in which stories can be structured. Most folktales, for example, are constructed as mere episodes in an ongoing narrative that seems to have no end: the Anansi stories, and the Brer Rabbit stories (however Joel Chandler Harris may have tidied them up for publication) are like that, as are some of the works of modern African novelists who use as models traditional African storytelling; Amos Tutuola and Ayi Kwei Armah come to mind. I have already mentioned soap operas, especially those endless confections that come to Spain from South American studios and are known, appropriately, as *culebrones*—big snakes. One might go so far as to guess that whenever the meta-narrative makes its appearance it is a sign that conscious literary artifice has been at work. Even in Western storytelling it is really only as old as the novel (the handful of ancient written stories that fit the meta-narrative, such as Apuleius's *Golden Ass* and Petronius's *Satyricon*, are frequently referred to as novels).

Thus, it must be that the use of the meta-narrative as a grand design for a symphonic work has in itself a meaning and a significance. The scene of triumph and celebration that most typically ends a symphonic work tells us unmistakably that what has been overcome has been overcome forever, that the new order that has been established is there permanently, and that there is no way within the context and the rules of the narrative that it can be disturbed. The excitement with which the finality of the victory is greeted in performance by the audience suggests that it meets and matches desires and needs for a similar kind of finality.

There are other questions we could ask of a symphonic work. Why is the overcoming of an antagonist of such importance? What is it in the lives of those who compose, those who play and those who hear the works that makes the protagonist's victory such an important event? And why is the level of violence in the overcoming frequently so high? Because those features of symphonic works cannot be denied; they are there by all the musical signs developed over the past four hundred years.

The second similarity to bedtime stories is the importance of repetition. Favorite pieces are played over and over again, and new works are assimilated into the repertory only grudgingly if at all. Two comments on this fact are in order here. The first is that this was not always so. In the heroic days of symphonic music, there was an insatiable demand for new works. The aristocracy and later the bourgeoisie, who gave the lead in these matters, demanded, and received new works as a matter of course. It was during the middle years of the nineteenth century that the momentum diminished somewhat as the idea of a canon of classics gradually took hold (Mendelssohn's Leipzig revival of J. S. Bach's *Saint Matthew Passion* in 1829 is generally regarded as a key event), but up to the time of the First World War the demand for and interest in new works remained strong.

Since then, as I have remarked before, practically nothing has become as essential a part of the symphonic repertory as earlier works, and in fact very little has entered the repertory at all. If the high point of creative energy in symphonic music was the period from about 1770 to 1830—the period, in fact, that more or less coincides with Beethoven's lifetime—the century and a half since then has seen a gradual decline, with a sharp cutoff after 1918. The First World War was, of course, a catastrophe to European bourgeois culture whose proportions are still not fully appreciated, and it seems to have put into abrupt reverse the new-worlds-to-conquer spirit of the Western industrial bourgeoisie.

It could even be that the superb new concert halls that have been built since the Second World War are not signs of growing but of waning self-confidence. Certainly, very little creation takes place within them; these great temples have been built to celebrate a past, not a present, explosion of creative energy. I quoted in an earlier book (Small 1987) the opinion of Northcote Parkinson (1957) concerning the buildings that organizations erect as headquarters for themselves, grand, opulent, and, like concert halls, planned down to the last detail. It is conceivable that Parkinson's dictum that "perfection of planned layout is achieved only by organizations on the point of collapse" may apply with equal force to the institutions of symphonic music.

The second comment is that, just as with bedtime stories, the endlessly repeaked performance of a symphonic work drains the work of any power it might once have had to disturb. I remember my father, who loved music of all kinds and was not at all sentimental, once asking me to put on his record of the "dear old Fifth Symphony"—meaning, of course, that of Beethoven. Noone would have described it in those terms in its composer's own day; it hit audiences like a fist in the face, and whether they enjoyed the experience or not they found it profoundly upsetting of all their musical presuppositions.

It is instructive in this regard to glance through Nicholas Slonimsky's collection of what he calls "critical assaults" on composers since the time of Beethoven, *Lexicon of Musical Invective* (1953). One is at first tempted to feel an amused contempt for the apparent obtuseness of many of the judgments; how *could* those critics have failed to perceive that the works on which they heaped such abuse and often ridicule are among the masterworks on which our entire culture of classical music is founded? How *could* anyone have suggested that the *Eroica* Symphony should be abridged "lest it fall into disuse," or that the scherzo in five-four time of the *Pathétique* Symphony could be rearranged "without the least inconvenience" into six-eight, or that Brahms might "for a change" put a little more melody in his work? But what makes many of the reviews most difficult for present-day readers to comprehend is the fact that what baffled, infuriated or distressed contemporary critics seems often to have been exactly the features of those works for which they are most admired today.

To take just two examples, from Beethoven. A persistent early complaint about the Fifth Symphony concerned that very same transition from the scherzo to the finale which is today thought of as one of his masterstrokes; one writer in the *Lexicon* complains that Beethoven chose to "suspend the habeas corpus of music by stripping it of all that might resemble melody, harmony and any sort of rhythm"—which seems to us today, minus an understandable slight exaggeration, to describe precisely the effect for which Beethoven strove and that he brought off so brilliantly. And what the same critic called the "deplorable ending" of the second movement of the Seventh, with its plangent momentary F-sharp and G-sharp against an A minor chord, is one of the memorable moments in the piece. Even Carl María von Weber, a great musician and no fool, protested after hearing an early performance of the same symphony that "Beethoven is now ripe for the madhouse!" which is about as sincere a tribute as could be paid to that Dionysian work.

Performing those masterworks today upsets nobody and cannot upset anyone. Any controversy that once raged around them has long since subsided, and they are beyond criticism. Analysis, yes, and exegesis, whole libraries of that, but their nature and their value are unquestioned and apparently unquestionable. Indeed, they have become the standard by which all others are judged.

It is not just that the "suspension of habeas corpus" in the Beethoven Fifth has become harmonic orthodoxy, though it is true that that and thousands of other once daring strokes have become commonplace through use and sometimes overuse. It is that the performance of the work has become incorporated into a ritual that has a different function, a different meaning, from the performance ritual of its own day. To perform them today is to send a message, not of subversion or of discomfort but of reassurance and of comfort. What else can the message possibly be, since each work has been validated over and over again by the admiration of generations and is being performed in these sumptuous surroundings backed by the full weight of social approval of the whole symphony concert ceremony?

Our sense of superiority over those seemingly imperceptive critics might be tempered if we remind ourselves that those judgments were made when the works were, to repeat a metaphor I used earlier, white-hot lava, straight from the creative volcano, and could burn. Beethoven's vision of the brotherhood of man in his Ninth Symphony, despite the obvious flaws we see today, was a real vision, and it frightened the authorities. Everyone knew that at their behest the word *Freude*, joy, in Schiller's *Ode*, which forms the text for the choral final movement, had been substituted for the original word, *Freiheit*, freedom.

Today the lava has cooled, and performance of the piece frightens no one; we could even say that it *belongs* to the authorities, as is suggested by the fact that the famous choral tune has been scouted as a national anthem for the new bureaucratic Europe. The work can be performed anywhere, even in the most oppressive states, without causing a moment's worry, and its once revolutionary sentiments have become a bedtime story for adults of the middle and upper classes. To perform this and other works of the Western classical canon in a symphony concert today is to give reassurance that things are as they have been and will remain so.

A third comment is that, like children at bedtime, we have become deeply concerned with the note-perfect accuracy of the stories we are being told. Not content with demanding of performers that they play not just every note but every ornament, accent and slur exactly as written in the score, we pursue the authenticity of the score itself back to the composer's manuscript and sometimes beyond, to his sketches, and even sometimes to some notional authenticating version that no longer exists, that perhaps never existed, or to a first performance that may or may not have gone according to the composer's wishes. The authenticity movement, such as I discussed briefly in chapter 6, with its period hardware, its obsession with texts and with composers' intentions, is at base motivated by the same desire for reassurance that makes the five-year-old correct his father's momentary stumble in the reading of a familiar bedtime story.

Bedtime stories, as I have suggested, are good for children, but I am not sure that they are so good for adults. Reassurance in too large a dose can be fatal, especially when it is clear from all around us that things are *not* as they have been and are *not* going to remain so.

The whole event that is a symphony concert as it takes place today might have been designed and indeed was designed, even if not necessarily consciously, as an instrument for the reassurance of the industrial middle and upper classes, for the presentation to themselves of their values and their sense of ideal relationships, and for persuading those who take part that their values, their concepts of relationship, are true and will last. From the moment of entering the great building one is presented in concrete form with those relationships; the very form and organization of the place embody them. The relationships among members of the audience; between the audience and the orchestral musicians; among the orchestral musicians; between audience, musicians, and conductor; between all three and composer, the hall staff, those who are outside the building and not taking part in the ceremony, even with their own past, are all displayed, and all represent ideal relationships as imagined by those taking part in the ceremony. I have tried in earlier chapters to dissect out some of these relationships. There also appears to be, if not a congruence, then at least a close relationship between these relationships between people as they encounter one another in the concert hall, on the one hand, and between the sound relationships as they are brought into existence by the musicians, on the other.

I emphasize the importance of relationships because it is the relationships that it brings into existence in which the meaning of a musical performance lies. What I have tried to show of a symphony concert is true of any musical performance anywhere and at any time: that it is possible to look as well as listen around us and ask what the nature of those relationships is. Broadly, the questions one might ask of any performance fall into three groups, and it might be useful as a kind of checklist if I were at this stage to give an outline of them:

1. What are the relationships between those taking part and the physical setting?
2. What are the relationships among those taking part?
3. What are the relationships between the sounds that are being made?

These three groups of questions themselves interrelate in complex ways, but let us first of all examine them in this order, one at a time, and then examine as well as words will allow us to do some of the interrelationships.

We have seen that the physical setting of the symphony concert has a profound effect on the human and the sonic relationships that are generated there. We can generalize from that to any musical performance and note whether it is taking place indoors, and is thus confined to greater or lesser degree within the built space, or outdoors. Indoors will, of course, make for greater concentration of the sounds and probably of the attention generally, whereas outdoors will allow the sounds, and the attention, to spread out and disperse. In addition, indoors will to a greater or lesser degree prevent the sounds of every day from mingling with the musical sounds; outdoors will allow them to mix. Then we may ask, is the space urban or rural? Is admission to the space free or restricted? How is one admitted? It may be through invitation, through simply belonging to the same group (a church congregation, for example, or a political party), or through the passing of money so that anyone who can produce the price of admission can attend.

If it is indoors, we may ask if the space is purpose-built or uses an existing space. Spaces that are in common use for other purposes, whether domestic or public, may well create different relationships from those which are used only for musical performances; the former may leave those taking part within the world of their everyday lives, while the latter may take them out of it. Is it soundproofed, or can sounds enter and leave freely from and to the outside world? Whom does it bring together and whom does it keep apart? Does it provide for one group of people to dominate another, perhaps but not necessarily by raising them onto a higher level, or are they all equal? That applies not only to the relationship between performers and audience but also to relationships within the audience and among the performers; among the audience, for example, boxes, stalls, and galleries—or as Americans say, orchestra and balconies—both affirm and enforce social distinctions within the audience, while among the performers the tiering of orchestral seats and the presence of a conductor's podium are concrete signs of distinctions within the performing group. Is the space opulent, simple, ornamented, plain, colored, colorless, warm and welcoming, or cold and off-putting? Are the musicians placed at the center of attention of the building or off to one side, even perhaps in a corner? Does the design of the building permit eating, drinking, talking, socializing in general, dancing? If there is dancing, is the whole space or just a part given over to it? Are there seats, and if so, how are they arranged? Does the design of the space allow those taking part to move around freely or does it enforce immobility?

Among those taking part the relationships can be divided into several groups, of which the principal ones are: those among the performers, those among the listeners, and those between performers and listeners.

Of the performers we may ask, what is their relation to their own bodies? Do they engage as they play in expressive bodily movement or reduce it to a minimum? Do they show outward signs of involvement in their performance, appearing to be moved or excited by it, or do they appear detached? How do they relate to one another? There is an enormous number of questions one could ask concerning this, all leading off into subquestions, and I shall outline just some of them. The first, from which a number of other questions stem, is, are they inventing for themselves or are they playing someone else's invention? If it is the latter, did they learn what they are to play from a written score or part or by ear?

The answers to those questions will affect the closeness or distance of the relationships between the musicians. In general, playing from a score places the musicians at a greater social distance from one another than does playing by ear. Playing by ear almost always leaves the performing musicians some latitude to invent for themselves and to respond directly to one another's actions; but when they play from a score or part their relationships are mediated through the notations the composer has provided. There are degrees of closeness and distance in this also; not all notated scores even attempt to specify in every detail what the performers are to do, and many styles of notation leave a great deal up to them to decide.

Inventing as they play leaves the musicians free to relate much more closely; in fact, it demands that they do so. But on the other hand, no invention is total, and no relation between performers can be completely unmediated; any relationship needs some form of mediation, even if it is only an agreed language in which to communicate and thus establish the relationship.

There are physical factors also: how close to one another the players stand or sit; whether they face one another or all face the same direction, maybe concentrically toward a director or conductor; whether their arrangement is formal, in rows perhaps, or informal; whether they move together or individually; how much they watch one another and pick up visual clues; whether they stay in the same place or are free to move around.

Then there is a group of questions centering on who is in charge. Is there a leader at all, and if so, what is the nature of his or her authority? Does that authority operate from inside or outside the group? How much control does the leader have? Whose decision is final? Is there an ultimate authority on what is played and on how it is played?

It is clear that many of the questions we ask of a performance will concern relationships of power: Who decides what is played and how it is played? Where does the authority of the person in charge come from? Who cedes it to him or her? Such questions involve not only the performers but also the audience and may extend beyond the walls of the concert hall. The conductor may dominate inside, but he is controlled by the composer, who in turn is dominated by the patron. We may ask, who dominates the commissioning committee of the broadcasting bureaucracy or the university music department?

Not even a patron always acts freely. Even those princes of the state and the church who commissioned works to be played in their palace or cathedral had to have in mind the importance of musical performances in the maintenance of their own power and prestige. The practical political importance of their role as artistic leaders and tastemakers cannot be overstated, and to be seen as favoring a musician whose style was inappropriate to their position—not grand enough perhaps or old-fashioned or out of line with the taste of allies or superiors in power—could undermine their authority as severely as could unwise decisions of state. Even Louis XIV of France, the Sun King, supreme in power in early-eighteenth-century Europe, calculated his decisions about the music, and the dance, that was to adorn his court as carefully as he did those of diplomacy and war.

Among the listeners there can be any number of degrees of intimacy or distance. We have seen how in large-scale public musicking in the modern West the audience comes together mainly as strangers, even if they do not always stay that way. But we saw also that there are many other kinds of relationship, an infinite gradation in fact. We also can examine the ways in which the listeners physically relate to one another: do they talk during the performance or remain silent? Do they move around or sit still? Do they communicate in any way or avoid contact? To what extent, in fact, are they a community and to what extent a collection of individuals?

Between listeners and performers there is also an infinity of nuances of relationship, not necessarily expressed by visible behavior in the performance space—who dominates, who controls, how much power do the listeners have over the course of the performance? Can they change it or terminate it, cause it to be lengthened or shortened? It may not be possible to answer those questions by simply observing the visible aspects of the performance, though the audience's visible and audible response to the performance, and the performers' response to that response, will give clues.

There is, for example, a power relationship expressed by the old saw "He who pays the piper calls the tune," and although those sitting listening silently and still to the performance may not appear to be exercising control over what is played, they may well be doing so through the control that being in a position to pay permits. Not that power necessarily resides in having the price of admission; being a member of a paying audience of perhaps twenty thousand at an outdoor performance or even one of two thousand at a symphony concert does not confer much power over it. Who actually pays the piper and is thus able to call the tune is a complex business, and in today's large-scale musical world the individual listener has no more control than he does over the design of his car or the flavor of his breakfast cereal. He is one consumer among many, no more.

We must not imagine, however, that power relationships, whether mediated by money or not, between performers and listeners are the only kind possible in a performance. Relationships between performers and listeners may be close, intimate, and even loving, as when the lover or the suitor sings or plays to the beloved or the sought. And in other kinds of performance the back-and-forth passing of energy from performers to listeners and back again in mutual amplification can carry the musicking to a tremendous pitch of excitement that can approach and even cross the threshold of possession.

That brings us to another possible set of relationships—between those present and those significantly absent or perhaps those supernatural beings that are being summoned by the musicking. In a symphony concert, as indeed in all forms of classical musicking, the principal of these significant absentees who is being summoned will probably be the dead composer, but we can also cite, in other kinds of performance, the ancestors, the unborn, deities, political and religious leaders, and even the rest of the human race if, for instance, those taking part consider themselves in any way an elect group. In any prestigious musical performance—a gala or command performance, for example, or one that is being attended by royalty or by political or religious leaders—or even a special performance by a great performer or group, the relation between those within the performance space and those outside it may also be important. On the other hand, small beleaguered religious or political congregations may be very conscious of their relationships to those outside the building where they sing or play, like, at the extreme, those civil rights protesters in southern churches in the 1950s and 1960s who sang not only to their God but also to the torch-brandishing mob they knew was outside.

The third group of questions concerns the sounds themselves and their relationships. Here we enter an area of enormous complexity that I can barely begin to cover. Such factors in the nature of the sounds themselves as the precision and constancy of pitch, the amount of "noise," and the nature of the attack and decay qualities are important in our perception of them; also the vocal and instrumental qualities, whether tense or relaxed, amount of vibrato, manner of attack and of moving between pitches.

The relationships between the sounds can be divided into two groups, those which occur successively and those which occur simultaneously. In the former category come the rhythmic relationships: how many rhythmic patterns are going at once, whether the different patterns share a common downbeat, whether the patterns of accents are additive or divisive and whether the downbeat, if there is one, is regular in its occurrence. There are also melodic qualities, which may include smooth or jagged, high- or low-tension, wide or restricted range, high or low tessitura, long or short phrases, fast or slow succession of pitches, diatonic or chromatic, and the mode of the melody. Other successive relationships include the speed of succession of the sounds, the amount of dynamic and textural contrast over time, and the rate of harmonic change, should there be harmony.

Simultaneous relationships include the number of sounds occurring at any one time, whether one voice is leader or all voices are equal, the amount of tension between the voices, whether the texture is unified and blended or whether individuals can all be heard, whether the texture is full or sparse, consonant or dissonant, whether dissonance matters, and if so, how much dissonance is tolerated.

There are also relationships between simultaneous and successive relationships: how many rhythmic patterns are going on at once, for example, and a whole slew of relationships between rhythm and melody and harmony.

Then there is the question of how much deviation is tolerated from "official" or notated norms of pitch and rhythm. In all cultures some deviation is tolerated, if not actively sought: slight flattening and sharpening of pitches—"pitch bending" and "dirty" sounds; an undulation in the pitch that produces an enriching of the sound—vibrato; placing notes slightly but systematically before or after the beat or taking a little from one beat in order to lengthen the following without distorting the underlying beat itself—rubato (robbing); trailing the vocal or instrumental sound between successive pitches rather than moving cleanly between them—portamento or glissando; as well as slowing down and speeding up at certain points. Charles Keil (1995) has called such deviations from the norms "participatory discrepancies" (PDs for short), and he points out that their presence is essential in any performance that lays claim to being anything other than a soulless procession of notes. But these PDs take place within strictly controlled limits; any of them engaged in to excess will destroy the coherence of the performance.

What counts as excess, of course, varies greatly. There are large intercultural differences in the amount of PDs that are called for and tolerated.

Bending of pitches that is regarded as stylish and musical in a jazz player will be dismissed as hopelessly out of tune in an opera singer, and even within one culture itself there are differences, both geographic and temporal. The wide vibrato that is cultivated among opera singers from Eastern Europe has been dubbed by one English critic the "vile Slavonic wobble," and the amount of portamento that one hears in old recordings by violinists and even whole string sections of symphony orchestras is heard today with a fastidious shudder by advocates of "authentic" performance, even though in the symphonies of Mahler, for example, it is more authentic than the cleaner sound of today.

Those sound qualities and relationships I have mentioned so far are what one might call small-scale relationships, but they themselves relate to form larger-scale, longer-term sound relationships, which leads to further questions: Is there a clear beginning and ending? Is there a tendency toward climax and resolution, or does the musicking take place entirely in the present?

These three, probably arbitrary categories of relationships do not exist in isolation but themselves interact in complex ways, in what Gregory Bateson calls second-order relationships, relationships between relationships, and even third-order relationships, relationships between relationships between relationships. When we try to express such third-order and even second-order relationships in words, the formulation comes out appearing so complex that we are led to think that they are too complex for our minds to encompass.

Let us take from our catalog one or two examples of second-order relationships. There is a relationship between the relations between composer and performers, on the one hand, and the relationships between the sounds, on the other; should the composer prescribe totally everything the performers do, the performers will lack the freedom to make their own sound relationships, and their relationships to one another will not be direct but will be mediated through the notations in the score.

There is a relationship between the relationships between the elements of the physical setting, on the one hand, and, on the other, the relationships between performers and listeners; as we have seen, performance spaces affect greatly the relationships that are created among those that are inside them. There is a relationship between the ways in which the performers relate to the listeners, on the one hand, and, on the other, the relationship between the performers and the sound relationships they create; the more prescribed the sound-relationships, the less control the listeners have over the course of the performance.

Those second-order relationships may take some figuring out but, again, are articulated perfectly clearly in the performance itself. It is when we come to third-order relationships that real verbal difficulties arise. For instance, one set of second-order relationships between the first-order relationships between, on the one hand, performers and composer and, on the other, between performers and audience relates in a third-order relationship to a second set of second-order relationships between the first-order relationships between the sounds, on the one hand, and, on the other, those between the sounds and the space in which they are played.

With that near-incomprehensible sentence we have come to what is really the crux of this book: while this formulation stretches the resources of verbal language about as far as they will go, if not further, it still does not begin to test the power of musicking itself to articulate extreme complexities of relationship. It does not matter whether or not we understand this or any other verbal formulation; in the act of musicking itself we shall be able to do it effortlessly. What I am arguing is that in musicking, in engaging in any capacity in a musical performance, we are articulating matters for which words are not only inadequate but are also unnecessary.

The pattern of relationships that is established during a musical performance and connects together its relationships, whether they be first-, second-, third-, or *n*th-order, models in metaphoric form, the pattern which connects us to ourselves, to other humans, and to the rest of the living world, and those are matters which are among the most important in human life. As in all human relationships the pattern is complex and often contradictory, and it is an image of our deepest desires and beliefs. If we would seek a reason for the central position that musicking occupies in human life, it is here.

Gregory Bateson said that the question "How do I relate to this creature?" is ultimately an *aesthetic* question. How right he was I hope I have succeeded in showing.

CHAPTER 13

A Solitary Flute Player

*

(I have to come clean about the following chapter and say that it is here against the advice of some of my friends who have read my manuscript. They caution me that the solitary flute player appears too much like a total-ized representation of the "other" that has beset European thinking about the rest of the human race—one thinks of Edward Said's eloquent protest (1978)—and that he appears to be an idealized and interchangeable crea-ture who has no real existence as a human being.

I bow my head to such comments and have to concede that they may well be right. But I am very fond of that flute player; to me he is no created "other" at all but a friend and respected fellow musician. If he appears in my account of him to resemble that "other," the fault lies not with him but with the imperfection of my representation. If we listen carefully and sym-pathetically, we shall find that he does have something to tell us about the nature of the musical act and about its social nature, and I cannot allow myself in all conscience to silence him.)

A herdsman is playing his flute as he guards his flock in the African night. Alone with his flock, playing his flute with no one but himself and his ani-mals to hear him, what relationships could he possibly be conjuring up, when there is no one within earshot to whom he might be relating? Surely, there is nothing there but his own solitariness?

But let us look and listen more carefully.

First let us look at the flute he is playing. Technologically speaking, it is a simple affair, made of cane or hollowed-out wood, with maybe three or four burned-in finger holes, capable of producing only a few notes. It is end-blown, and the flutist holds it angled slightly to one side as he blows against a notch in the end of the tube. He may well have made it himself, or perhaps someone in his village, known to him, made it for him. Although one of a type, it is a unique individual because every piece of wood or cane is unique, and it has been fashioned into an instrument by following the natural shape of the material. Its individuality may be emphasized by carved, painted, or burned decoration. Like all wind instruments it is animated into life by the breath from his body, the most intimate relationship one can have with a musical instrument. He may well feel it to be a valued friend and colleague rather than an inanimate sounding object.

Simple it may be in its construction, but primitive it is not. Rather, it is the outcome of constant experimentation through generations, of choosing the right kind of reed tube, cutting it at the right time of year, burning out the finger holes in exactly the right places, and cutting the notch to exactly the right size and shape. Nor is the technique of playing it primitive. We should remember that the elaborate key and valve mechanisms of Western orchestral instruments are there to make them easier, not harder, to play. The simplest instruments are often the hardest to play, needing constant care if the sound produced is to be properly under control.

So between the herdsman and his flute there already exists a complex set of relationships before he ever uses it to make a note of music. Like all musical instruments it does not exist in a social vacuum, but in its design and making, its tuning and sound quality, it is a product of the society of which he is a member. It represents in tangible form the society's technology and its ways of thinking and especially its concepts of human relationships.

This flute, in fact, is as much a product of technology and of technological attitudes and choices as is the Western orchestral instrument that goes by the same name, and it is as finely adapted as the Western instrument to the musical and social purposes for which it is intended. Neither flute is a better or worse instrument than the other; each is the result of different technological and musical choices. This flute is made from what lies to hand, keeping as nearly as possible the natural forms of the wood, with a minimum of shaping. The technology that made it is not crude or underdeveloped but is the result of an attitude toward the natural materials that is the opposite of what is generally found in industrial societies. The one likes to disturb the natural materials as little as possible, while the other prefers to transform them.

What is the flutist playing on his instrument? We hear an endless stream of tones, many of them sounding out of tune to our ears, accustomed to Western tempered pitches, and the number of notes the instrument makes available may seem pitifully small. It will produce, of course, only one note at a time, but the player does not seem to feel the need for more because he has learned to hear in the melody and its intricate rhythms enough complexity to satisfy him. It is a different style of complexity from that which musicians in Western industrial societies enjoy, which tends to involve a large number of tones sounding together.

If we listen carefully, we shall hear delicate inflections in the sounds. By changing his embouchure, by varying the power of his stream of breath, and by small movements of his fingers over the finger holes he can change the pitch of the notes, sliding and smearing them as well as changing their quality in subtle ways. We shall hear also curious inflections on the beginnings and ends of tones and phrases, as well as hesitations, hiccups, arabesques, and graces, gestures that are full of meaning in his musical universe if not in ours.

The rhythms he is playing are enormously complex, too complex at times for us to follow, but we may be sure that they are always being measured against a rhythm that is going on in his head, which he may even be tapping out with one foot as he plays. That rhythm is almost certainly not a procession of equally spaced pulses such as Western musicians use to guide their performance but may be a repeated twelve-beat cycle of 2, 3, 2, 2, 3 beats, against which he pits the rhythms of his melodies, for he needs a clash of rhythms as much as a Western musician needs harmony and its tensions.

We cannot, of course, know what he is thinking as he plays or what he imagines he is doing. He may be inventing a new melody, trying it over and over until its sound relationships are coherent and satisfying to his ears, and also perhaps practicing getting his fingers around a tricky passage, for musicians the world over like to set themselves technical problems. It is quite likely that the shape of the melody he is making will be owed at least in part to the way his fingers move over the holes, and that its phrase lengths and its rise and fall will come at least in part from the way he breathes.

He may be playing a familiar melody, one composed perhaps by someone in his village or by someone whose name is forgotten in time. Or he may just be letting his fingers and his breath wander over the instrument, thinking with his muscles, guided by impulses whose nature neither he nor we can fathom, forming melodic and rhythmic shapes that appear and disappear, as ephemeral as smoke.

But whatever it is he is playing, it will not be invented from nothing. No human being ever invents anything from nothing but is guided always in his invention by the assumptions, the practices and the customs of the society in which he or she lives—in other words, by its *style*. A person may rebel against the assumptions of the society, but the style of the rebellion will inevitably continue to reflect those assumptions. It is inescapable. And since style is concerned with the way in which things relate, it is itself a metaphor for the way in which the society conceives of the pattern which connects.

So the way in which the flutist brings the sounds into relation with one another as he plays is in a general way determined by the set of ideal relationships that he holds in common with the other members of his social group, whether village, tribe or nation. How he plays will be within the limits of the style he has received from the group, and in playing in that style he will be exploring, affirming, and celebrating the concepts of relationship of the group, as well as his own relationships within it and with it.

Relationships, of course, can be of many kinds. They range from love to hate, from dominance to submission, from dependence to independence, from respect to contempt, and any of those in complex combinations. The flute player might play entirely in the received manner, perhaps a received melody played entirely in the manner in which he received it. Or he may use the melody as a basis for innovation in small ways, ornamenting it with graces and variations, or he might reconstruct it completely but always within the limits of the style. Or he may launch out in new ways, which, by violating the norms of the style, will criticize it while still relating to it.

Thus, his relationship to the style, which is the community's way of doing things, may be respectful, submissive and dependent or disrespectful, dominant and independent—or more probably, it will be somewhere on a scale between one extreme and the other, perhaps even both at the same time, for human beings are rarely clearly one thing or another but are contradictory and paradoxical. Through musicking, humans have the power to explore and articulate those contradictions and paradoxes simultaneously, in ways that verbal language cannot.

The flutist's way of playing, then, will contain within itself ways of mediating change with continuity, stability with instability, stagnation with renovation, in complex relationships with one another. So it is that he will be articulating not just his solitariness but his relationships with the entire population of his conceptual world. Although physically alone, he is surrounded as he plays by all the beings that inhabit that world, not only humans, animals and plants but also the land itself, the ancestors and the yet unborn, and even the illimitable population of the spirit world; and through the sounds he makes he is exploring, affirming and celebrating the ways in which he relates to them.

Because his world is not a literate one, his relationship with the ancestors and the past of his people is mediated not through written records, with their fixity, their appearance of objectivity and the distance they place between the reader and the subject of the writings, but through the recollections of older people, through stories and myths that have been told to him, and through dances, songs and melodies passed down to him by elders. Some of the songs of the ancestors have to be carefully learned and repeated exactly if their force is to be retained, but others are flexible and can be changed, added to and varied. And of course, because there is no fixed written record of those songs any more than there is of the people's history, and because people's memories are fallible, even those songs which are supposed to be fixed are subject to constant drift. They can even be forgotten, leaving space for new creation. The ancestors, though respected and frequently summoned for consultation through musicking and dancing, are not allowed to dominate the present generation, which has to be free to work out its own destiny.

Nor does the flutist live in an isolated, self-contained society. Those of us who live in modern nation-states isolated from one another by passports, quotas and visas may welcome, for every good reason, the kind of international musical "dangerous crossroads" described by George Lipsitz (1994); but in fact, over the course of human history there have been few human groups, however small and remote, that have not been in regular contact with members of other groups, that have not interacted and spoken one another's language. The self-inflicted isolation of modern nation-states, each within its own frontiers, is a recent phenomenon; Benedict Anderson (1983), in his analysis of nationalisms, calls them "cultural artefacts of a particular kind" and dates them from no earlier than the late eighteenth century.

The flutist's world is much less circumscribed than members of literate societies like to think, and because it is not literate, it is flexible. He is free to absorb directly from those outsiders with whom he is in constant contact what he needs to make his own life, and his musicking, more interesting and satisfying to himself. He may even master the styles of one or more of his neighbors, becoming musically multilingual (after all, bi- or even multilingualism is the rule rather than the exception among most of the human race), as long as he can find in those styles musical relationships with which he can empathize.

All human beings are about as complex as one another. We speak verbal languages that linguists assure us are all about as complex as one another, and we all live within networks of relationships that are as complex as one another, even if they are not all complex in the same ways. The networks of functional relationships in the industrialized world may well appear brutally simple, if not crude, to those who are accustomed to the subtle and complex patterns of a village society. Wherever they have gone, human beings have used the language of sonic gesture to articulate those relationships, to model the pattern which connects, and have developed that language in ways that can deal with the pattern's complexity. Even to play a homemade flute, alone, with no one but oneself to hear, is an act that can define relationships that are just as complex as that of taking part with two thousand others in a symphony concert.

As he plays, the flutist is bringing into existence a sonic space that is defined by the limit of audibility of his flute in each direction, upward toward the skies as well as outward on the earth around him, into which he is projecting himself. It is his own sonic territory, in which his ideas of relationships are valid. And because how we relate is who we are, he is in effect saying, to himself and to anyone who may be listening, *Here I am, and this is who I am*. Who that "I" is, is complex and even multiple, endlessly developing and unfolding, as are the sonic relationships that the lone herdsman, with no one but himself to hear, is creating in the night.

Postlude

Was It a Good Performance
and How Do You Know?

What, then, are the implications of all this for our everyday musical practice?

The first is that if musicking is indeed a facet of the great unitary performance art we call ritual, and is thus an aspect of the language of biological communication that every living thing, as a condition of survival, has to be able to understand and to use, then it must follow that all normally endowed human beings are born with the gift of musicking, no less than they are born with the gift of speaking and understanding speech. Both gifts, of course, have to be cultivated; while in the West today we take for granted the informal learning and practice in speech that all but the most desperately deprived young children receive within their families and peer groups long before the formal process of schooling begins, there are, alas, few parallel opportunities for such informal and continuous cultivation in musicking. True, many parents encourage their children to perform, on occasion, and in the early years of schooling, at least, musicking plays a part; but what no longer exists in industrial societies is that broader social context in which performance, as well as listening, is constantly taught and musicking is encouraged as an important social activity for every single member of the society. Many people are taught to play, but very few are encouraged to perform.

By way of contrast, in traditional African societies a child's musical experience and development may well begin with hearing and sensing multiple bodily rhythms as it rides on its mother's back while she dances or with being dandled and bounced in time with the drums, and they continue through multiple socially sanctioned and encouraged musical and dance activities, some of which, according to J. H. K. Nketia, are specific to the young while others are shared with adults. Children not only learn traditional songs and dances but also learn from an early age that they can make their own, and adults help them to do this, just as they help them to learn the appropriate music for their ceremonies.

This is done on the assumption that they will eventually assume those musical roles which are expected of all responsible adults within the various social organizations to which they belong. In African societies it is taken for granted, still today, that everyone has the ability not merely to perform someone else's songs and dances but also to make creative gestures of their own. Through the constant stimulation of the musical faculties that takes place in day-to-day interaction, everyone does indeed develop such abilities. Their social and conceptual world is not divided into the few "talented" who play and sing and the many "untalented" to whom they perform but resembles more a spectrum that ranges from little musical ability to much, but with every single individual capable of making some contribution to the communal activity of musicking.

I report this, not to demonstrate any inherent superiority that Africans may have in this regard (it happens, in fact, to various extents and in various ways, in most traditional societies), and certainly not in any sentimental spirit of harking back to imagined "simpler" times, but to show that the universal distribution of musical ability is not a fantasy but is in many societies and cultures an everyday reality. It does not imply that everyone is a musical genius, even a potential one. Just as they recognize that, while everyone has a bedrock ability to talk, some are more gifted with words than others, those societies recognize that some people are more gifted in music than others; those who are so become the leaders and the pacemakers in the communal work of musicking in which everyone is able to and does take an active performing part. The big challenge to music educators today seems to me to be not how to produce more skilled professional musicians but how to provide that kind of social context for informal as well as formal musical interaction that leads to real development and to the musicalizing of the society as a whole.

An example from another art may be helpful. As a first-year zoology student in university, I learned to dissect dead animals of various kinds. We were told before our first lab session that we were to bring sketch pads and pencils in addition to our scalpels, forceps and scissors; and when we had finished our dissections, the lab assistant told us that we were to draw the dissections we had just done. When several of the students protested that they could not draw, the reply came back, implacably, "Draw it." "Can't I bring a camera and just photograph it?" "Draw it." So we set to and somehow managed to produce drawings that represented, with various degrees of clarity and accuracy, the relationships of the sundered animal tissues we had on the tables before us.

As we went on, from worms to insects to starfish and finally to rats and rabbits (undergraduate zoology in those days was almost entirely comparative anatomy), I found I got better at drawing, and I even began to enjoy and to be a little proud of that part of my work. But I began to realize also that the aim of the drawing was not to produce artistic masterpieces; it was simply a way of learning to look and to see relationships. Its value lay not so much in the finished drawing (if I did treasure one or two particularly good efforts, it was more as a reminder of a job well done) as in the *act* of looking and drawing, as a technique in the complex and difficult task of learning to understand not only the relationships of the internal organs of each species I was studying but also the second-order relationships between analogous and homologous organs in the various species, classes and phyla, and even some third-order relationships between second-order relationships, which are, as we have seen, resistant to being verbalized but can be visualized, at least in part, by drawing them.

It was, of course, a very specific and limited kind of understanding, based as it was on the killing and cutting up of those unfortunate creatures (I have to admit that it never occurred to me in those days to feel sympathy for them), but what we were learning about was one version, if a strictly impersonal scientific version, of the pattern which connects, and our drawing was a tool for exploring, affirming, and ultimately maybe celebrating (a little) its relationships. In that laboratory it was assumed that everyone could draw, and indeed, as far as the course was concerned, everyone had to draw as a condition of survival; and second, drawing was a way of learning about relationships, and the reason for doing it lay not in the finished drawings but in the act of drawing. It took me many years to grasp what this implied: that all art, even laboratory drawing, is ultimately performance art.

It was not only from the internal relationships of each individual drawing that we learned; we learned also from the (second-order) relationships *between* the drawings, by comparing the relationships revealed by one with those revealed by another. Nor did we do that in silence and solitude; we looked also at one another's work and compared one set of drawings with another, discussing and analyzing, assessing and evaluating them, not necessarily in any spirit of competition (it was a less competitive age) but in order to widen our experience of the (third-order) relationships that the comparisons revealed.

Similarly in musicking; our exploration, affirmation and celebration of relationships does not end with those of a single performance, but can expand to the relationships between one performance and another, and, for those who are prepared to explore farther afield, to the relationships between performances in different styles, genres and even whole musical traditions and cultures. It is an ever-widening spiral of relationships, and each twist of the spiral can widen our understanding of our own relationships, of the reality that we construct and is constructed for us by the society in which we ourselves live.

We do not, of course, carry out our exploration alone; the responses of other people to performances in which we have taken part create also a reciprocal set of relationships. On the one hand, the responses of people with whom we stand in a positive relationship will affect our own response to the performance, while on the other our relationships with others are affected by the way in which they respond; a similar response to our own will create a bond between us. Verbal discourses about musicking thus play an important part, not as substitutes for, but as adjuncts to, musical experience; talking about musicking and comparing musical experiences is not only an inexhaustible source of conversational and literary topics but can enrich the relationships which taking part in performances has created.

If musicking is indeed an aspect of the language of biological communication, then it is part of the survival equipment of every human being. To music is not a mere enhancement of spare-time enjoyment but is an activity by means of which we learn what are our ideal social relationships, and that is as important for the growth of an individual to full social maturity as is talking and understanding speech. Speaking and musicking, as we have seen, resemble one another in many ways, but they differ also, in even more important ways, especially in the power that musicking gives to articulate human relationships, in all their multilayered and multiordered complexity and quicksilver changeability, in ways that words cannot do.

But if everyone *is* born capable of musicking, how is it that so many people in Western industrial societies believe themselves to be incapable of the simplest musical act? If they are so, and it seems that many genuinely are, it must be either because the appropriate means for developing the latent musicality have been absent at those crucial times of their lives when the nervous system is still in the process of completing its formation (those who are deprived of speech opportunities at that crucial time also never fully develop their speech capacities) or more often, I believe, because they have been actively taught to be unmusical.

The agencies militating against the musicality of ordinary people are many and varied. They include the system of stars and superstars that, as we have seen, lives on the assumption that real musical ability is as rare as diamonds and as hard to cultivate as orchids. Individuals are assumed to be unmusical unless they show evidence to the contrary. This assumption, which is widely disseminated through the media of socialization and of information, places the stars, whether of popular or classical music, in a world of glamour and privilege from which everyday people are excluded. It reveals itself also, perhaps most damagingly, in the day-to-day assumptions of social life; families and their power relations can be the very devil in that respect.

If the number of young people of student age who have passed through my classes is any indication, there must be millions of people in Western industrial societies who have accepted the judgment passed upon them and classed themselves as unmusical and even as something called "tone-deaf." Where that odious term came from I do not know, and what it can really mean I am not sure. I can only assume that it means something like "unable to distinguish one pitch from another," but if that is so it must be a very rare and socially crippling affliction, since anyone unable to distinguish pitches would be unable to speak or to understand speech. The ability to speak and to understand speech depends in fact on a very sophisticated pitch discrimination, not only in order to recognize the formants that distinguish one vowel sound from another but also, and just as important, to recognize the very complex forms of vocal intonation and inflection that are used in the most ordinary conversations, which we have seen to be an essential element in the articulation of relationships.

An enthusiastic student of mine in London some years ago did an imaginative piece of research, even if its formal methodology and approach were rudimentary. She had no difficulty in finding among her fellow students (not, I hasten to add, music students) a number of people, mostly women, from a variety of backgrounds (though all were of course united by being engaged in higher education), who believed themselves to be tone-deaf, and she undertook to teach a dozen or so of them to sing at least a simple song. I spent a fascinating afternoon listening to some of her taped interviews, which all followed a remarkably similar scenario.

After a good deal of coaxing and cajoling she would manage to get a song from nearly all, simple things to be sure, like "Three Blind Mice" or "Twinkle Twinkle Little Star" or, in one surprising case, an old popular song from the 1920s called "Ramona." Most of them were quite decently in tune and one or two actually rather beautifully sung, I thought. But the crunch would come when, on the tape, she would say something like "There! I *told* you you could sing." Instantly there would come a reply, always something like "Oh, but that isn't *real* singing." What real singing might have been like I was left to imagine, since, maddeningly, she would switch off the recorder at that moment, believing she had made her point. But it was clear that someone had set before these people an ideal of "real" singing to which they believed they would never attain. Who that someone could be I was unable to find out either, but the overall uniformity of the response was such that it was obviously no freak outcome. Somebody had taught those otherwise intelligent and articulate women that they could not, must not, sing.

Schools themselves, alas, and the music tuition they provide, can contribute to this process of demusicalization. Music teachers too often regard themselves more as agents for the discovery and selection of talented potential professionals than as agents for the development of the musicality that lies within each child. A hidden logical chain, or syllogism, underlies much (though fortunately not all) school music practice. It goes like this:

1. Our music (which may be classical music, marching band music, show band music, choral music, or big band jazz but rarely improvised or self-composed music, which is difficult to control) is the only *real* music.
2. You do not like or are not proficient in or are not interested in our music.
3. Therefore, you are not musical.

The logic is impeccable, and the syllogism's force is irresistible—once you accept the premise in the first statement. It is also very destructive. The whole chain is, I believe, a fabrication of those music teachers who care more for what people will think of their ensemble than for the real musical development of their students. Some children do indeed have difficulty in learning to sing in tune, but the difficulty will be overcome by practice and encouragement, not by telling the child that she should open and shut her mouth and make no sound, a practice that seems to be as common today as when I was at school. The voice is at the center of all musical activity, but it is all too easy to silence and very hard to reactivate, since those who have been silenced in this way have been wounded in a very intimate and crucial part of their being. In my opinion any music teacher caught doing such a thing or using the epithet tone-deaf of a pupil should be sacked on the spot.

Second, if to music is to explore, affirm and celebrate one's link with the great pattern which connects the whole living world, then all musicking is serious musicking. Whoever engages in a musical performance, of whatever kind, is saying to themselves and to anyone who may be taking notice, *This is who we are*, and that is a serious affirmation indeed. From performers and audience at a symphony concert to drunken ol' pals singing bawdy or sentimental songs in rustic harmony, to the teenager in the street with a Walkman across her ears, to the aspiring group of young musicians trying to catch the attention of a record company executive, to the seven-year-old picking out her first little pieces on the piano, to the group of aunts and uncles summoned to hear her doing so—all those who engage in musicking are engaging in a very serious activity. The pieces that are played may be judged to be frivolous (the creation of a good piece of frivolous music, however, is a serious business), but the act of performing is never so.

And if all musicking is serious musicking, then no way of musicking is intrinsically better than any other; all are to be judged, if they are to be judged at all, on their success in articulating (affirming, exploring, celebrating) the concepts of relationships of those who are taking part. We may not like those concepts of relationships, and we are surely entitled to say so if we wish, but we should understand that our opinions are as much social as they are purely aesthetic—if anything can be judged to be purely aesthetic. That is to say, we are passing an opinion not merely on a musical style but on the whole set of ideal relationships that are being articulated by the musical performance.

I, for example, have discovered that I do not much like the relationships that are articulated by those events called symphony concerts; they are too hierarchical, too distant, and too one-dimensional for my taste. Again, those recorded performances which fill the aural space of an average shopping mall—and not only in the United States these days—seem to me to be manipulative and serve to reinforce my dislike of such places and their rituals. Those which are to be heard through the PA system of public transport, especially trains and airliners, also seem to me manipulative, intrusive and domineering, like a pacifier forcibly shoved into my mouth to keep me docile.

In all of these situations, and an infinity of others, it is not so much the style of the sound relationships themselves that we may or may not like—in another context I might well find many of them pleasurable—but the relationships of the performance space themselves. Any performance, in fact, that the hearer has no choice but to hear affirms a relationship of unequal power that leaves the hearer diminished as a human being; for whatever else it might be, all musicking is ultimately a political act.

Until the advent of recording, event and performance were inseparable; to hear the performance one had to attend the event. One consequence of the availability of recordings is that those who do not wish to or for other reasons cannot take part in the ritual event that is a "live" performance can use the recordings to create their own event, their own ritual, based on the sounds in their combinations that they hear from the records. This fact has led to the creation of many new contexts for recorded performances, and that in turn has encouraged many musicians to create performances on record that will serve the purposes of those new contexts.

The first of these to achieve widespread popularity was probably that of discotheques, whose rituals then provoked the creation of recordings designed especially for them. This in turn gave rise to a new musical style, which today, twenty years later, we take for granted, forgetting that it was the ritual that gave rise to the style, not the other way around. The same is true of other subsequent styles such as acid house, rap, and hip-hop. When the records created to serve those rituals are then used to serve the needs of a different ritual, the cycle begins once more, all without anyone necessarily noticing what is going on. An observation by the sociologist Simon Frith (1983) has always intrigued me. He says: "The usual theory is that the star is an extraordinary fellow who brings excitement and glamor into the lives of his fans, ordinary people, but the process works the other way around too; stars, dull professionals, are made glamorous by the imagination and wit and excitement of their fans."

What makes this constant recycling possible is the openness of the gestural language that musical sounds employ. The gestural language of a musical performance never means one and only one set of relationships but is open to reinterpretation over and over again as listeners create new contexts for their reception and their ritual use of it. We have seen how this has happened over the history of the works that are played today in symphony concerts. If we were to extend our study to recorded performances of those same works, we should doubtless find many other new ritual uses that have been made of them, though I doubt very much if we should find the same vigorous inventiveness that is found in the forms and rituals of popular musicking.

But if the link between the notated work (or the recorded performance) and the ritual uses made of it is flexible, it is not infinitely so. There need not be total congruence in the (second-order) relationship between the relationships articulated by a musical work itself and those that are articulated by the ritual of its performance, but there does need to be some link, some accord between them; that is why each ritual has its own repertory, and also perhaps why there is overflow from one ritual to another and from one repertory to another. When the link becomes too attenuated, it will break, and either the ritual or the repertory will no longer be performed. I suspect that this may be happening today with the ritual of the symphony concert.

It is clear, then, that the two assertions—first, that all musicking is serious musicking, and second, that everyone is capable of musicking well—depend on each other, and both depend upon the fact that musicking is, first and foremost, performing and listening. The word *well* in this context is, of course, open to a number of interpretations. In the modern West it generally implies above all else a high degree of technical skill or virtuosity, but I wish to suggest a different approach to the question of musical quality. If the function of musicking is to explore, affirm, and celebrate the concepts of ideal relationships of those taking part, then the best performance must be one that empowers all the participants to do this most comprehensively, subtly and clearly, at whatever level of technical accomplishment the performers have attained. Such subtlety, comprehensiveness and clarity do not depend on virtuosity but reflect, rather, the participants' (that is, both performers and listeners) doing the best they can with what they have.

In this sense the word *best* applies not only to technical skill but also to all the other relationships of the performance, which is carried out with all the loving care and attention to detail that the performers can bring to it. Doing the best one can with what one has is a recipe, not, as may at first be thought, for smug mediocrity but for constant advance into new territory, since those who persist in doing the best they can with what they have will get better, will find new nuances of relationship, and new skills with which to articulate them. Indeed, it may be the only way in which balanced improvement in performance will take place, since it is clear that concentration on the development of virtuoso technique will not of itself produce good performances. And if only the best performance of which the performers are capable will enable the participants to articulate properly their concept of the pattern which connects, then many of the performances in which I myself have taken part as listener, often by famous performers—including conductors and orchestras—have little of value to say in that regard.

Doing the best one can with what one has can apply with no less force to the development of the performance of a specific musical work than it does to general musical development. If one tackles its problems with all the care one can bring to it, with patience and without hurry (here the amateur performer has an advantage over the professional, in that for him or her time is not money), performance will gradually improve; I cannot see the need to waste time and musicality practicing scales, exercises, and studies. When, for example, I work at my performance of material provided by J. S. Bach under the title *Italian Concerto* in F, it is amazing how my playing of the scales of F, B-flat, C major and D minor improves. And we have it on the authority of his sister that Wolfgang Amadeus Mozart never practiced the fortepiano after the age of seven but relied on his everyday musical activities to keep him in trim.

From our examination of the ceremony of a symphony concert we have seen that not all musical performances expand or alter our concept of the pattern which connects. Most performances, in fact, merely confirm our feelings about the pattern and of our place in it; it is, of course, more comfortable that way. The audiences that attend the average symphony concert are not seeking any such expansion, are not looking for new experiences that will expand their concept of the relationships of their world. Rather, they are seeking confirmation of a habitual pattern of relationships.

We need not, however, despise performances that merely serve to confirm those habitual patterns. They are needed if we are to reassure ourselves that *this* is how the world really is and that *this* is our place in it, that our values, our idea of the pattern which connects, are real and valid. But we also need performances that expand our concepts of relationships, that present relationships in new and unfamiliar light, bring us to see our place in the world from a slightly different point of view. It is not just those performers who are called great who can do this for us; it is open to anyone to use his or her powers to descend into the underworld and return with new visions. Everyone can be his or her own shaman.

It may seem too obvious to mention, but all those who engage in the practice of musical performance, famous and unknown, amateur and professional, skilled and unskilled, work always from a base in the firmly known sets of musical relationships we call a tradition, or a style, and most of what they do will already have been done many times before. As Bateson remarks, a book will tell you nothing unless you already know nine-tenths of it, and the same is true of musical performances. In any performance whatsoever, the vast majority of what is heard and experienced by both players and listeners will be familiar, if not in substance at least in style, to all its listeners; if this were not so, comprehension would be impossible. Even the revolutionary Beethoven was firmly rooted in the European traditions of the eighteenth century, and throughout his life he remained at a very deep level faithful to their conventions, while Charlie Parker's innovative improvised performances, which seemed so incomprehensible to many of his contemporaries, were equally firmly rooted in traditional blues and black folk song.

What was possibly the biggest stylistic break in the history of European concert music, that which followed the Second World War and gave rise to what is still, nearly fifty years later, known quaintly as the avant-garde, took place within a set of performance conditions and conventions that had changed hardly at all since the nineteenth century (the first six chapters of this book could equally well be describing a concert of avant-garde music) while the actual sound combinations become with every year that passes more plainly linked to the traditional styles of Western concert music, especially with the dramatic representation that we have seen has been its central concern since the early seventeenth century.

One thing we do not need in order to bring about a good performance is the kind of obsessive concern for the authenticity of the composer's written text and the equally obsessive concern for fidelity to it that seems to characterize so much contemporary concert performance. What we have in those coded sets of written instructions we call a score are not sacred master texts but something more like constructor toys by means of which we can build our models of the universe. All constructor toys, of course, impose limits on what can be modeled; you can only build what the Meccano or Lego allows you to build, and there are as many assumptions built into those toys as there are in any other human artifact. But if you work within the rules, the range of models that can be built is wide indeed.

Similarly, those constructor toys we call musical scores can provide a wide range of models of the pattern which connects. Nevertheless, the kind of story we can make up from them is constrained by the limits of the style. Those stories may tell of triumph and the apotheosis of the human spirit, and the emotions that they evoke in us may be lofty and broad, but the fact is that there are vast areas of human experience with which they do not concern themselves, and those are precisely the areas that fall outside the common experience and relationships of members of the industrial middle classes of the past two centuries or so. The densely packed and highly purposeful sequence of events with which they present us cannot allow us to use them to model the conceptual universe of a poor black woman in the United States or that of a Zen Buddhist or that of a Tibetan peasant or that of a Spanish Gypsy.

Nevertheless, we are free, as performers and as listeners also, to use these works of music in any way we like. There is nothing in the rule book that tells us that the score is a sacred text that must not be altered in any way or that it must be performed in a way that approximates as nearly as possible to the way it was performed in the composer's time. Or if such a rule does exist, it was invented in the twentieth century by composers and musicologists as part of the contest for control of the musical texture, which we have seen has been a feature of the Western concert tradition since the seventeenth century at least. We who wish to play those works are under no obligation to obey it. Performance is for performers and for listeners, not for composers and certainly not for their works and not for musicologists either. The performer's obligation, in other words, is not to the composer (who is quite likely dead anyway and can make no protest) or to the work but to his own enjoyment and to that of his or her listeners, if there be any. The performer has the right to make any changes he or she feels like making in the work and to interpret the written or printed score any way he or she chooses. The listeners (who may, of course, include other performers as well as composers and musicologists) have the right to reject those changes, but that does not affect the performer's right to make them.

But we are also free to construct our models of the universe from our own materials, rather than relying on musical kitsets of relationships provided by others. We shall, of course, not be starting from scratch but will be drawing on our memories of what has sounded right to us in the past as well as on our imagination of what is going to sound right in this place, at this moment, and with these fellow musickers. There need be no opposition or antithesis between the two modes of performing. They reinforce and strengthen each other, as they did in the performances of great European musicians of the past, whose performances in the nonliterate mode were as much admired as their literate performances.

But we should never forget: first came performance, whether we speak historically, in terms of what we can know of the musical history of the human race; ontogenetically, in terms of the development of musicking in the life of the individual human being; or aesthetically, as I have argued throughout this book. Music is performance, and pieces, or works, of music, whether on the smallest or the grandest scale, whether written down or not, exist in order to give performers something to perform. Unperformed, only the instructions for performance exist.

When we perform, we bring into existence, for the duration of the performance, a set of relationships, between the sounds and between the participants, that model ideal relationships as we imagine them to be and allow us to learn about them by experiencing them. The modeling is reciprocal, as is implied by the three words I have used persistently through this book: in exploring we learn, from the sounds and from one another, the nature of the relationships; in affirming we teach one another about the relationships; and in celebrating we bring together the teaching and the learning in an act of social solidarity. The simultaneous inward and outward flow of information that goes on throughout the performance is made possible by the fact that the language of the information is not that of words but of gestures. There is thus a continuity of communication, from the most highly elaborated human musical gestures and patterns of gesture, through the gestural languages of mammals and insects and plants, to the minute signals that are sent and received by microorganisms. The ancient means of communication unites the whole living world, including ourselves, in the pattern which connects.

This brings us to the consideration of that other word whose signification has puzzled philosophers for centuries, namely, *beauty*. Here we find a comparable confusion to that which was have seen surrounds the word *music*, for just as there is no such thing as music, neither is there such a thing as beauty. There are only qualities in an object or action that arouse in a perceiver a pleasurable response and make him or her perceive it as beautiful.

Like any other stimulus, it requires active work on the part of the perceiver to convert the raw stimulus into meaning. Like all knowledge of the world outside the individual, it is not absolute but is a relationship between the perceiver and the perceived, and the sensation of what we call beauty is the representation in consciousness of that relationship. As those emotional states we call love, hate, joy, grief, dependency, and so on are representations in consciousness our perception of certain relationships, so with the sensation of beauty. Like those emotions, the sensation of beauty is not an end in itself but a sign that the relationship is occurring.

So our question becomes *What kind of relationship is it between object or gesture, on the one hand, and perceiver, on the other, that gives rise in the perceiver to the sensation we know as beauty?* As Bateson has shown us, that question is really two, the first concerning the nature of the object or gesture and the second concerning that of the perceiver: "What is man . . . ?" Such an investigation would require volumes; here it is only possible to draw attention to a possible line of inquiry and propose a possible answer.

The answer I propose, again following Bateson, is that the sensation of beauty is a sign that the gesture or object relates to the perceiver in such a way as to reveal the workings of the pattern which connects as it is conceived as a set of ideal relationships by the perceiver. It is as if the perceiver has in his or her mind a grid of relationships that appear as ideal and that the regularities in the perceived object or gesture are somehow mapped onto the regularities in the mental pattern; and where they fit, they create the sensation we call beauty.

Since not everyone has the same mental grid or set of ideal relationships, we find that not everyone's conception of what is beautiful is the same. The old saw, that beauty resides in the eye of the beholder, makes sense as far as it goes; certainly beauty does not reside in any absolute sense in an object or gesture but occurs only when the perception of the internal relationships of an object or gesture arouses a response of a certain kind in a perceiver (the perceiver, of course, may be also the one who creates the object or the gesture).

In musicking, of course, our response is never to an object but always to that pattern of gestures we call a performance. Those people who can imagine from study of the instructions for action contained in the score how the piece will sound are still imagining a performance, even if a very abstract and attenuated one, with all the human relationships, which we have seen to be such a vital part of the meanings generated by any performance, short-circuited out. When we take part, whether as performers or listeners or in any other capacity, in a musical performance that we find beautiful, it must because the inner relationships of the performance accord, or fit, in some way with those relationships which we imagine to be ideal.

Our sense of beauty, our aesthetic sense, then, is by no means a free-floating or functionless source of pleasure but is an important element of the way in which we explore, affirm, and celebrate our sense of how the universe is put together and of how we relate to the other elements of it. It seems that Bateson's observation that "The question 'How do I relate to this creature?' is an *esthetic* one" is not only true but of profound significance in the development of our own relationships. For it is in those activities, those fractured shards of the great performance art that is ritual, which are called the arts, and, I submit, especially that of musicking by reason of its closeness to being pure relationship without specific referents, that we develop best our sense of how we relate not only to those other creatures with which we share our planet but to the whole conceptual universe that shapes our lives and our actions. How we like to music is who we are.

That leads us finally to the question that I framed to myself in the Prelude to this book: *Was even Mozart wrong?* Is there something in the nature of the works of the classical concert repertory that makes the acts of performing and listening to them under any circumstances go counter to the way I believe human relationships should be?

The late John Cage, when asked in interviews questions he did not want to answer, used to say, "I don't find that a very interesting question," and go on to the next. I wish I could do the same, for I find the question a remarkably painful one to have to answer; playing and listening to these works has been for me a source of pleasure and satisfaction since my earliest days. But I think I have to answer yes; after writing chapters 9 through 11, I could hardly say otherwise. And if I answer yes, and at the same time admit that playing and listening to these works has been a source of pleasure and satisfaction, then I have to ask myself the reciprocal Batesonian question: Who am I that I should go on wanting to play and hear the works of this repertory?

As a style of musicking that is and has always been cultivated by the holders of power, first in Europe and later in its colonies and outposts, the acts of composing, performing, and listening to these works have reflected and shaped the perceptions of those who have held power. If I myself have not the slightest desire to hold power, nevertheless, my acceptance of my fortunate position in this society as a white, middle-class male academic on a comfortable pension places me willy-nilly—and however I might at the conscious level reject their values—at least to some degree in debt to those power holders and thus to some extent by their side.

I have to hedge my question and point out that there is a decreasing number of such works that I do like to play and to hear as the years pass, partly perhaps because so many of them have exhausted their interest for me (I believe that the number of possible nuances of meaning that can be extracted from even the greatest of musical works is not inexhaustible) and partly because of my increasing distaste for the violence and the egotism that I hear in so many of them.

But there remains a small repertory of pieces that to hear and especially to play gives me endless satisfaction. It seems that the relationships that are articulated in playing or listening to these pieces (and of course, we must never forget that the player is always the principal listener), fit, for better or worse, the grid of ideal relationships that, without realizing it or at least without verbalizing it, I hold in my mind. I do not even know that I *could* verbalize them, either my own grid of relationships or those which are articulated by the performance, at least not any more satisfactorily than I have done with the two symphonies I discussed in chapter 11.

But although I do not verbalize them, it seems that I do musicalize them, at a deeper level than that of speech. If I am right about the values, which is to say, the concepts of ideal relationships, that are articulated by the rituals of performing and listening to these works, then I have to admit to a contradiction between those values and beliefs about relationship which I consciously hold and verbally express to anyone who will listen and those that I hold at a deep level, those which resonate with those articulated when these pieces are performed.

Well, that is my affair, and I mention it only to show how the act of musicking can articulate and reveal to us some of our deepest values, not excepting many that run counter to those we consciously believe ourselves to hold. All human beings carry around within themselves any number of contradictions and paradoxes, and we need not worry ourselves too much about that (I am comforted also by Walt Whitman's superbly confident "Do I contradict myself? Very well, I contradict myself!"). In musicking we have a tool by means of which our real concepts of ideal relationships can be articulated, those contradictions can be reconciled, and the integrity of the person affirmed, explored, and celebrated.

Bibliography

Anderson, Benedict. 1983. *Imagined Communities: Reflections on the Origin and Spread of Nationalism*. London: Verso and NLB.

Bateson, Gregory. 1972. *Steps to an Ecology of Mind: Collected Essays in Anthropology, Psychiatry, Evolution and Epistemology*. New York: Chandler Publishing Co.; St Albans: Paladin (1973).

———1979. *Mind and Nature: A Necessary Unity*. London: Wildwood House; Fontana / Collins (1980).

Bateson, Gregory, and Mary Catherine Bateson. 1987. *Angels Fear: Towards an Epistemology of the Sacred*. New York: Macmillan.

Berger, John, with Sven Blomberg, Chris Fox, Michael Dibb, and Richard Hollis. 1972. *Ways of Seeing*. London and Harmondsworth: British Broadcasting Corporation and Penguin Books.

Berger, Peter, and Thomas Luckmann. 1967. *The Social Construction of Reality: A Treatise in the Sociology of Knowledge*. Harmondsworth, England: Penguin Books.

Blacking, John. 1976. *How Musical Is Man?* London: Faber and Faber.

Boulez, Pierre. 1964. Alea. Translated by David Noakes and Paul Jacobs. *Perspectives of New Music* 3 (fall-winter) 42–43.

Campbell, Meredith. 1989. Cultural Oasis in the Desert. *Daily Telegraph*, London, June 24.

Chernoff, John Miller. 1979. *African Rhythm and African Sensibility: Aesthetics and Social Action in African Musical Rhythms*. Chicago and London: University of Chicago Press.

Dalhaus, Carl. 1983. *Foundations of Music History*. Translated by J. B. Robinson. Cambridge and London: Cambridge University Press.

Daniélou, Alain. 1943. *Introduction to the Study of Musical Scales*. London: The India Society.

Debord, Guy. 1983. *The Society of the Spectacle*. Detroit: Black and Red.

Delaby, Laurence. 1991. Siberian Master Spirits and Shamans. In *Asian Mythologies*, compiled by Yves Bonnefoy. Chicago and London: University of Chicago Press.

Edelman, Gerald. 1992. *Bright Air, Brilliant Fire: On the Matter of the Mind*. London: Allen Lane, Penguin Press.

Frith, Simon. 1983. *Sound Effects: Youth, Leisure and the Politics of Rock*. London: Constable.

Geertz, Clifford. 1973. *The Interpretation of Cultures*. New York: Basic Books.

Hobsbawm, Eric, and Terence Ranger, eds. 1983. *The Invention of Tradition*. Cambridge and London: Cambridge University Press.

Jacobs, Jane. 1961. *The Life and Death of Great American Cities: The Failure of Town Planning*. New York: Random House.

Johnson, James H. 1995. *Listening in Paris: A Cultural History*. Berkeley: University of California Press.

Johnson, Mark. 1987. *The Body in the Mind: The Bodily Basis of Meaning, Imagination and Reason*. Chigago and London: University of Chicago Press.

Keil, Charles. 1995. The Theory of Participatory Discrepancies: A Progress Report. *Ethnomusicology* 39, no. 1.

Kenyon, Nicholas. ed. 1988. *Authenticity and Early Music: A Symposium*. Oxford and New York: Oxford University Press.

Lang, Paul Henry. 1941. *Music in Western Civilization*. New York: Norton.

Lebrecht, Norman. 1991. *The Maestro Myth: Great Conductors in Pursuit of Power*. London: Simon and Schuster.

———. (1996). *When the Music Stops: Managers, Maestros and the Corporate Murder of Classical Music*. London: Simon and Schuster.

Lipsitz, George. 1990. *Time Passages: Collective Memory and American Popular Culture*. Minneapolis: University of Minnesota Press.

———. 1994. *Dangerous Crossroads: Popular Music, Postmodernism and the Politics of Place*. London and New York: Verso.

Loesser, Arthur. 1954. *Men, Women and Pianos: A Social History*. New York: Simon and Schuster.

Lovelock, J. E. 1979. *Gaia: A New Look at Life on Earth*. Oxford and New York: Oxford University Press.

McClary, Susan. 1990. *Feminine Endings: Music, Gender and Sexuality*. Minneapolis: University of Minnesota Press.

McCulloch, Warren. 1965. *Embodiments of Mind*. Cambridge, Mass.: MIT Press.

Malm, William P. 1967. *Music Cultures of the Pacific, the Near East, and Asia*. Englewood Cliffs, N.J.: Prentice-Hall.

Nketia, J. H. K. 1975. *The Music of Africa*. London: Victor Gollancz.

Parkinson, C. Northcote. 1957. *Parkinson's Law, or the Pursuit of Progress*. London: John Murray.

Rose, Tricia. 1994. *Black Noise: Rap Music and Black Culture in Contemporary America*. Hanover, N.H., and London: University Press of New England / Wesleyan University Press.

Roszak, Theodore. 1972. *Where the Wasteland Ends: Politics and Transcendence in Post-Industrial Society*. London: Faber and Faber.

Said, Edward. 1978. *Orientalism*. London: Routledge and Kegan Paul.

Slonimsky, Nicholas. 1953. *Lexicon of Musical Invective: Critical Assaults on Composers since Beethoven's Time*. Seattle and London: Washington University Press.

Small, Christopher. 1977. *Music, Society, Education*. London: John Calder; New York, Riverrun Press (1982). Reissued (1996) Hanover, N.H., and London: University Press of New England / Wesleyan University Press.

———. 1987. *Music of the Common Tongue: Survival and Celebration in Afro-American Music*. London: John Calder; New York: Riverrun Press (1988).

Sterne, Jonathan. 1997. Sounds Like the Mall of America: Programmed Music and the Architectonics of Commercial Space. *Ethnomuscology* 41 (winter): 22–50.

Stravinsky, Igor. 1947. *Poetics of Music*. Cambridge, Mass.: Harvard University Press.

Taruskin, Richard. 1995. *Text and Act: Essays on Music and Performance*. New York and London: Oxford University Press.

Taylor, Rogan P. 1985. *The Death and Resurrection Show: From Shaman to Superstar*. London: Anthony Blond.

Thompson, Robert Farris. 1966. An Aesthetic of the Cool: West African Dance. *African Forum* 2, pt. 2 (fall).

Williams, Raymond. 1976. *Keywords: A Vocabulary of Culture and Society*. London: Fontana.

Index

UNIVERSITY PRESS OF NEW ENGLAND
publishes books under its own imprint and is the publisher for
Brandeis University Press, Dartmouth College, Middlebury College Press,
University of New Hampshire, Tufts University, and Wesleyan University Press.

ABOUT THE AUTHOR
Christopher Small is the author of *Music, Society, Education* (Wesleyan, 1996),
Music of the Common Tongue (1987), and *Schoenberg* (1978). He was Senior
Lecturer at Ealing College of Higher Education in London until 1986.
He lives in Sitges, Spain.

LIBRARY OF CONGRESS CATALOGING-IN-PUBLICATION DATA
Small, Christopher, 1927–
    Musicking : the meanings of performing and listening
/ by Christopher Small.
        p.   cm. — (Music/culture)
    "Wesleyan University Press."
    Includes bibliographical references (p.   )
    ISBN 0–8195–2256–2 (alk. paper). — ISBN 0–8195–2257–0 (pbk. :
alk. paper)
    1. Music—Philosophy and aesthetics.   2. Music—Performance—
Psychological aspects.   I. Title.   II. Series.
ML3845.S628   1998
781'.1—dc21   97–49996